IMAGES
of America
HARWICH

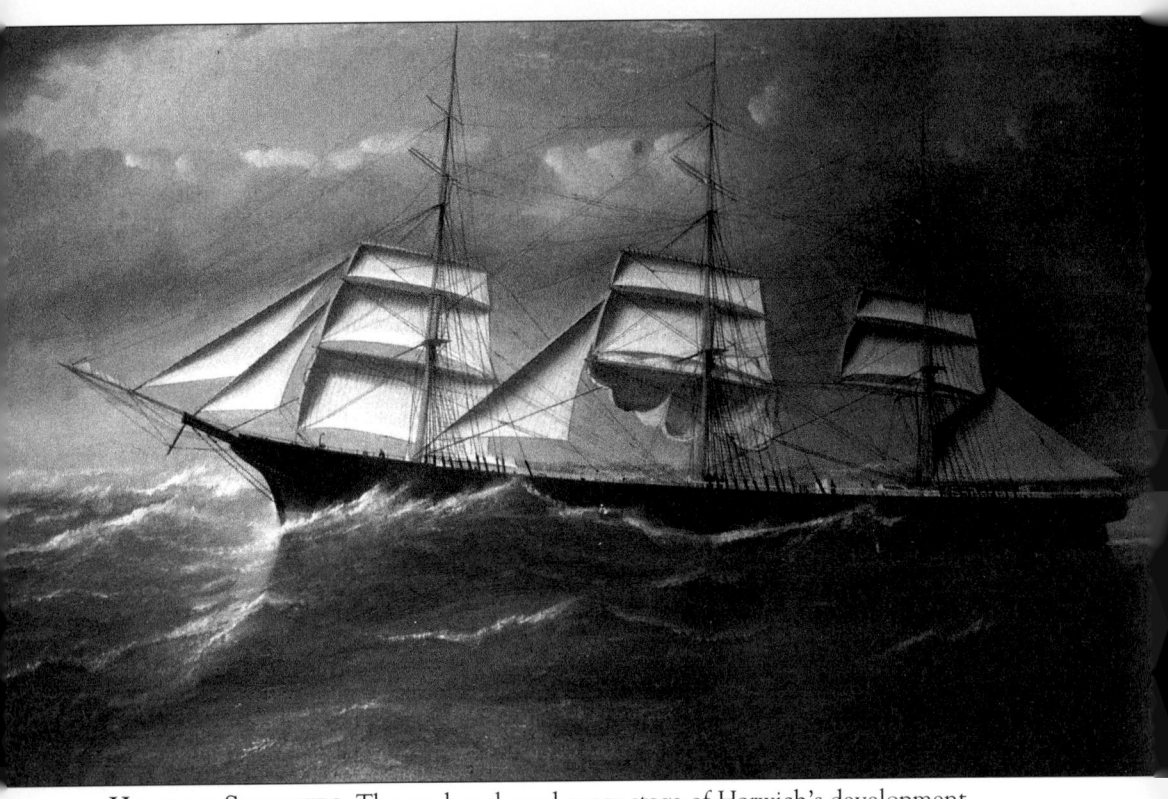

HARWICH SEAFARERS. The sea has shaped every stage of Harwich's development.

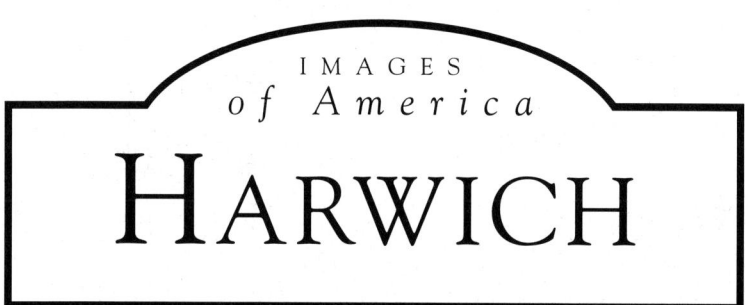

IMAGES of America
HARWICH

Joan M. Maloney

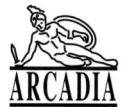

Copyright © 2001 by Joan M. Maloney.
ISBN 0-7385-0524-2

First printed in 2001.

Published by Arcadia Publishing,
an imprint of Tempus Publishing, Inc.
2A Cumberland Street
Charleston, SC 29401

Printed in Great Britain.

Library of Congress Catalog Card Number: 2001088717

For all general information contact Arcadia Publishing at:
Telephone 843-853-2070
Fax 843-853-0044
E-Mail sales@arcadiapublishing.com

For customer service and orders:
Toll-Free 1-888-313-2665

Visit us on the internet at http://www.arcadiapublishing.com

CONTENTS

Acknowledgments ... 6

Introduction ... 7

1. The Society and the Sea ... 9

2. Salvation by Cranberries ... 43

3. A Vacation Mecca ... 77

4. Harwich Remembers ... 113

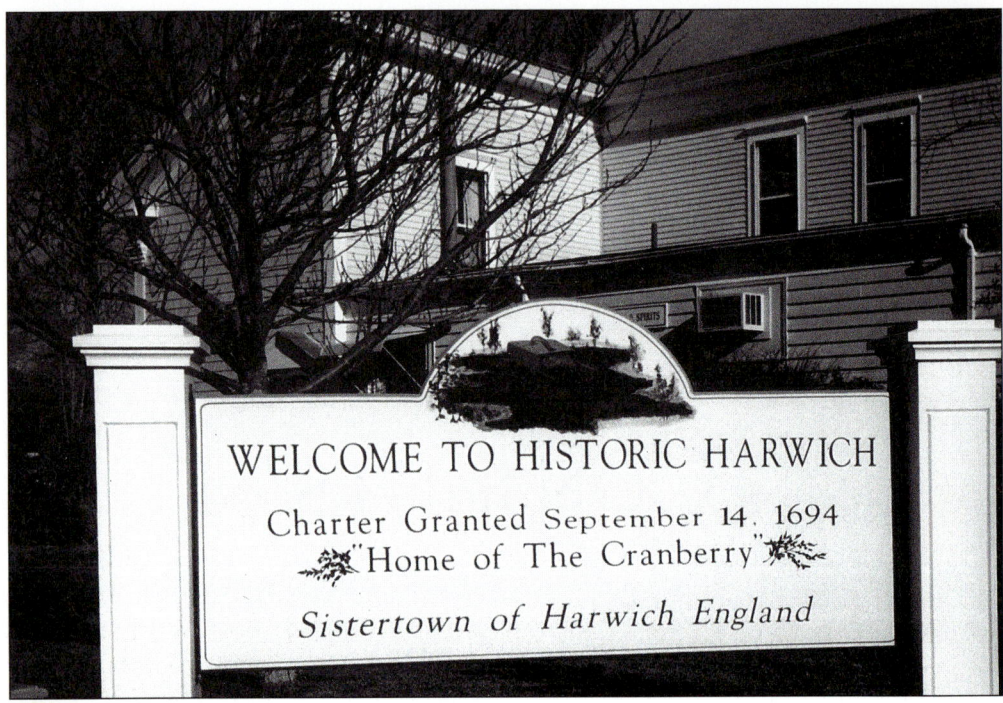

CROSSROADS. At the crossroads is the Harwich Historical District.

Acknowledgments

I extend my thanks to the officers and volunteers of the Harwich Historical Society—Gertrude Cutler, Fran Geberth, Louise Archambault, Walda Szopa, Betty Szeberenyi, and Marlene Vagenas—for their help and encouragement. Special thanks go to its director, Jim Brown, for his varied and always enthusiastic assistance and for opening the society's large collection of historical photographs. All the photographs used in this book are from the society's collection unless otherwise indicated. Adele Geraghty graciously loaned photographs related to Asa L. Jones. Kathy Peterson and Blanche Hunnewell kindly furnished scenes from the Harwich Cranberry Festival Committee. Sr. Aureen Rose Behrend, camera in hand in the best tradition of Clement Cahoon, captured the subjects needed to round out this account. Francis B. Larkin provided colorful anecdotes of his Harwich ancestors, and Eileen Krause of the Brooks Free Library scoured the library's files. Thanks are also due to those predecessors who cared enough to preserve these glimpses of Harwich's past. Without each of them, my quest to capture the town's history would have been folly.

INTRODUCTION

In 1864, prosperous cranberry-grower Cyrus Cahoon tried to purchase a small lot at the busy intersection of Main Street and the Market Road (now Route 124) in Harwich Center. Cahoon intended to build a small photographic studio to provide employment for his crippled son. Rejection of his bid surely relieved Nathaniel Robbins. For years, Robbins had been the town dentist, advertising his talents in making customized rubber dentures, but he also dabbled in photography. The distinction of opening the first town studio, however, properly belongs to Clement Cahoon. From rooms over Harwich Center's drugstore, Clement Cahoon invited parents to bring their children for portraits on sunny days. He captured many local personalities and scenes, some of which are included in the following pages.

Harwich, of course, has changed enormously since those days. With the new millennium, its tax base has exceeded $2 billion. If some magic process would permit Cahoon to revisit his hometown, he would be shocked that oxen and horse-drawn carriages have given way to streams of automobiles. He would be soothed, however, that so many of the familiar landmarks—churches, schools, banks, and parks—still remain.

Chartered to several colonists from Plymouth Plantation in 1694, Harwich attained its present geographic boundaries in 1803, after the northern half separated to become the town of Brewster. Left with some 20 square miles of land and an abundance of fresh water in its ponds and rivers, these early settlers scratched their livings from the sandy soil. By about 1850, however, two-thirds of the male workforce had turned to the riches of the sea, serving as mariners and fishermen.

The arrival of the railroad in 1865 was a mixed blessing. Local residents could now get to Boston in a few hours, and a wide variety of goods could be delivered at reasonable charges. Conversely, the packet ship became obsolete and, when people began to heat their homes with coal brought in by rail, the market for timber almost disappeared. At the same time, the Civil War had claimed the lives, health, or fortunes of many local men. It also decimated the town treasury, requiring much higher tax rates.

The town population suffered an alarming decline: each census from 1870 to 1920 showed a decline in residents. By 1920, Harwich's population was only about half of what it had been before the Civil War. The principal means of support for many families became the cultivation and marketing of the lowly cranberry. Cranberries flourished in the acidic bogs. Harvest meant employment opportunities for every man, woman, and child. The cash they earned sustained many families through the winter.

A few native sons realized that the town's stability depended on refocusing their efforts on the sea and on the town's quaint villages. This time, the accent would be placed on bathing at the town's beaches and on sailing pleasure boats from its harbors. Town voters were convinced of the merits of this vision by the offers of matching funds. Tax money helped pave roads that, in turn, encouraged the construction of hotels and inns to accommodate visitors. The strategy lured—and lures—vacationers.

Caught in the swirl of all this activity, some residents determined in 1901 to honor the old, simpler times by beginning an annual celebration of Old Home Week. This tradition is evident today in the annual Cranberry Festival, which marks the harvest each September by carnivals and fireworks. It is the same motivation that has led to the preservation of many town landmarks and efforts to pass on these traditions to today's children.

One
THE SOCIETY AND THE SEA

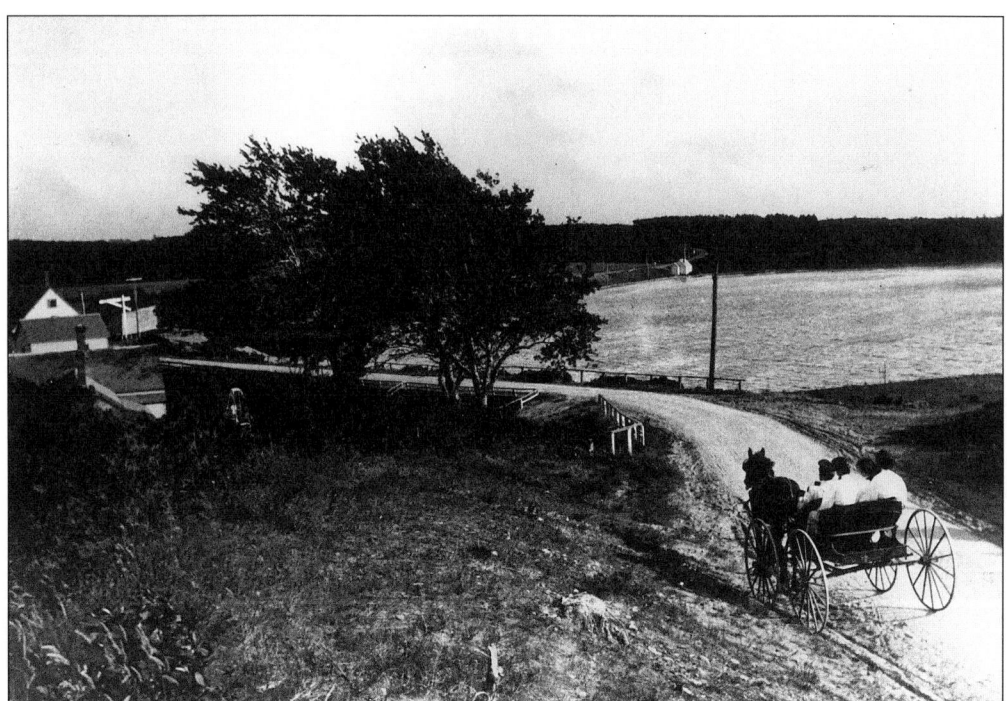

THE JOURNEY BEGINS. A dirt roadway (now Route 124) winds from Harwich Center to Pleasant Lake. The general store in the background is now a favorite stop with those using the Cape Cod bike trail.

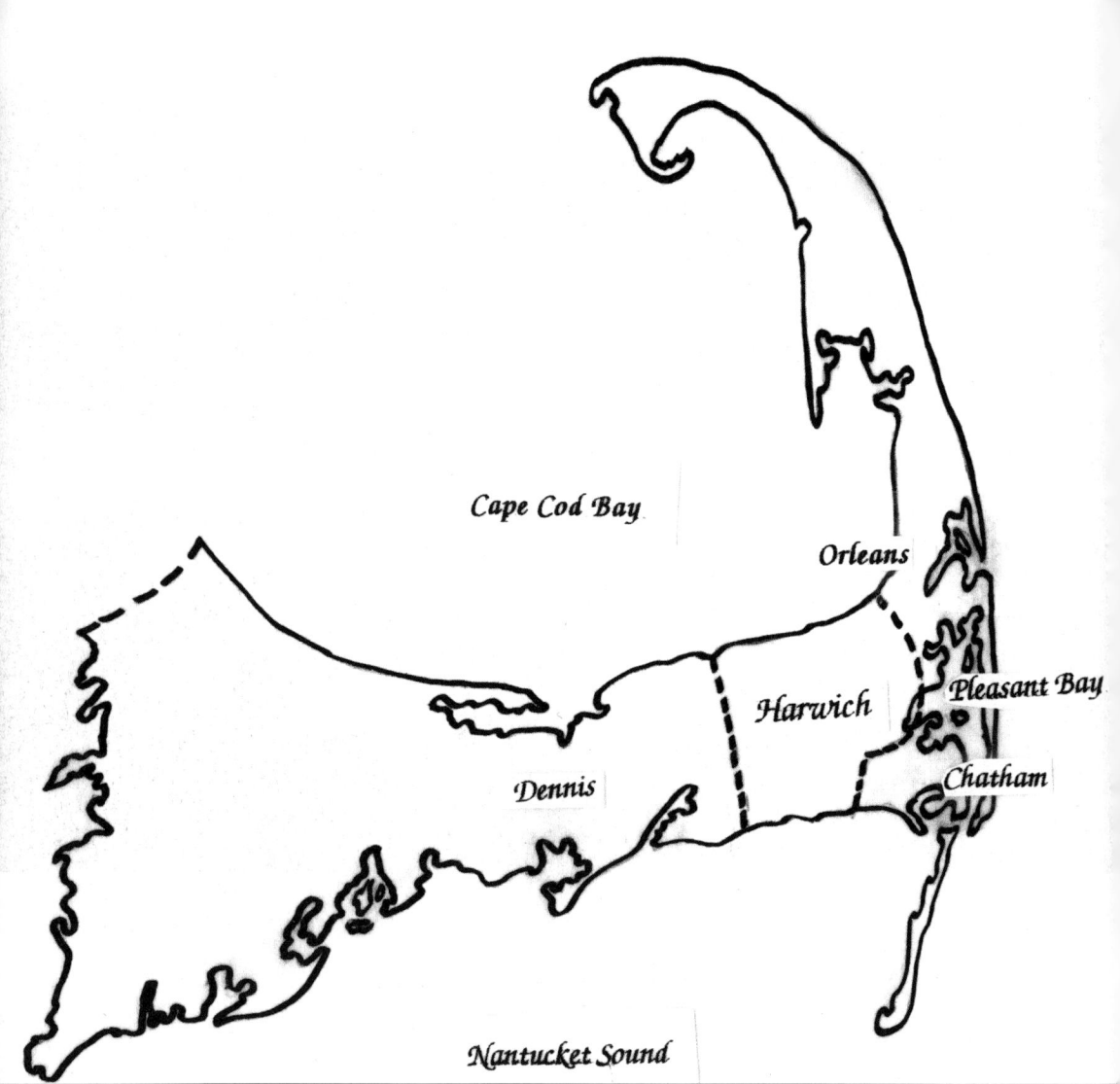

HARWICH BEFORE 1803. Prior to Brewster's breakaway in 1803, Harwich was bounded by Cape Cod Bay to the north, Nantucket Sound to the south, Dennis to the west, and Chatham and Eastham to the east. (Sr. Aureen Rose Behrend.)

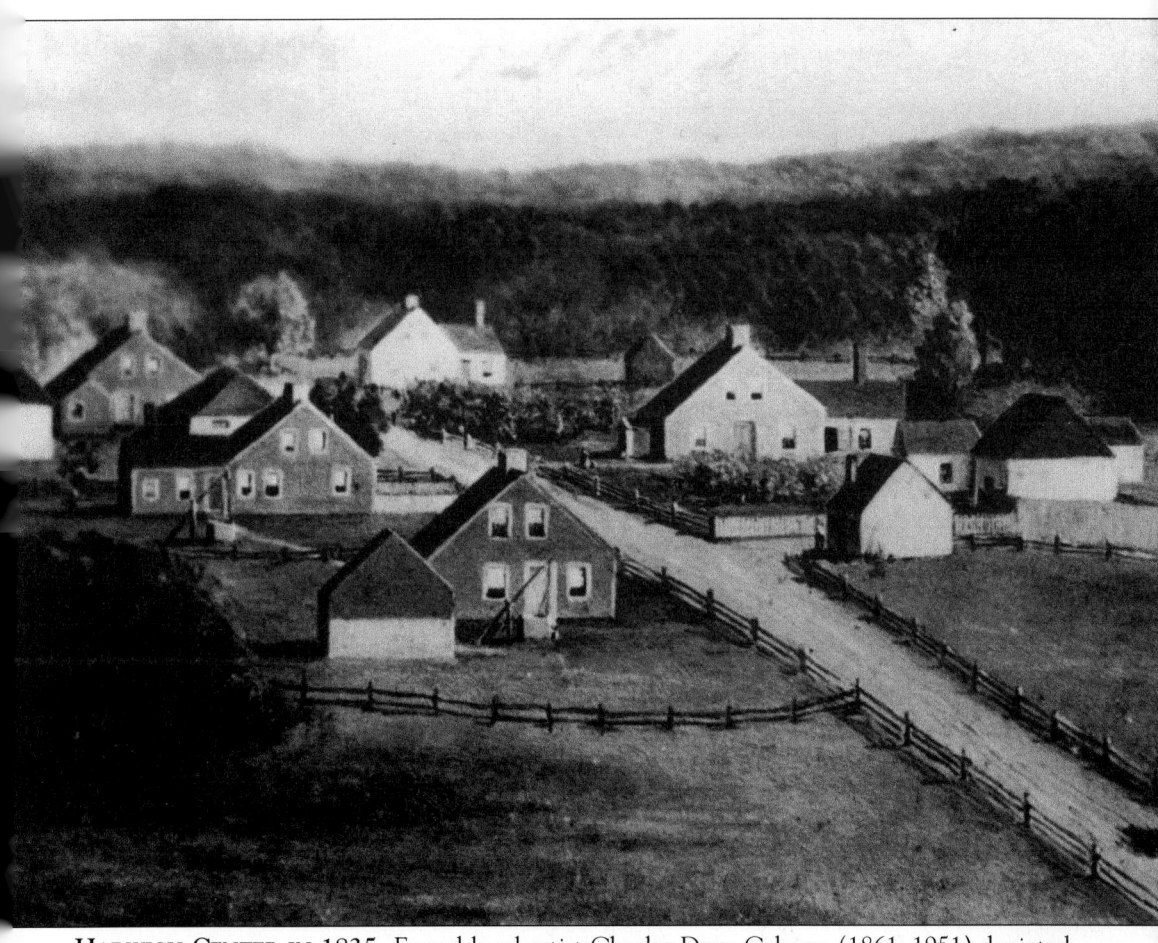

HARWICH CENTER IN 1835. Famed local artist Charles Drew Cahoon (1861–1951) depicted Main Street in this view looking west to the Bank Street corner. At the time, Harwich Center had only about 10 dwellings.

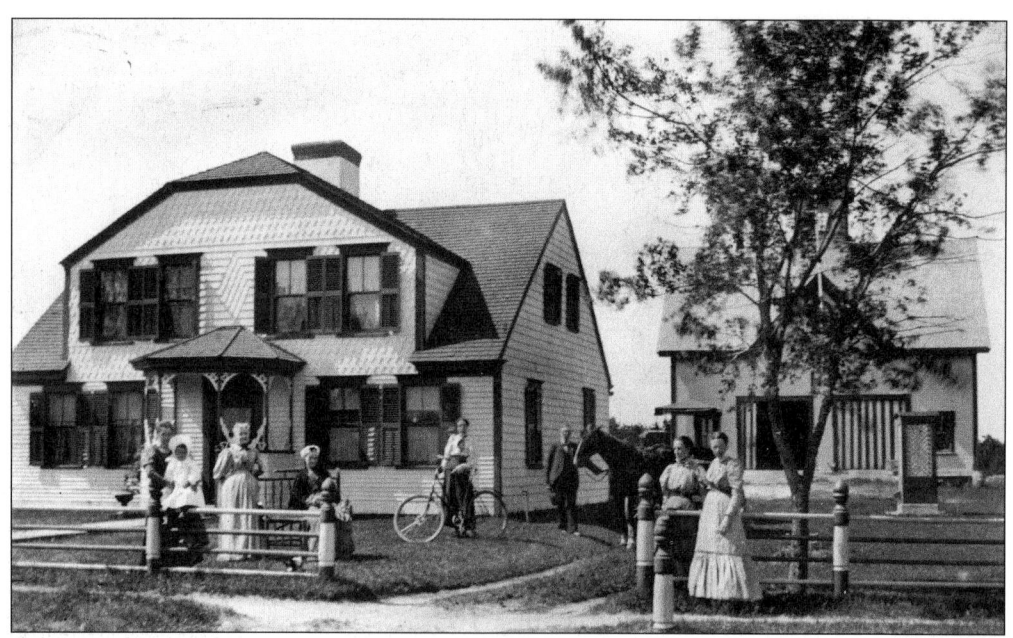

THE OLDEST HOUSE. This dwelling in South Harwich is believed to be Harwich's oldest house. The double Cape was constructed c. 1750, and the facade was added much later. Identification of old houses is complicated by the common practice of moving them from one site to another.

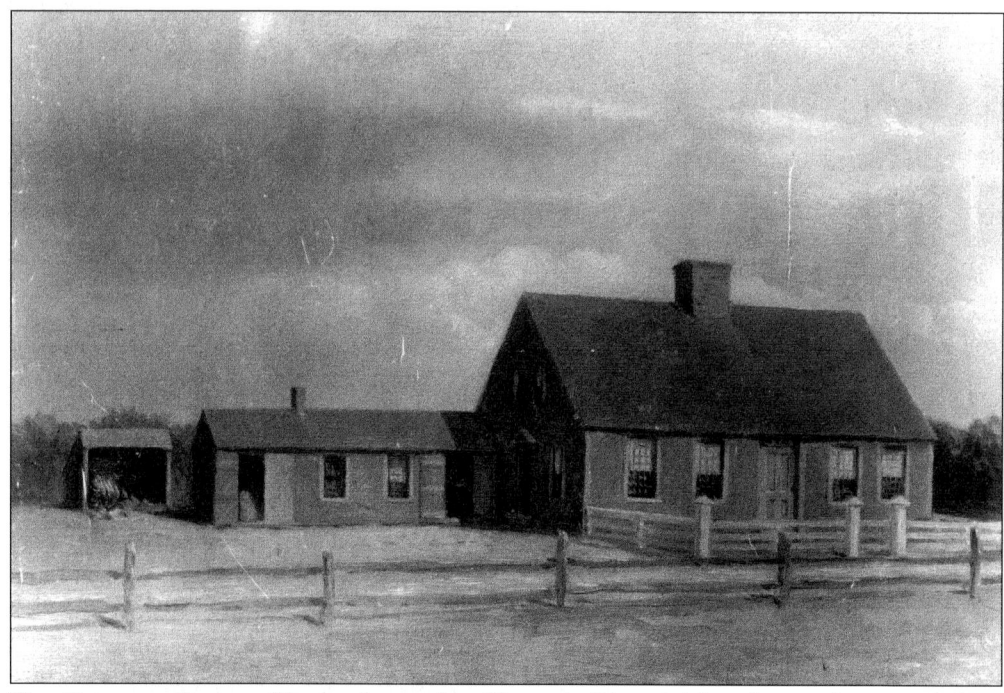

THE EBENEZER BROOKS HOUSE. Located on Harwich Center's Main Street, this typical Cape house, with a small side addition, was the first post office.

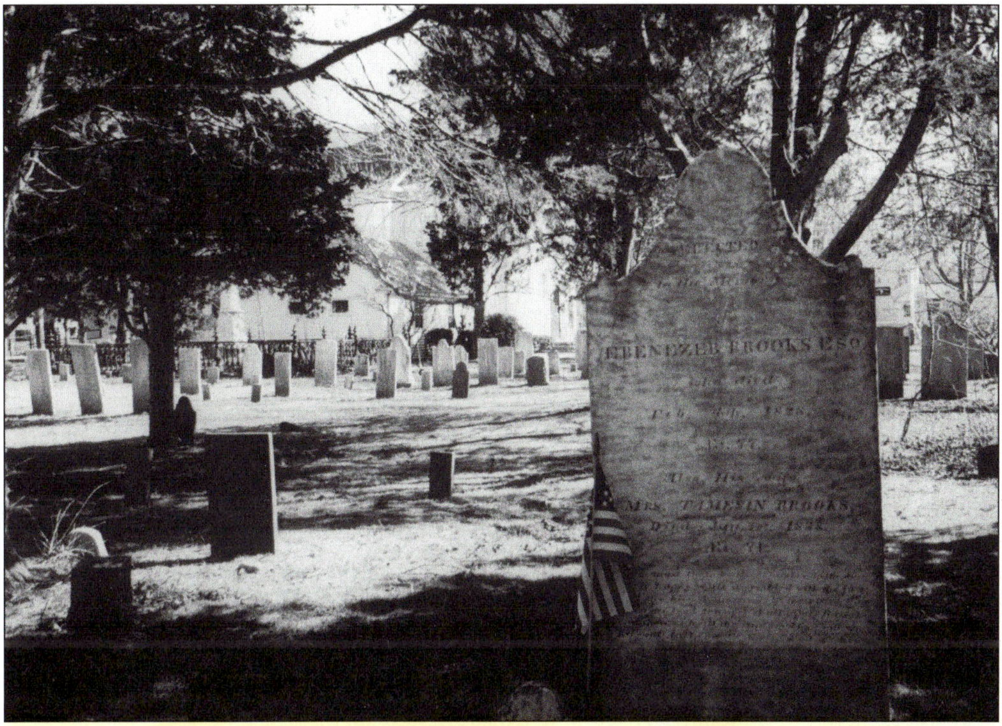

THE FIRST CEMETERY. Many of the town's early settlers are buried in the shadows of the Congregational church.

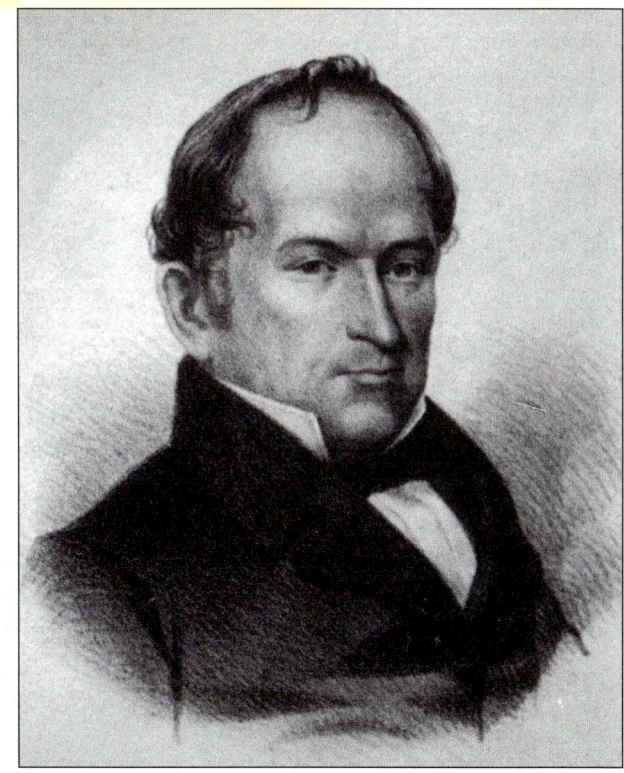

OBED BROOKS SR. (1781–1856). Obed Brooks Sr., son of Ebenezer Brooks, was kept from going to sea by the family's decision to build a general store in Harwich Center. Obed became a successful merchant, a justice of the peace, and a local political force.

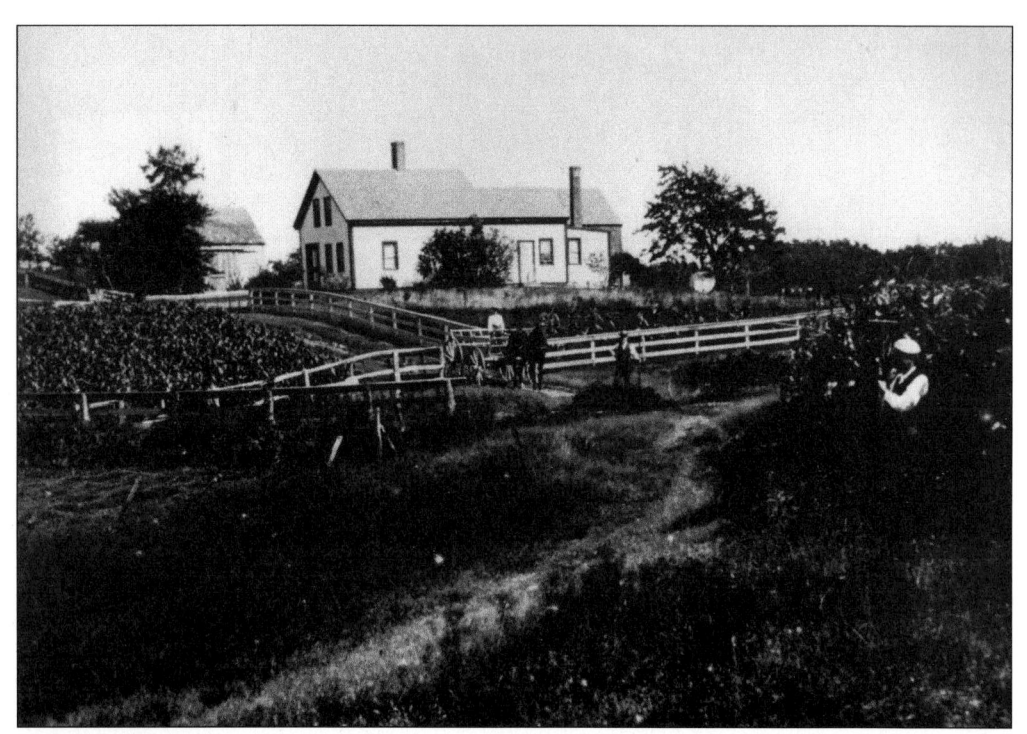

FARMING. Small farms abounded. The one shown here belonged to the Moody family. Most households maintained extensive vegetable gardens and meadowlands for animal fodder. Oxen were used not only for farming but also for transportation.

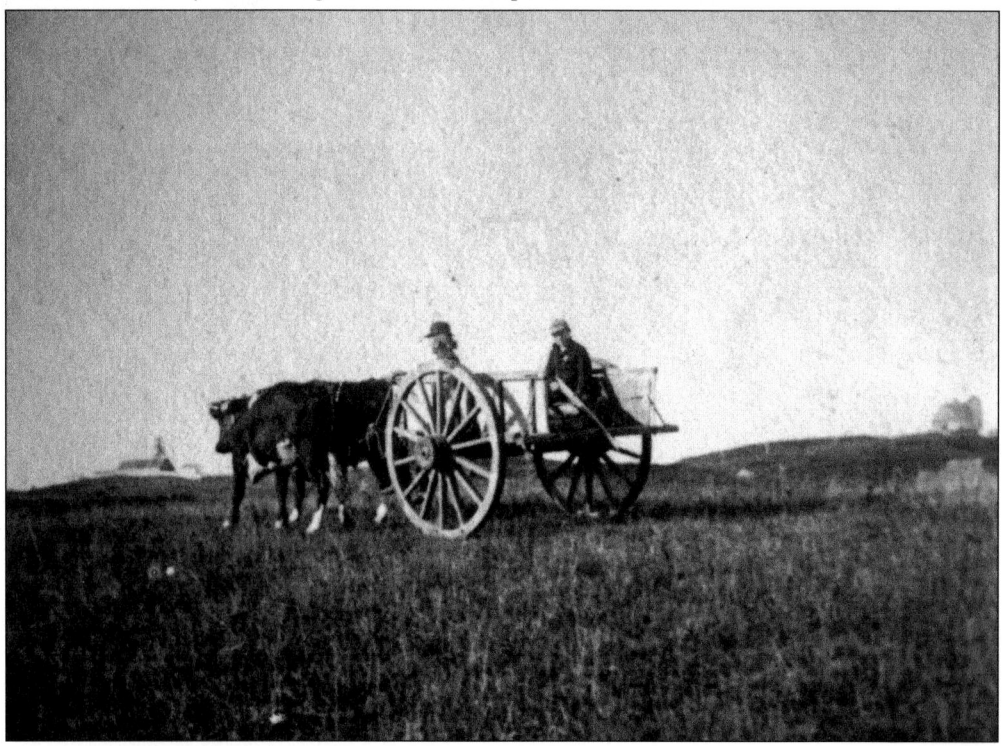

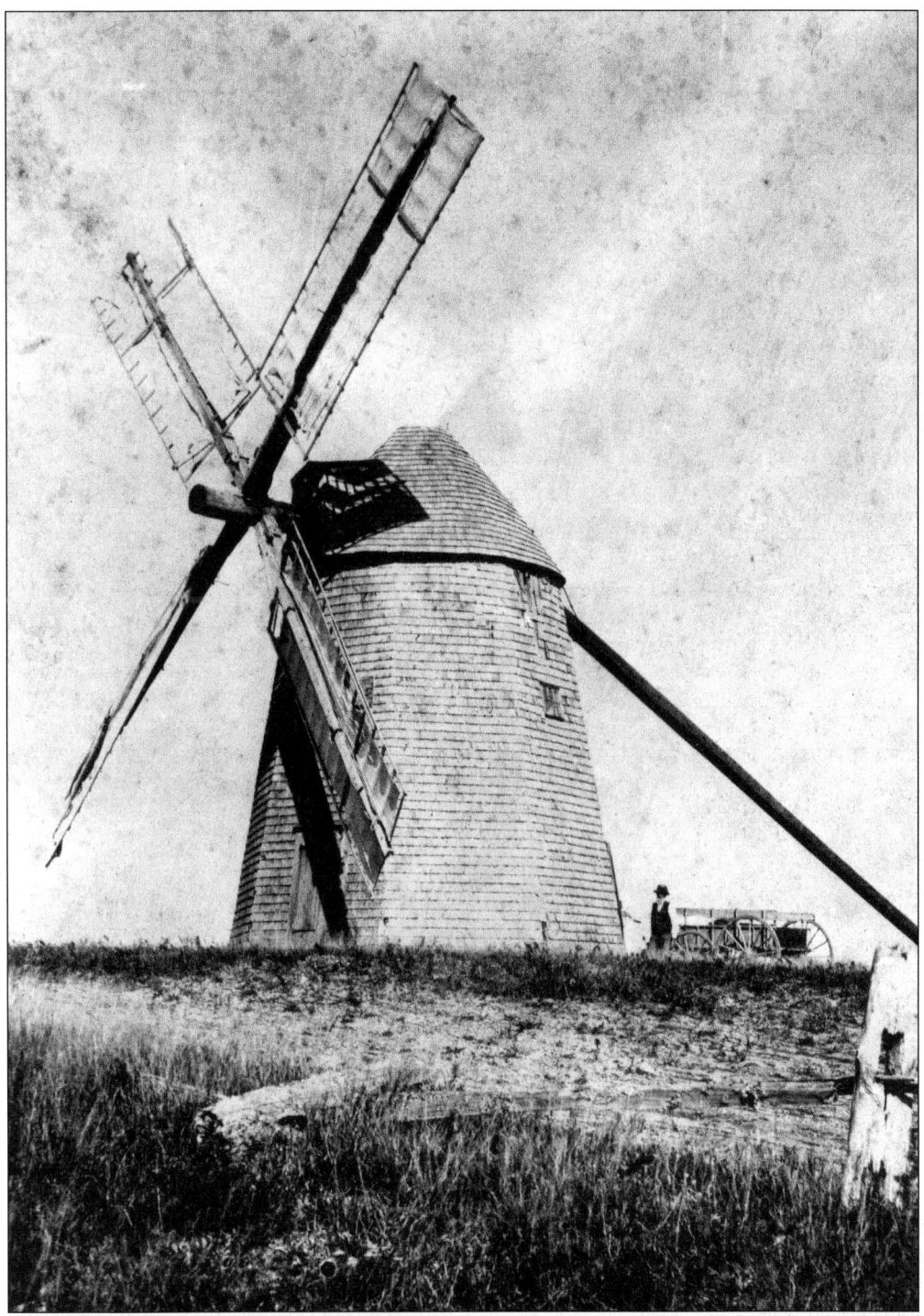

NICKERSON'S MILL. Windmills were vital assets to the community for grinding flour and for providing power to the saltworks. Seawater was distilled in wooden troughs, which were then scraped for salt to preserve fish. This mill was moved to its present location off Upper County Road *c.* 1903.

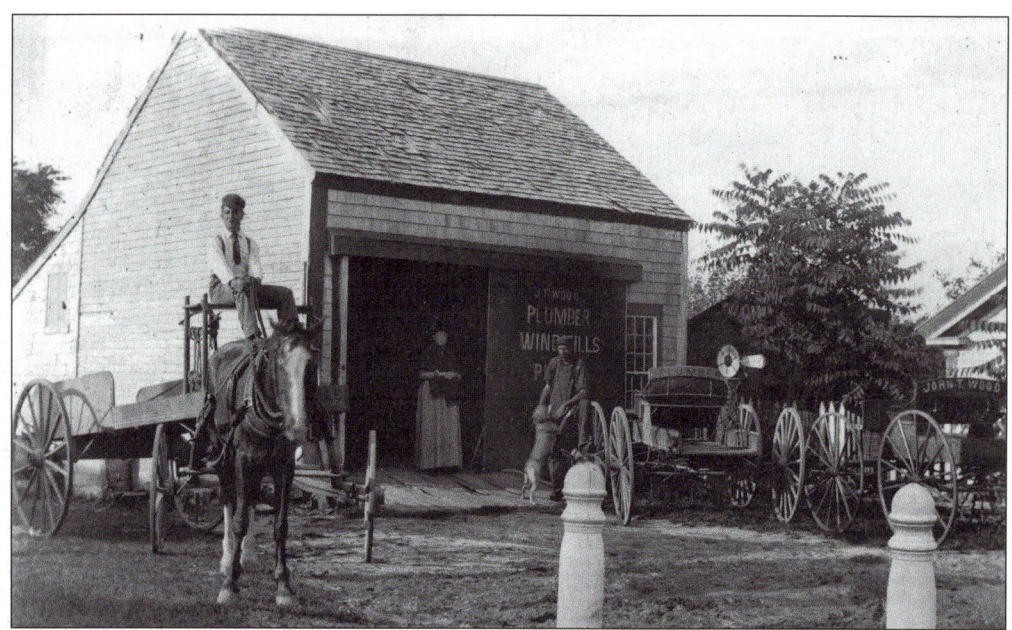

THE PLUMBER. From his establishment on Main Street in West Harwich, John T. Wood provided a vital service—repairing the windmills and pumps.

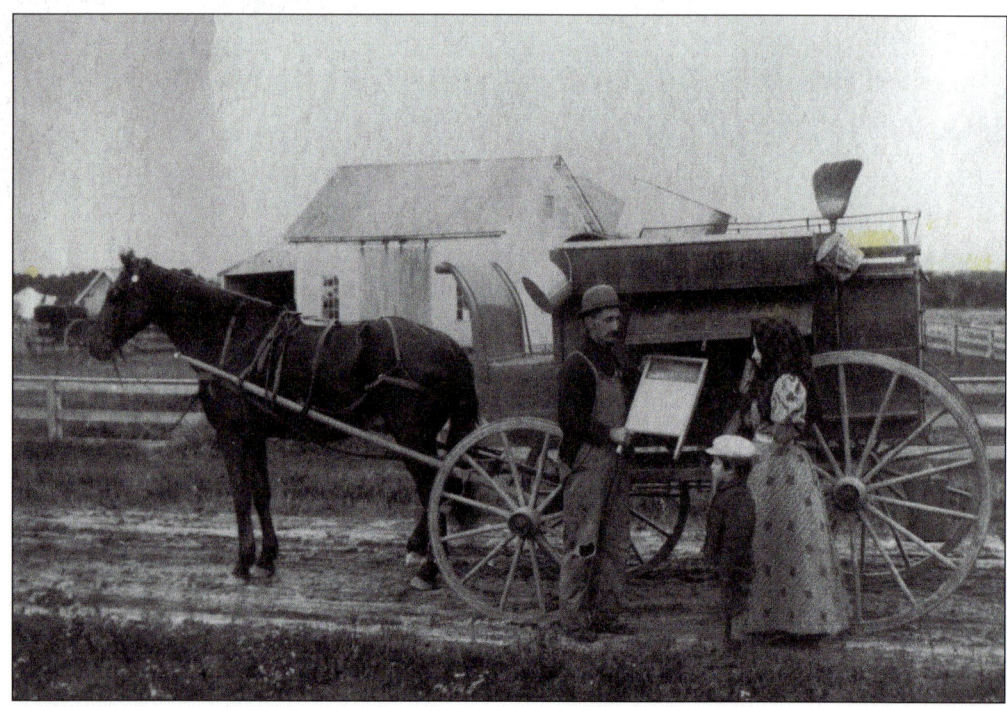

PEDDLERS. As the Cape's first itinerant salesman, the peddler offered goods that were not produced locally. He was also a source of news and gossip for many a farmer's wife.

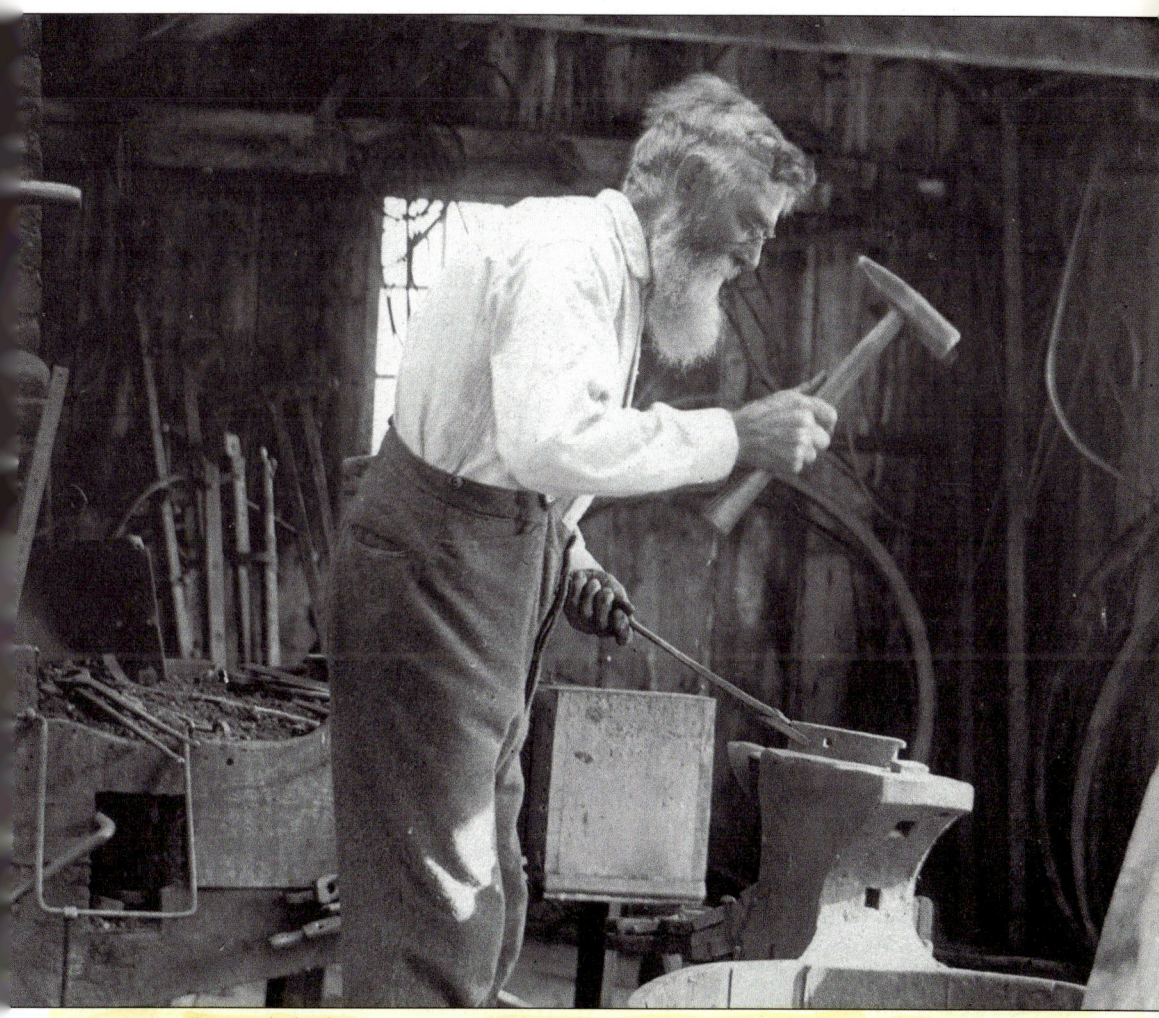

ARTISANS. Harwich had 96 artisans in 1860. Benjamin F. Robbins, shown in his shop on Parallel Street, was a skilled wheelwright. Robbins was also admired by some and opposed by others for his freethinking.

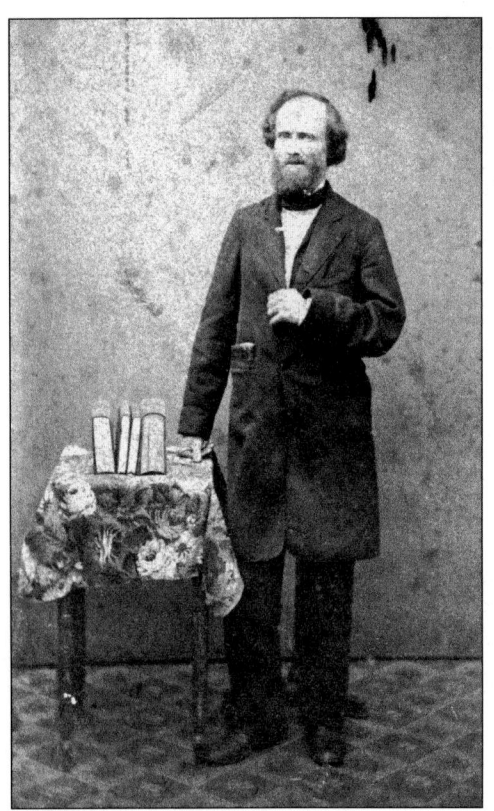

PROFESSIONALS. Harwich had 94 professionals in 1860, including Dr. Franklin Dodge (1809–1872), who operated his extensive practice from his home in Harwich Center. In the 1850s, Dodge charged 50¢ for an office visit and 68¢ for a house call.

OBED BROOKS JR. (1808–1882). Obed Brooks Jr. inherited much of his father's business acumen. He was a prime force in bringing the first two banks to Harwich in 1855 and, for many years, was simultaneously the cashier for the Cape Cod Five Cents Savings Bank and the Cape Cod Bank (now CCBT). As a widower with small children, Brooks married the daughter of his neighbor Dr. Dodge.

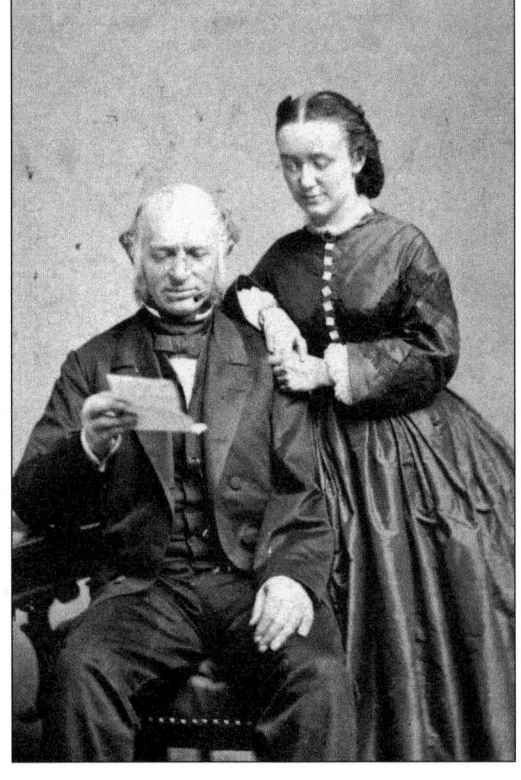

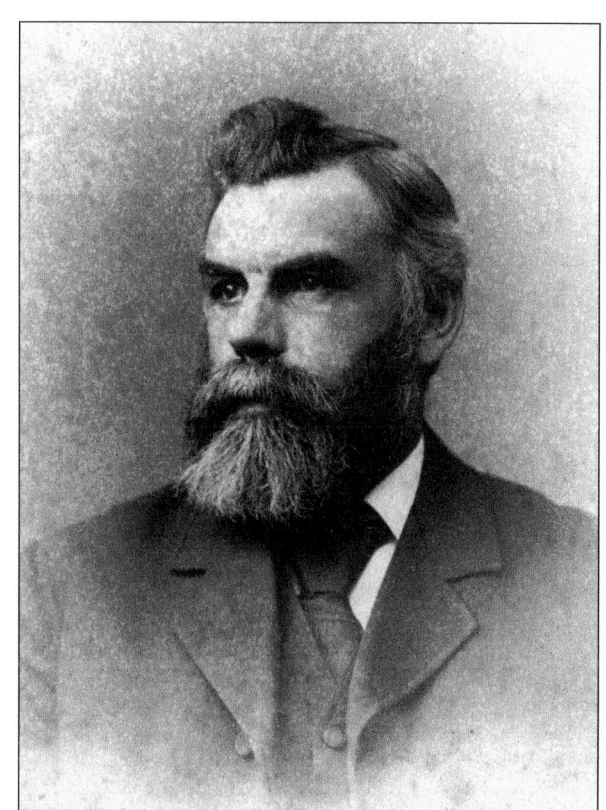

VALENTINE DOANE JR. Valentine Doane Jr. inherited the fortune made by his father, who had been a sea captain before investing in Harwich's first wharf and purchasing interests in several ships. In the mid-1850s, Doane built a large home facing his father's on Harwich Port's main road.

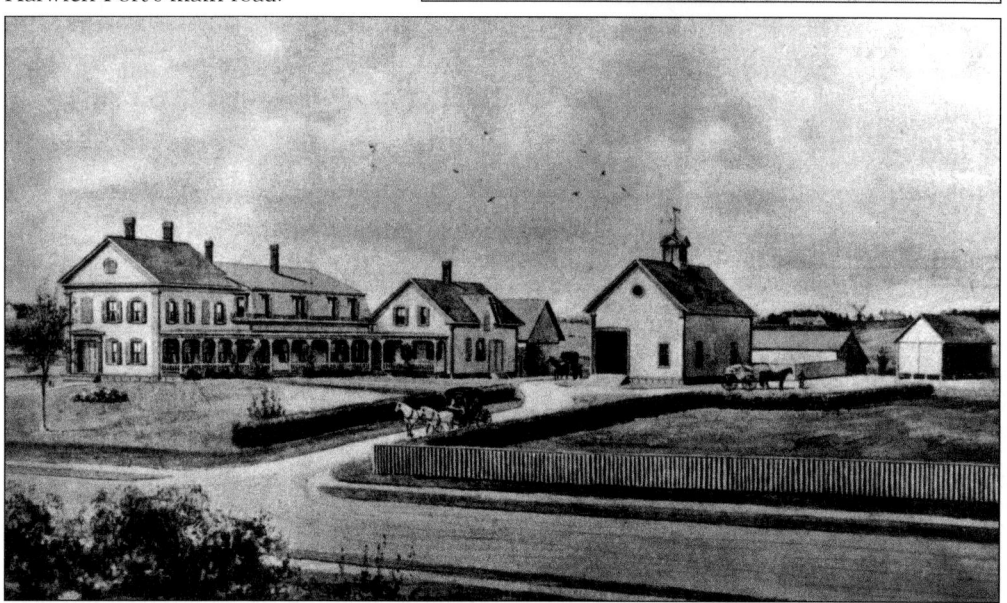

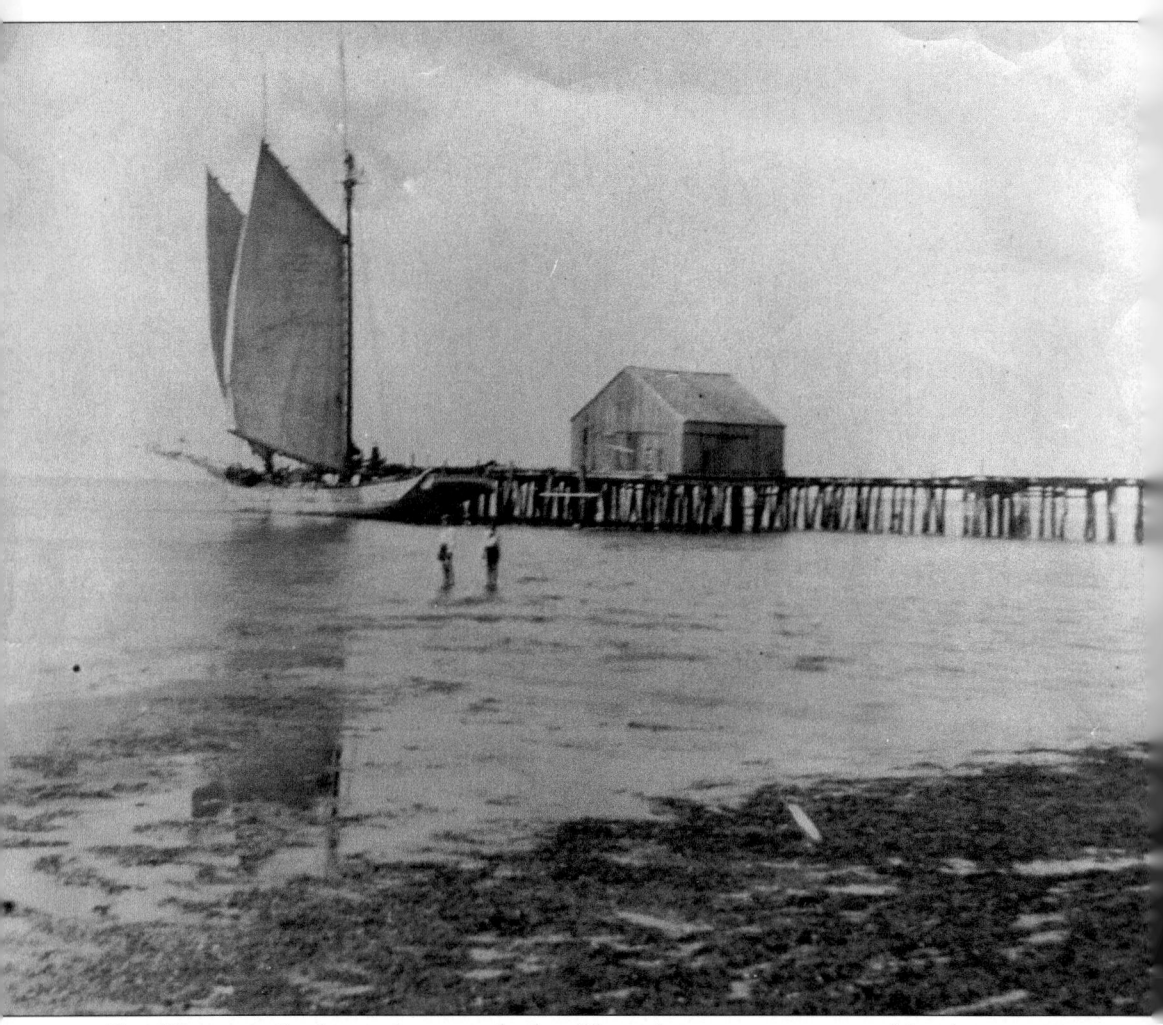

THE WHARVES. Lacking a deepwater harbor, Harwich mariners constructed four long piers into the waters of Nantucket Sound. This pier, Marsh Bank Wharf, was the first. It was built in 1844 just east of the Herring River. For many years, Henry Kelley (and then T.B. Baker) operated a thriving lumber and coal business. By the 1890s, all the wharves had been destroyed.

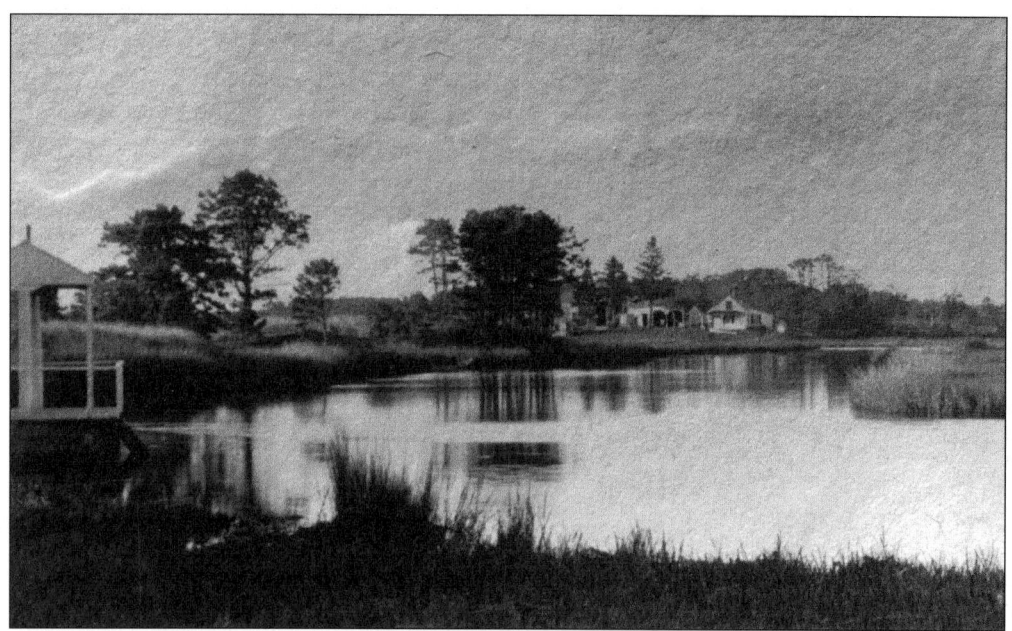

THE HERRING RIVER. The peaceful Herring River winds from Hinkley's Pond to the sea in West Harwich. The marsh hay growing on its banks in abundant meadows was a major source of fodder. In the early 19th century, boats were built on its shores. Although there was some experimentation, the absence of white water made it unsuitable for factories. The river was first bridged in 1804, when a small footbridge was built.

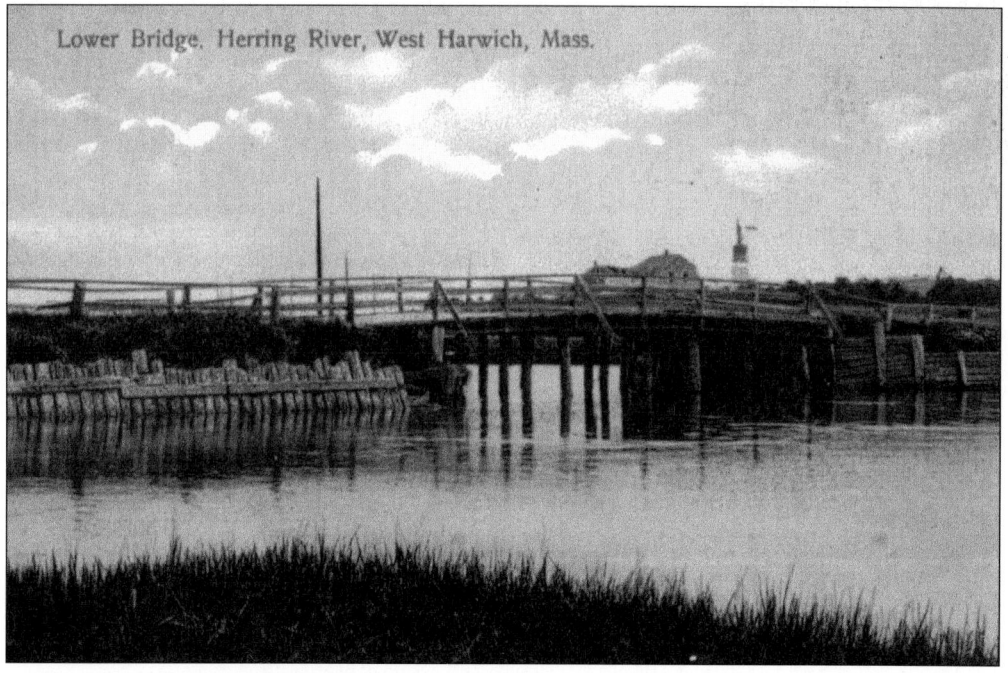

21

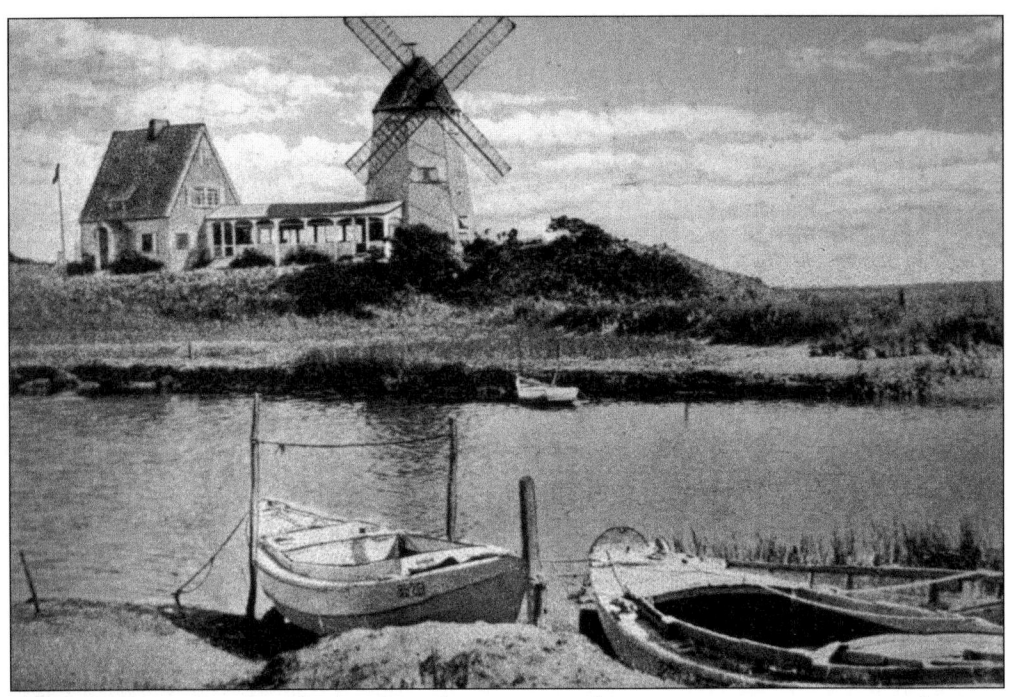

HERRING RIVER INLETS. The bends in the river provide many picturesque scenes and attract many people in kayaks and canoes to sample these charms.

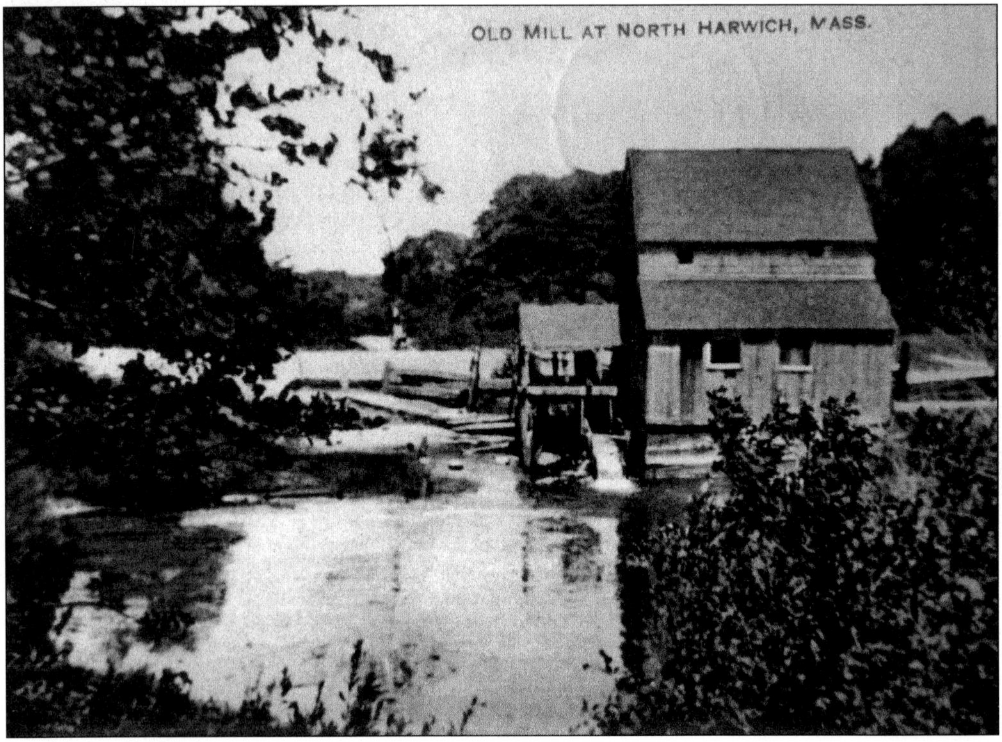

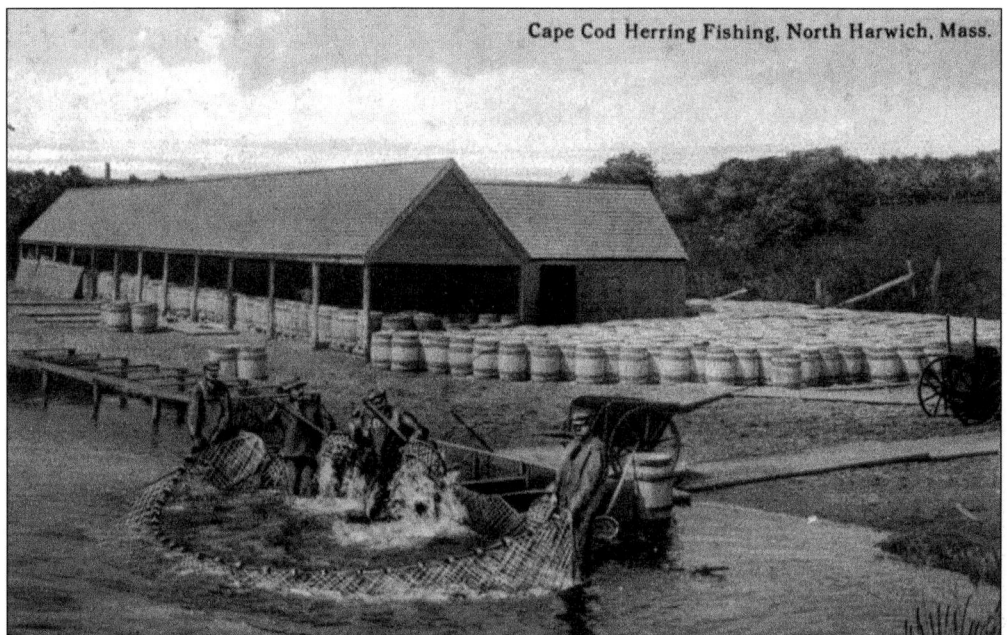

SEINING THE HERRING. When the herring headed upstream to spawn, they were easily gathered in purse nets, or seines. In earlier times, the fish were so plentiful they were often used for fertilizer. For many years, town meeting awarded the rights to seine to the highest bidders.

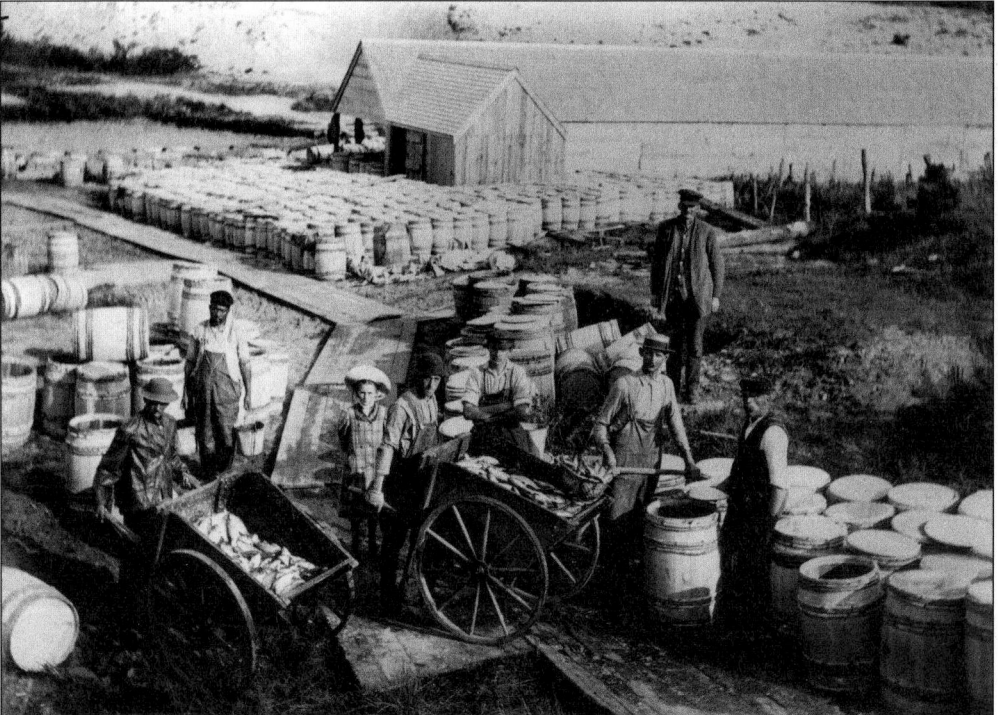

PACKING HERRING FOR MARKET. The herring catch was a major money provider. In 1863, for example, over $10,000 was derived from selling these fish. Coopers were kept busy preparing the barrels that carried the catch to the New York market.

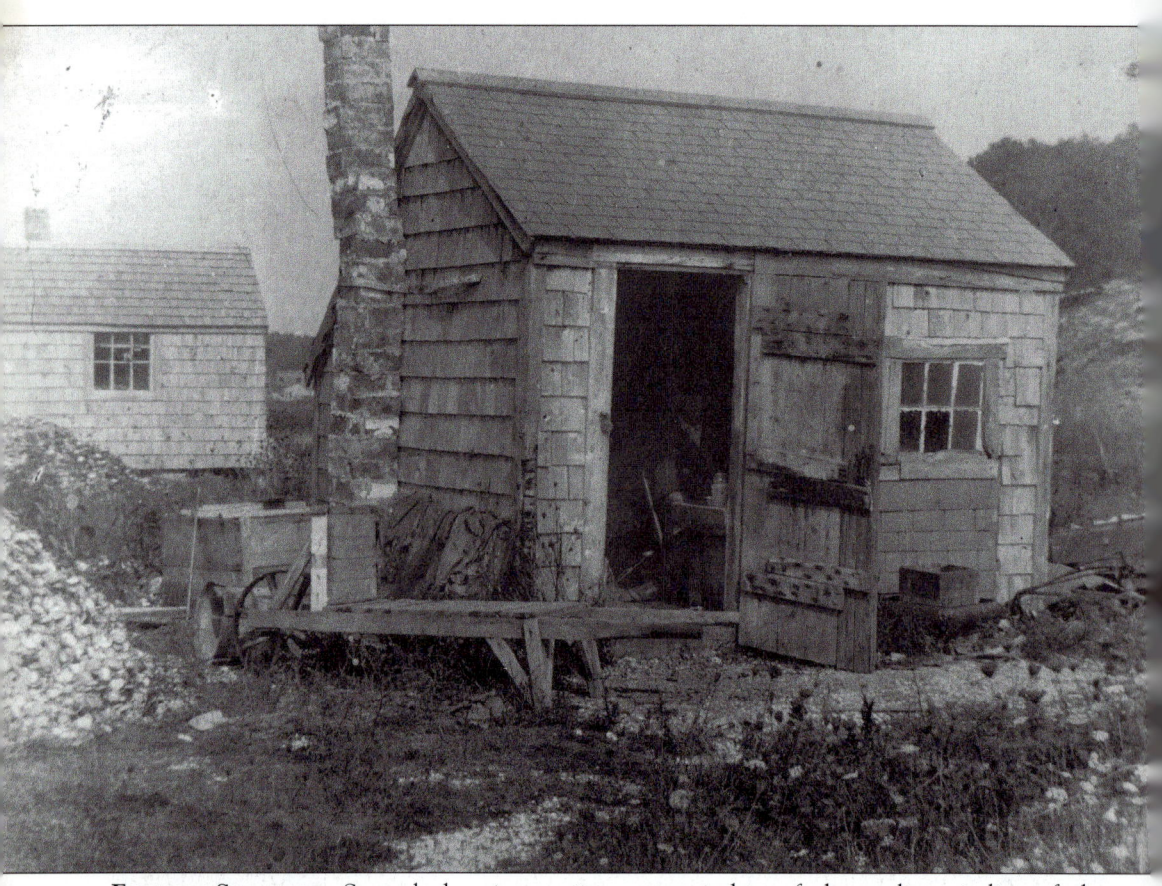

FISHING SHANTIES. Several shanties survive as reminders of the earlier vitality of the commercial fishing industry in Harwich.

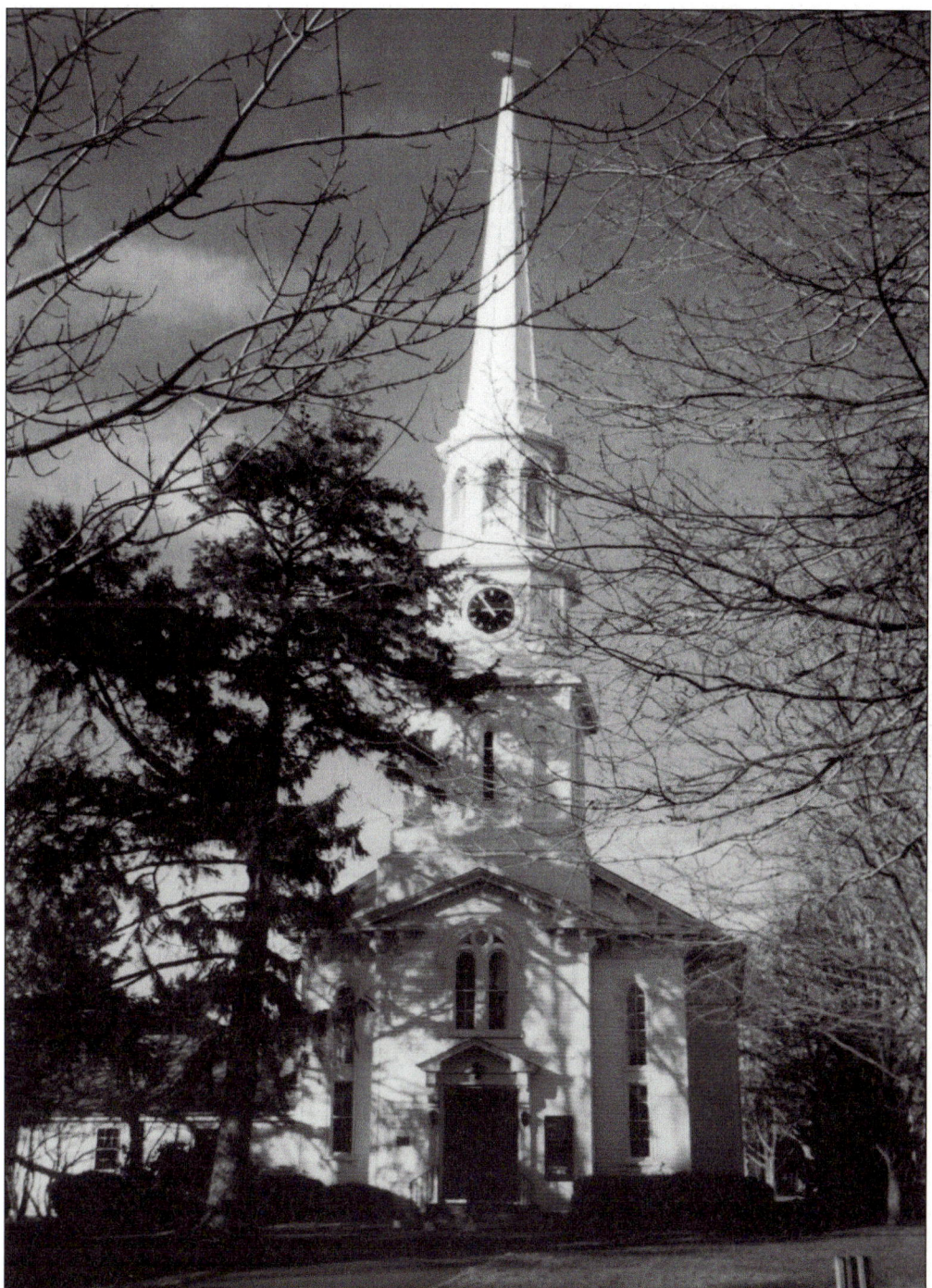

THE FIRST CONGREGATIONAL CHURCH, THE UNITED CHURCH OF CHRIST. The present church was built in the 1830s on the site of the first meetinghouse, which was erected in 1747 on Harwich Center's Main Street. Until the 1834 disestablishment, all residents were required to support it financially. The church has been a vital force in the Harwich community. (Sr. Aureen Rose Behrend.)

THE PILGRIM CHURCH. In 1855, a number of worshippers at Harwich Center's First Church left to form their own congregation in Harwich Port. On Sundays, wagons carried families in both directions, according to their religious convictions.

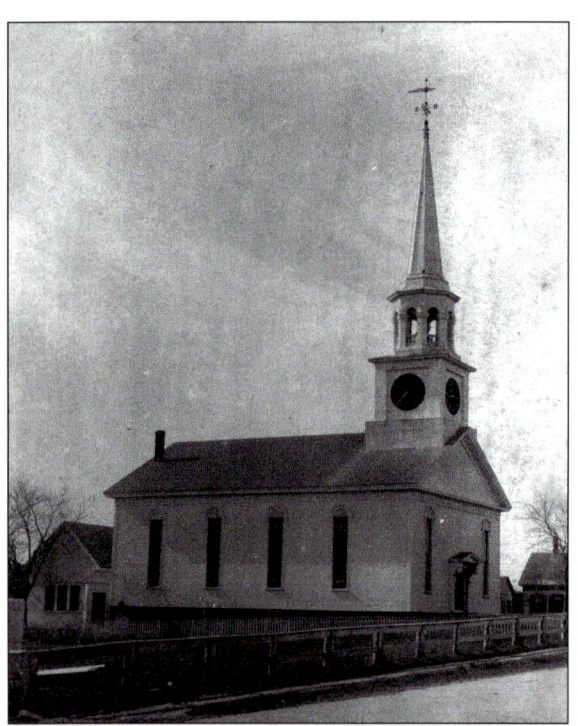

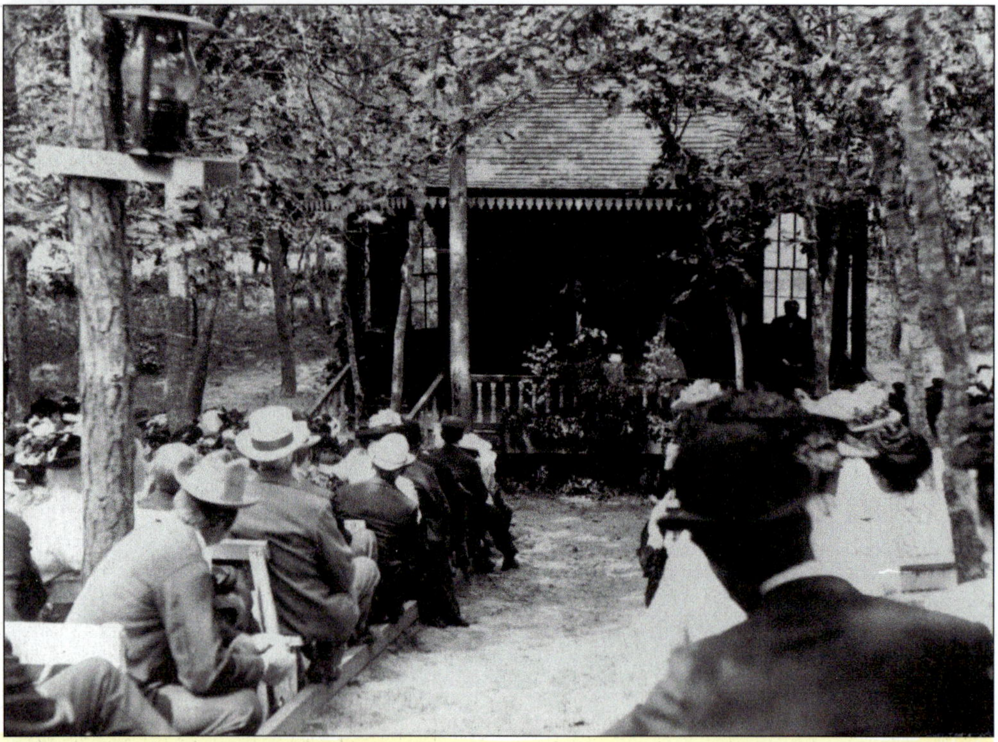

OCEAN GROVE CAMPGROUNDS. The late 19th century fostered a major religious revivalist movement. Ocean Grove, off Sea Street in Harwich Port, developed an entire community of small cottages for participants in the religious activities.

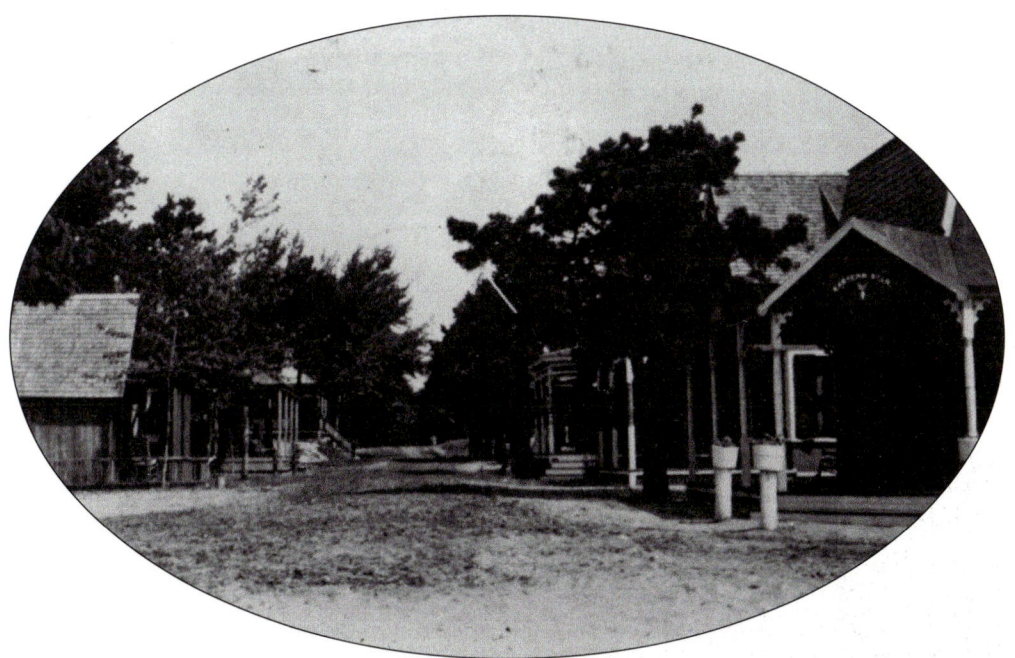

TYPICAL CAMPGROUND COTTAGES. The strictly seasonal homes were often decorated in Victorian or gingerbread styles. The lots, arranged in neat rows, were barely large enough to contain a dwelling.

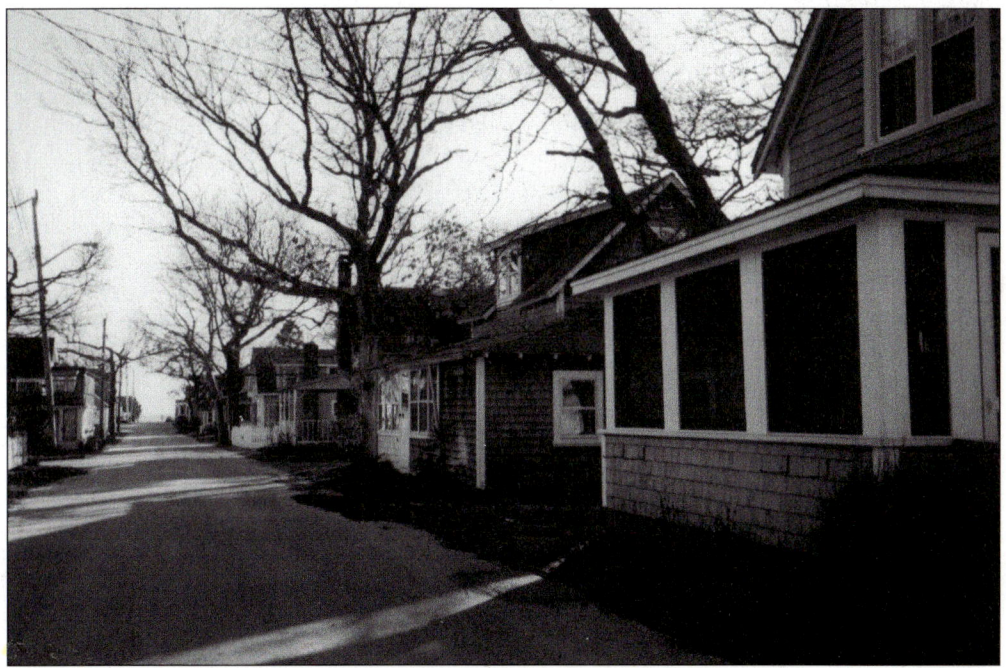

OCEAN GROVE TODAY. Many of the small cottages have been restored and winterized. They share access to a small beach and are now prized summer dwellings. (Sr. Aureen Rose Behrend.)

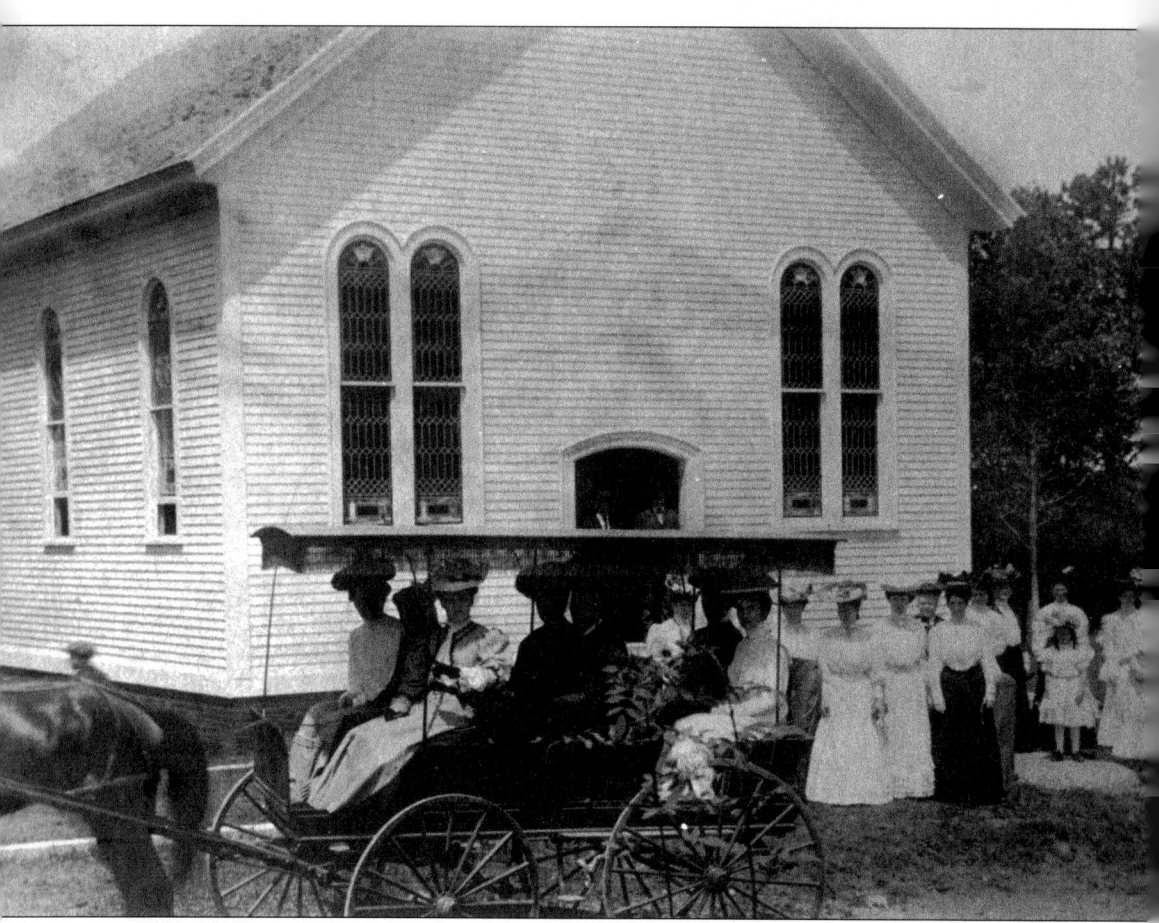

THE FIRST CATHOLIC CHURCH. The Irish were the first immigrants to come to Harwich. Welcomed for their labor, they often encountered hostility because of their religion. They built their own house of worship in Harwich Center in the mid-1850s. The priest arrived from Sandwich by horseback to serve worshipers from the neighboring towns.

SIDNEY BROOKS (1813–1887). Sidney Brooks, the second son of Obed Brooks Sr., graduated from Amherst College, taught briefly in Chatham, and then opened Pine Grove Seminary (later Pine Grove Academy). Pine Grove was coeducational and was the first secondary school in Harwich. Brooks had to give up the school after 20 years because of financial reverses.

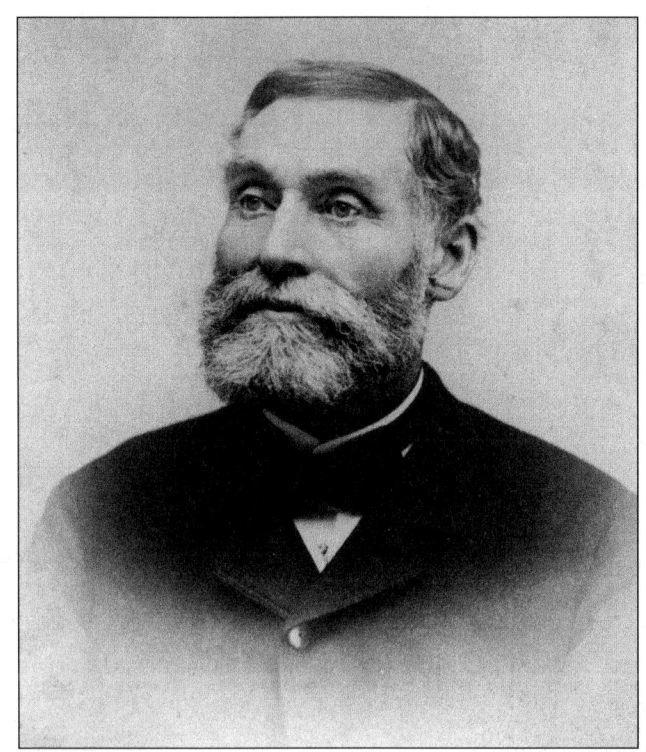

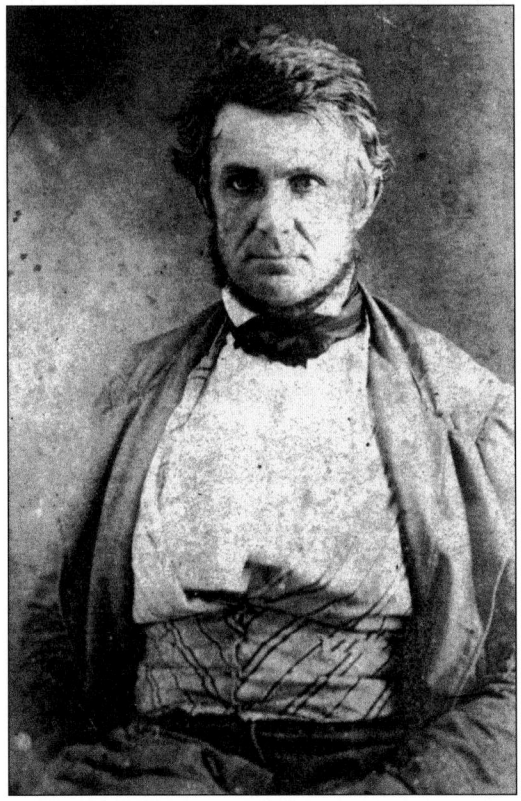

LUTHER GIFFORD. Luther Gifford, a first cousin of Sidney Brooks, became a noted architect. Gifford designed Pine Grove Seminary and oversaw its construction. He planned simple but elegant classical lines for the building.

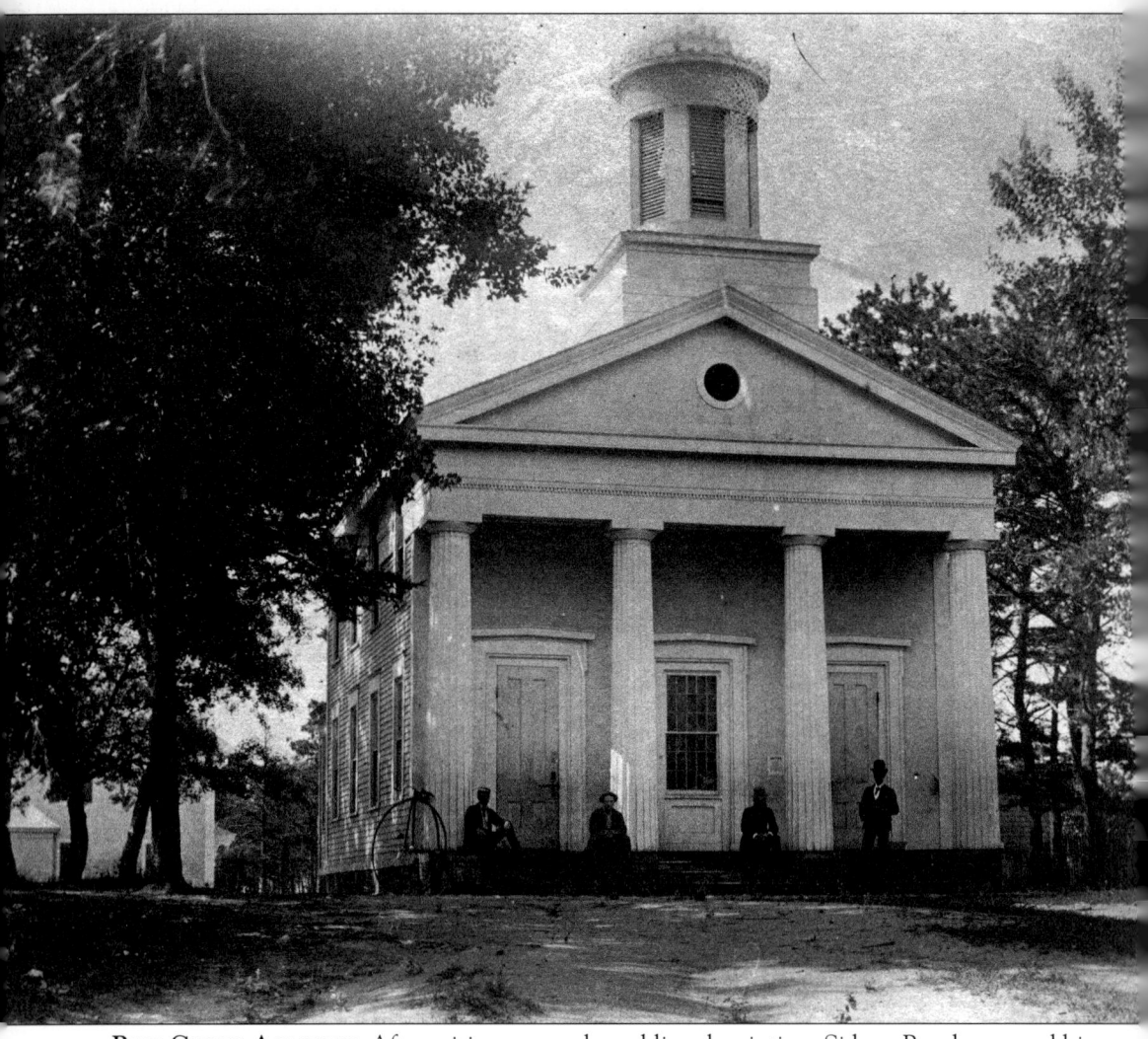

PINE GROVE ACADEMY. After raising money by public subscription, Sidney Brooks opened his school, which was situated on two acres of land and faced the Congregational church. The town purchased the building in 1880 for use as the first public high school. The building is now the home of the Harwich Historical Society and its museum.

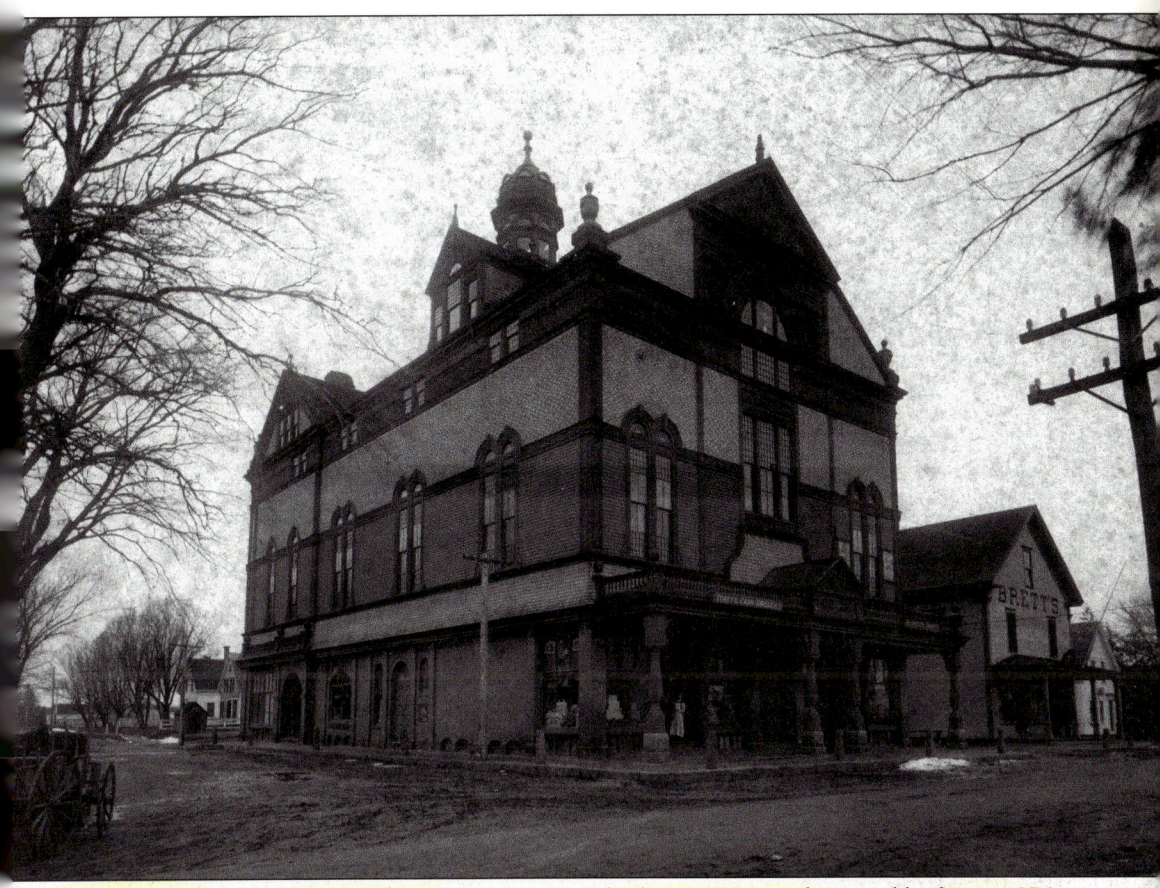

THE EXCHANGE BUILDING. This massive structure, built in 1855, was destroyed by fire in 1876 and was rebuilt on an even grander scale in 1884–1885. It was the largest building on Cape Cod for many decades and served as a beacon for ships at sea.

CHESTER SNOW (1816–1896). This likeness was taken by famed photographer Matthew Brady. Snow, who was orphaned at age nine, moved to New York and made a fortune in a forerunner company of Western Union. He returned to Harwich and was instrumental in bringing the first telegraph lines the length of the Cape and the railroad as far as Orleans. The Exchange Building was his dream to unite the entire community.

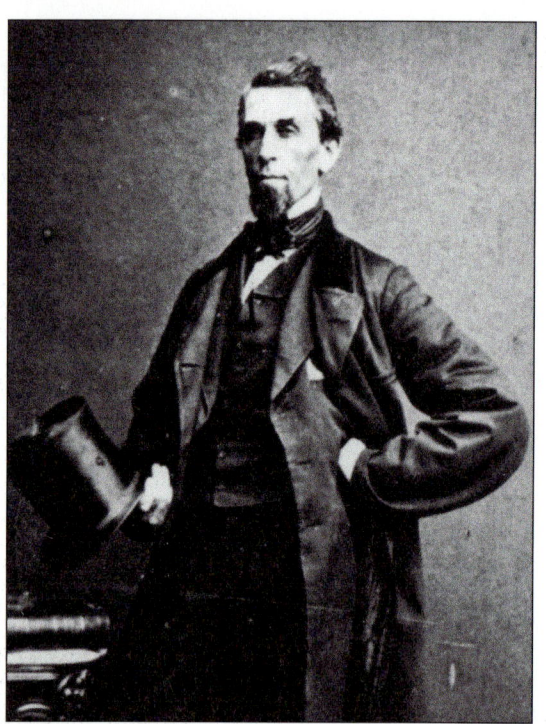

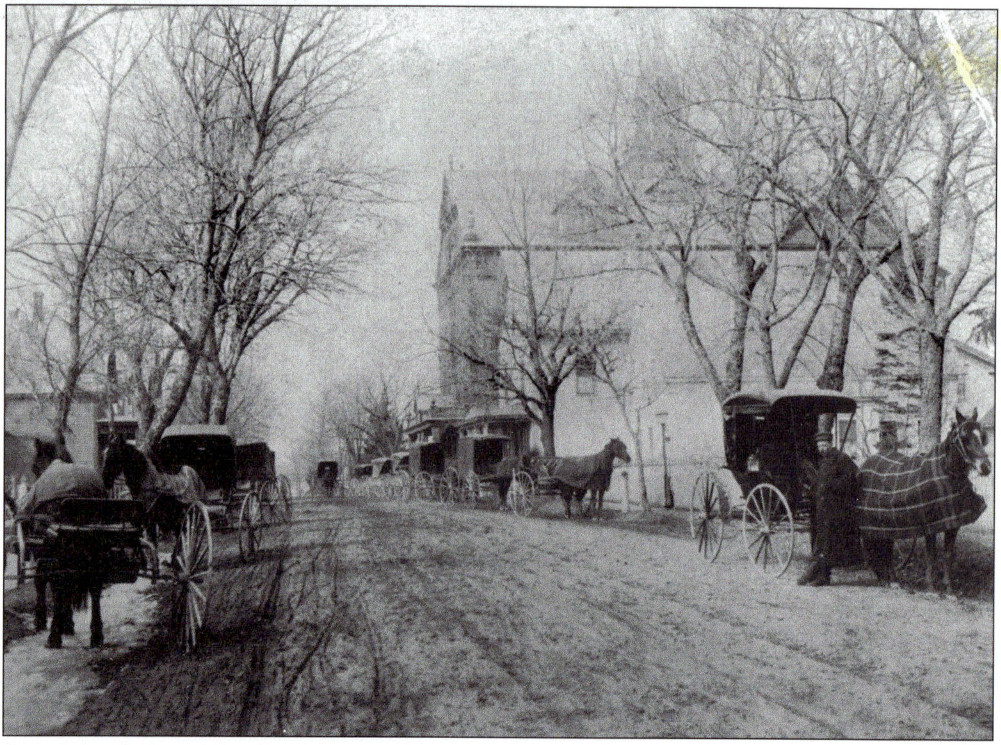

SHOPPING DAY AT THE EXCHANGE. The Exchange Building faced the Congregational church across Market Street. Its many shops provided for area customers. Later, fire wardens stood watch from the cupola and, during World War II, spotters searched for enemy planes.

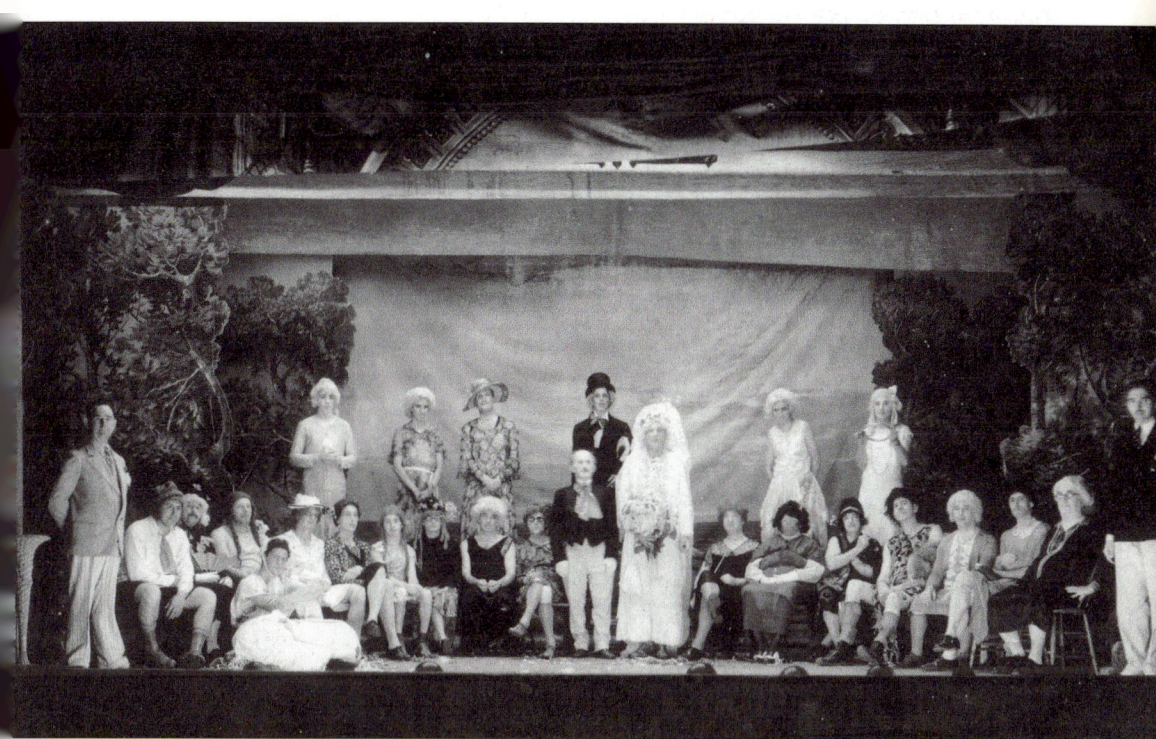

THE EXCHANGE BUILDING THEATRE. This splendid room, with a seating capacity of 1,200, had many uses. Besides providing a stage for theatricals, it held town meetings and conventions. Other amenities included a skating rink and a basketball court.

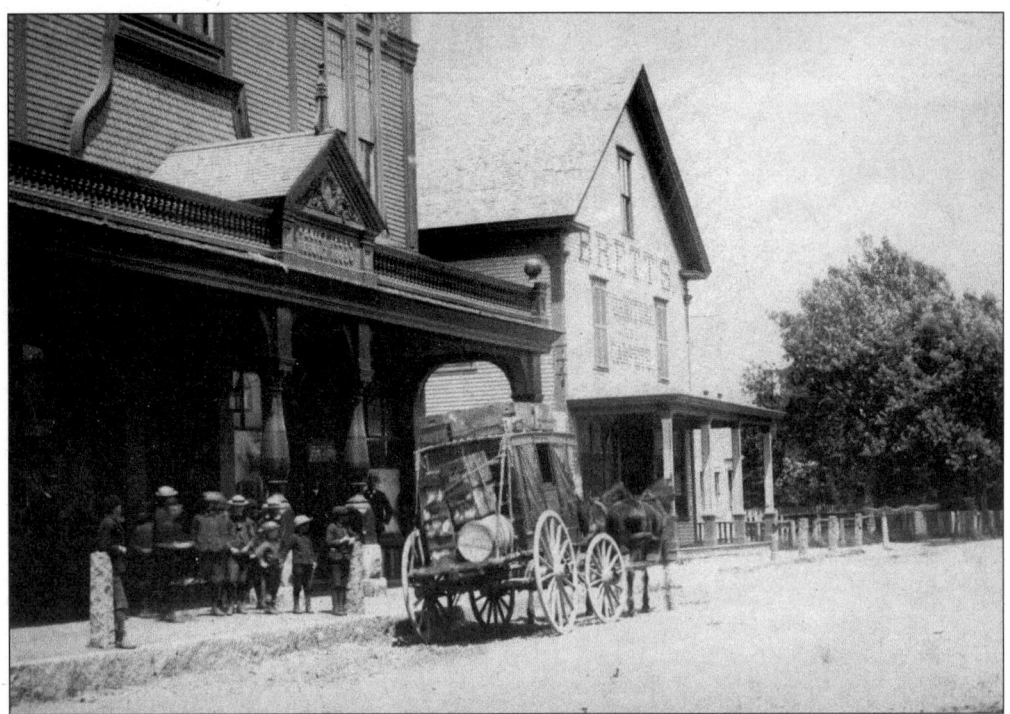

BARNEY TAYLOR'S STAGECOACH. Visitors to Harwich Center often relied on the services of one of the local stagecoaches, which departed from the front of the Exchange Building.

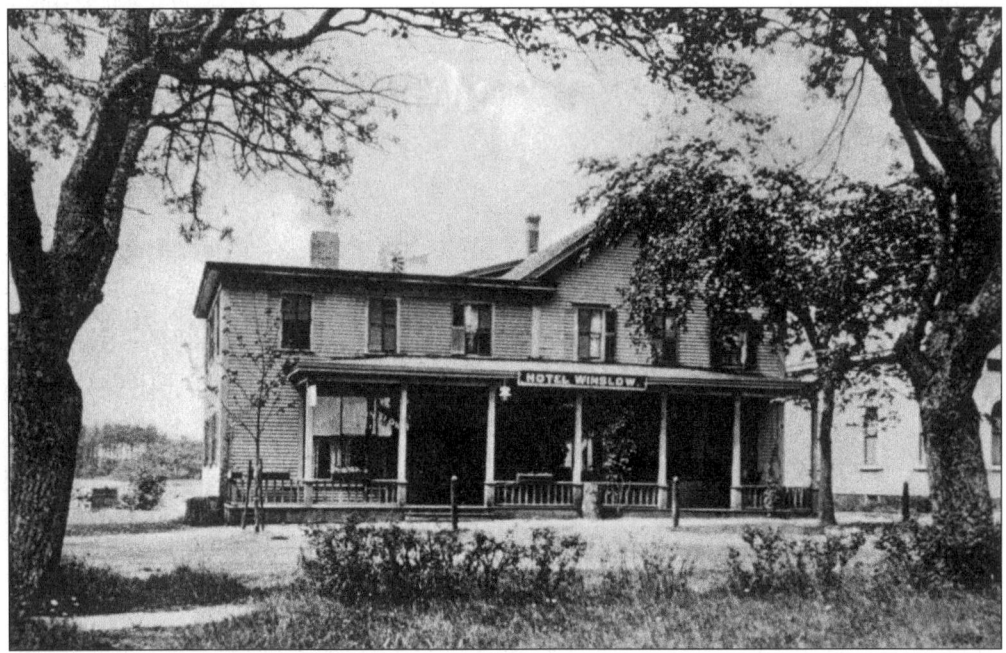

THE HOTEL WINSLOW AND THE FIVE CENTS SAVINGS BANK. The Winslow, which was Harwich Center's only hotel for many years, was only doors away from the Exchange. The first building of the Five Cents Savings Bank was just east of the hotel. Both were destroyed in the fire of 1912, which began in the Winslow and spread down the street.

HENRY COBB BROOKS (1824–1886).
Henry Cobb Brooks, the youngest son of Obed Brooks Sr., made a fortune in Boston in various enterprises, including his own shipping line to Australia. A confirmed bachelor and bon vivant, he planned to retire to Harwich.

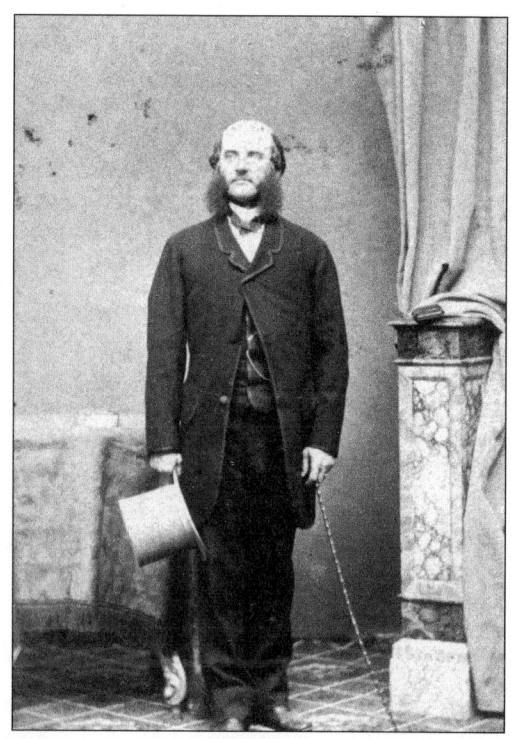

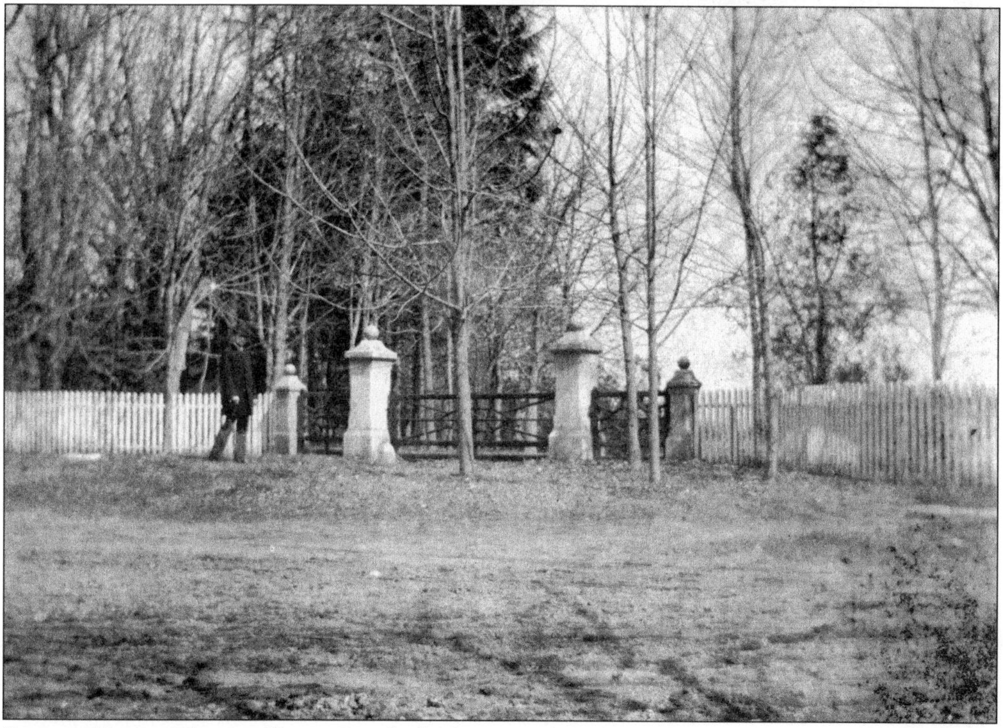

BROOKS PARK. The site Henry Brooks had prepared for his estate was carefully planted with a variety of species of trees. The land passed on to his relatives after his death. Through their generosity, it became a town park in 1908.

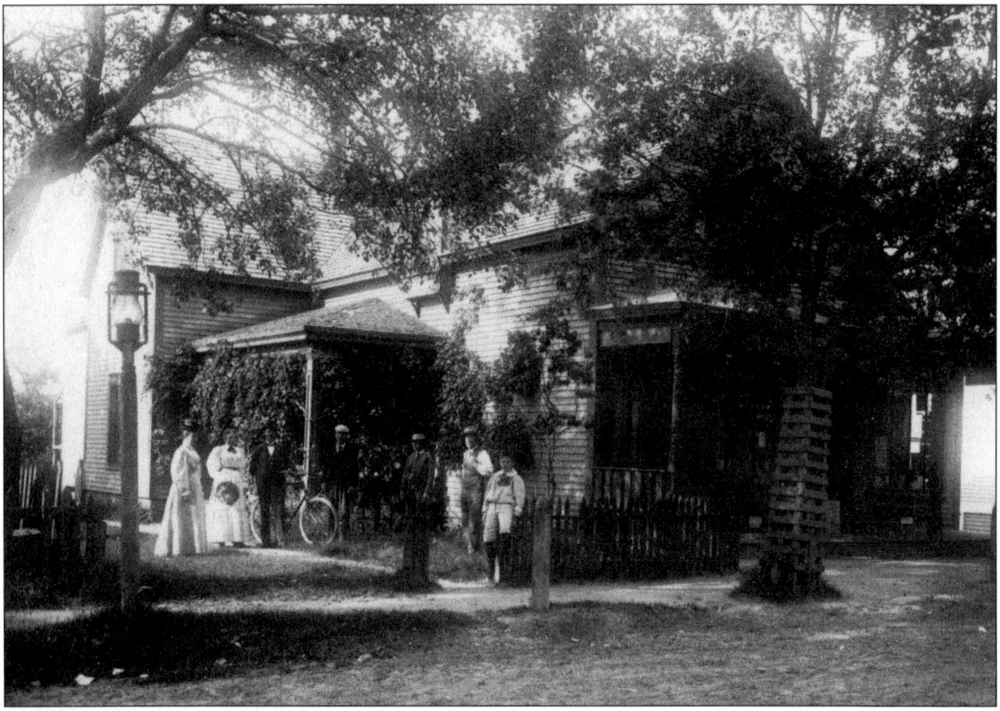

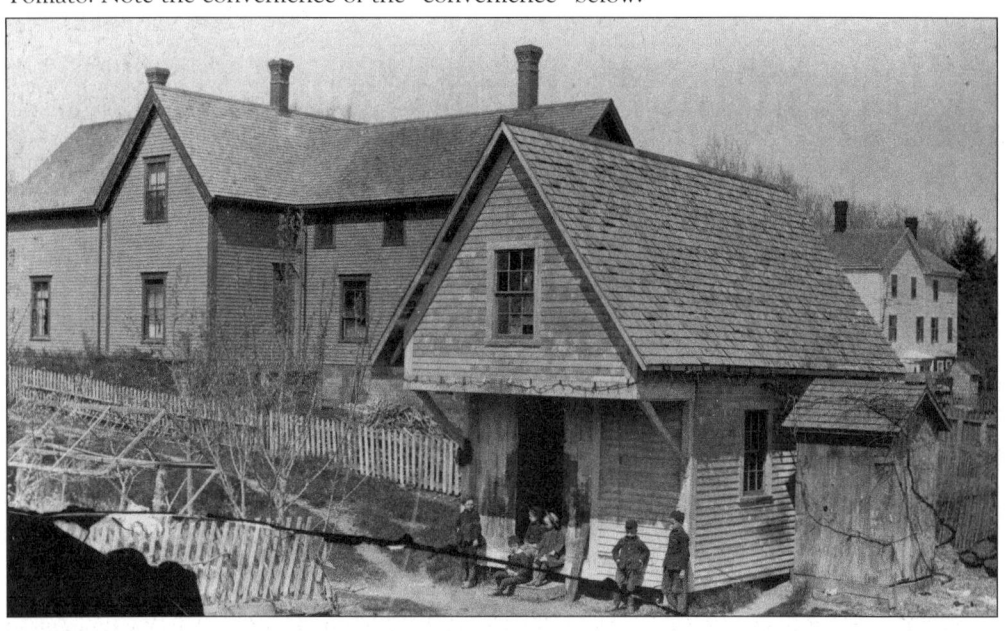

THE MOODY HOUSE. Samuel Moody, a respected blacksmith, raised his large family of 16 in this house facing on Harwich Center's Main Street, just to the east of what is now the Stewed Tomato. Note the convenience of the "convenience" below.

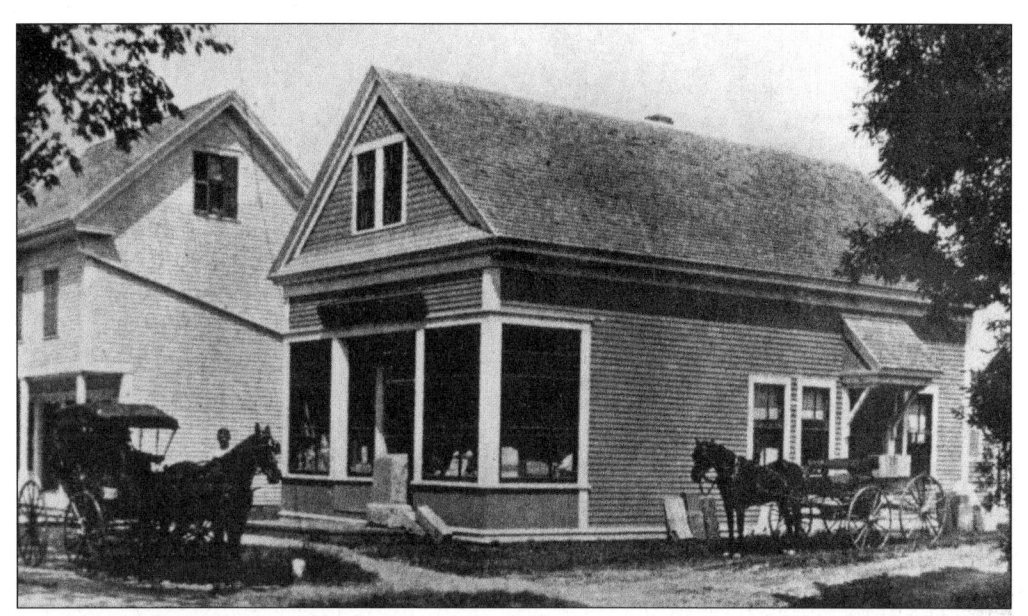

CROSBY'S MONUMENTS. This shop was originally constructed in 1865 for Jonathan Buck's boot-making business. In 1873, it was purchased by Henry T. Crosby for use as his stone monument business and his residence.

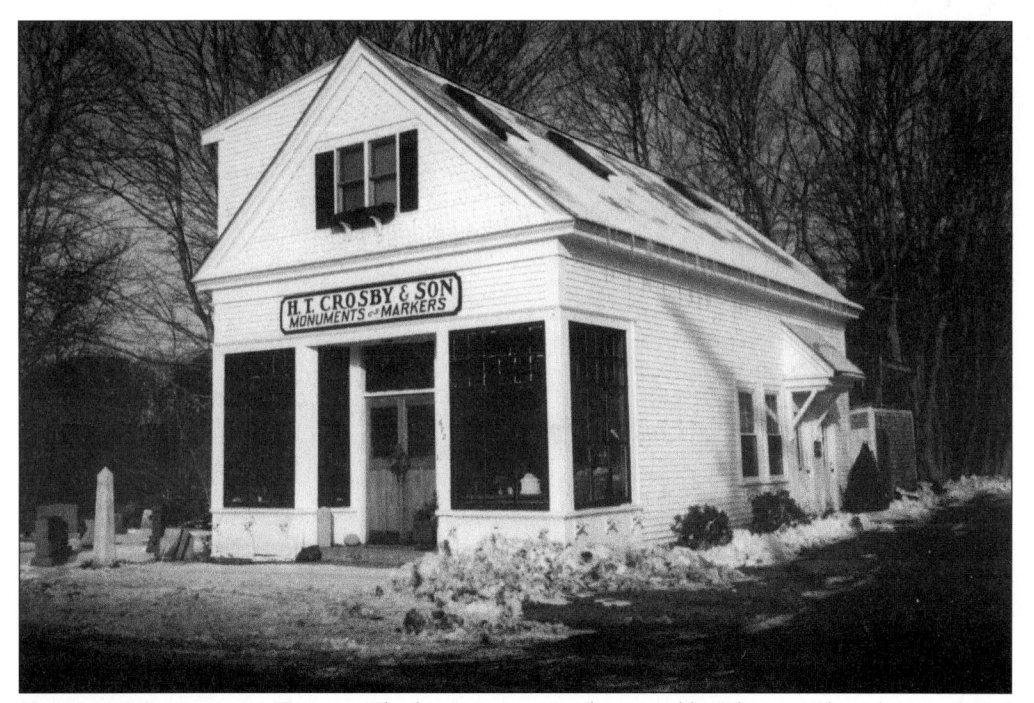

CROSBY'S MONUMENTS TODAY. The business, currently owned by Thomas Blute, has produced memorials for over a century and a quarter. (Sr. Aureen Rose Behrend.)

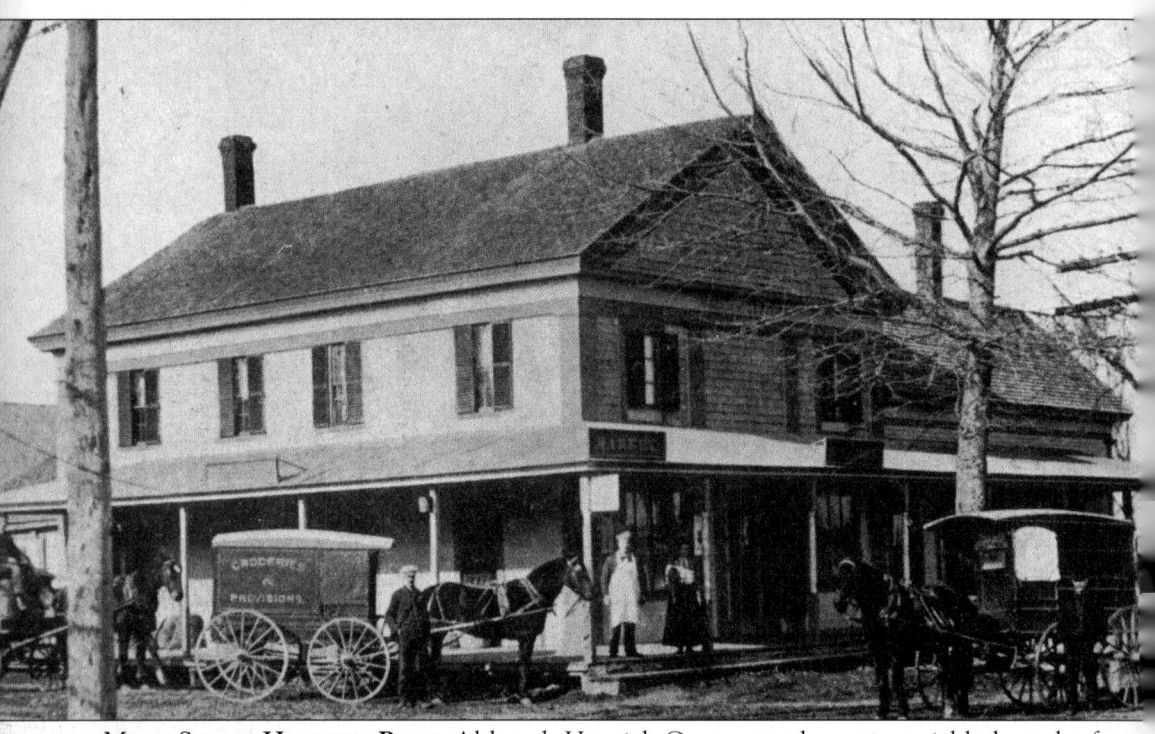

MILES STORE, HARWICH PORT. Although Harwich Center was the commercial hub, each of Harwich's villages maintained its own general store. Samuel Miles, like other owners, provided for public meetings on the second floor of his establishment.

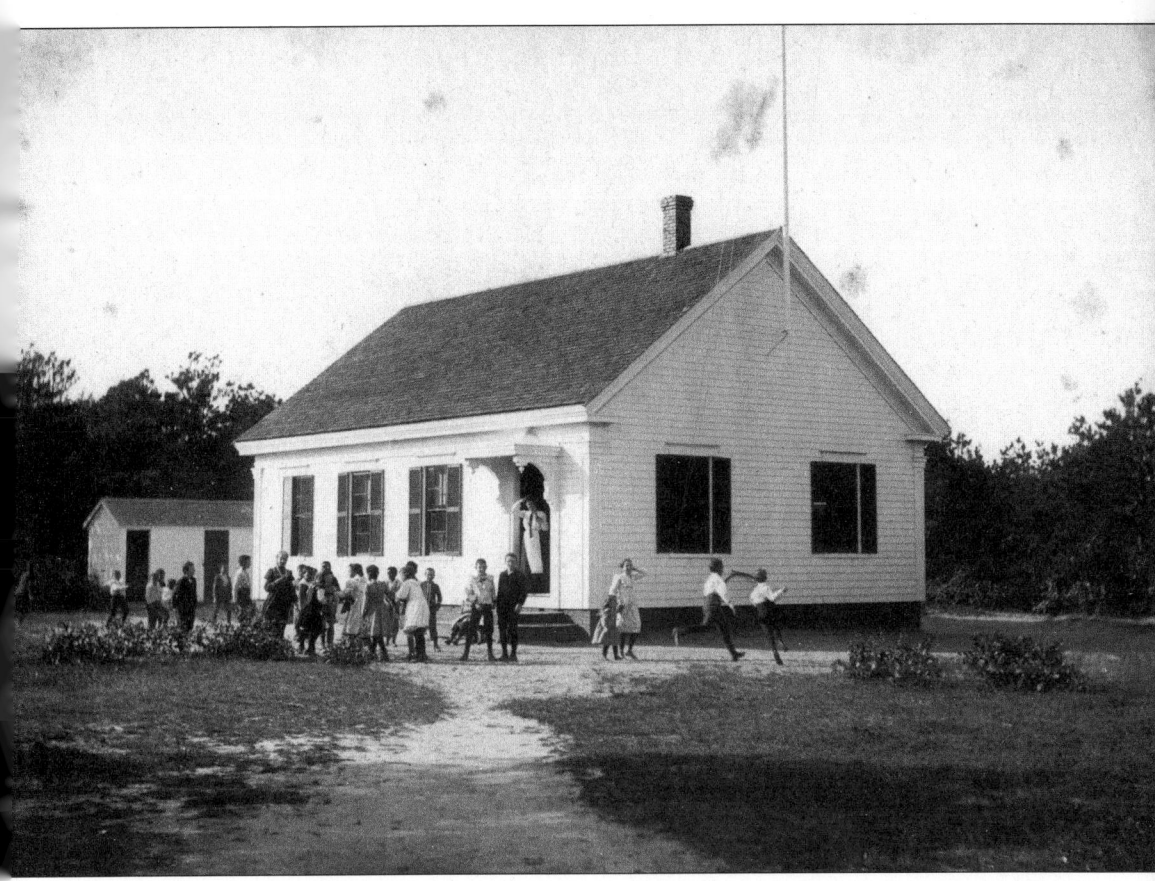

The Pleasant Lake Village School. Each of the seven villages—Harwich Center, Harwich Port, Pleasant Lake, North Harwich, South Harwich, East Harwich, and West Harwich—maintained its own elementary school.

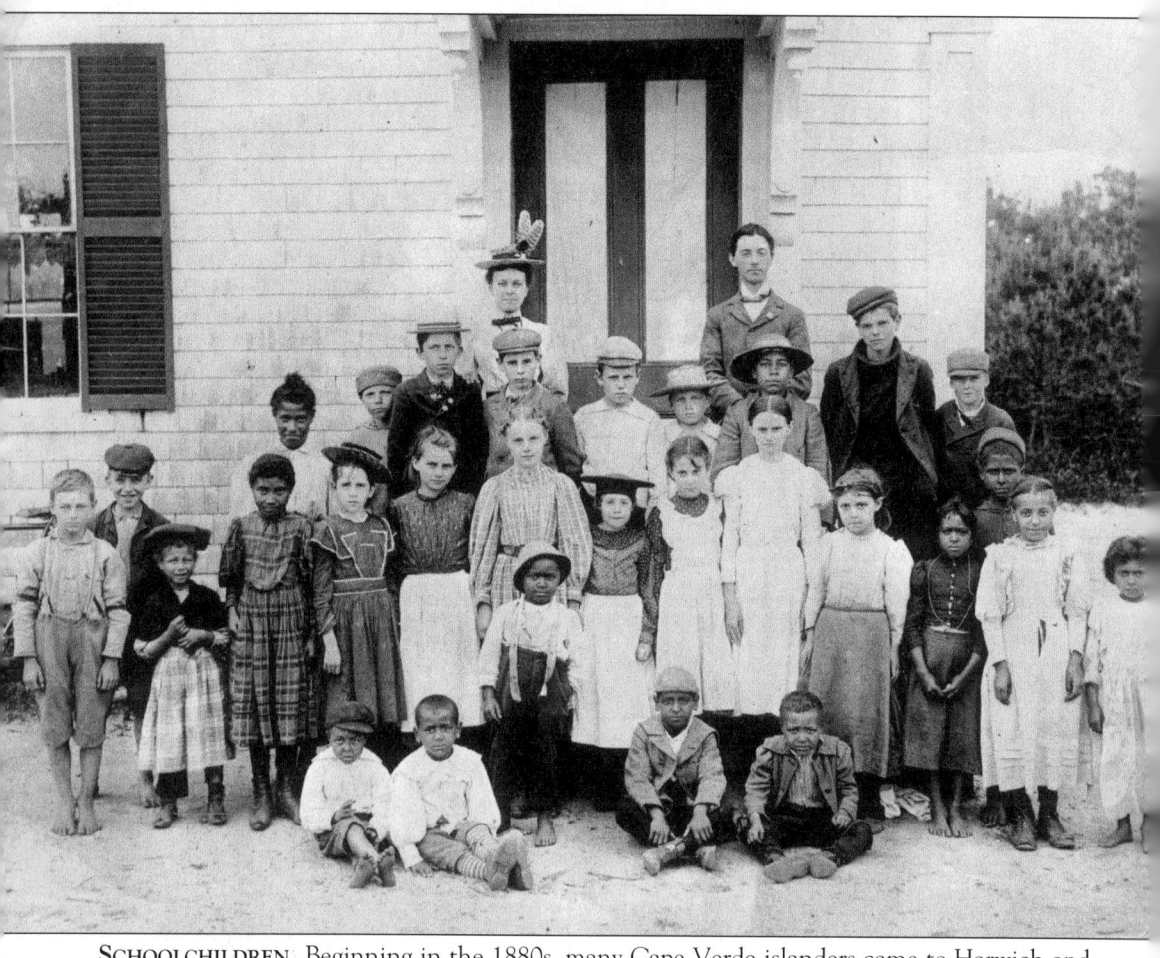

SCHOOLCHILDREN. Beginning in the 1880s, many Cape Verde islanders came to Harwich and found work in the bogs. An indication of the general poverty of the times is seen in the number of children sent to school without shoes.

HENRY C. BROOKS. As he made plans to retire, Henry C. Brooks erected the impressive Brooks Block next to the family homestead on Harwich Center's Main Street.

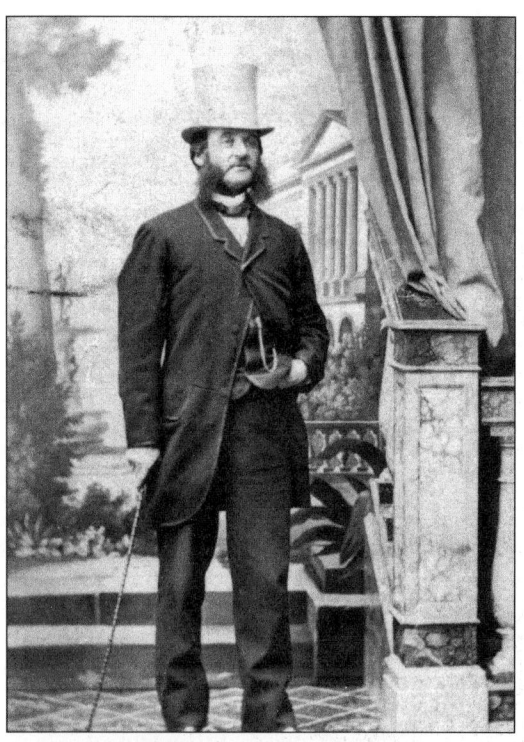

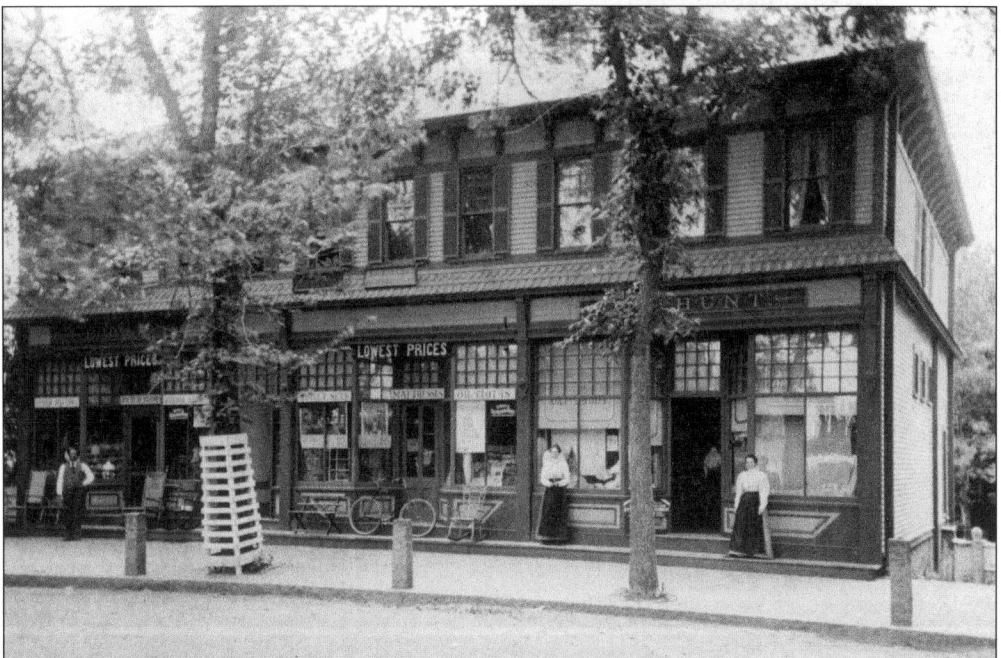

THE BROOKS BLOCK. Brooks used the rent from the first-floor shops to help establish Harwich's first free library, housed on the second floor. He donated his own extensive collection of books and willed the property to the town. For many years, the library was financed primarily by receipts from book fines and the dog licenses. The ladders surrounding the trees prevented damage from nibbling horses.

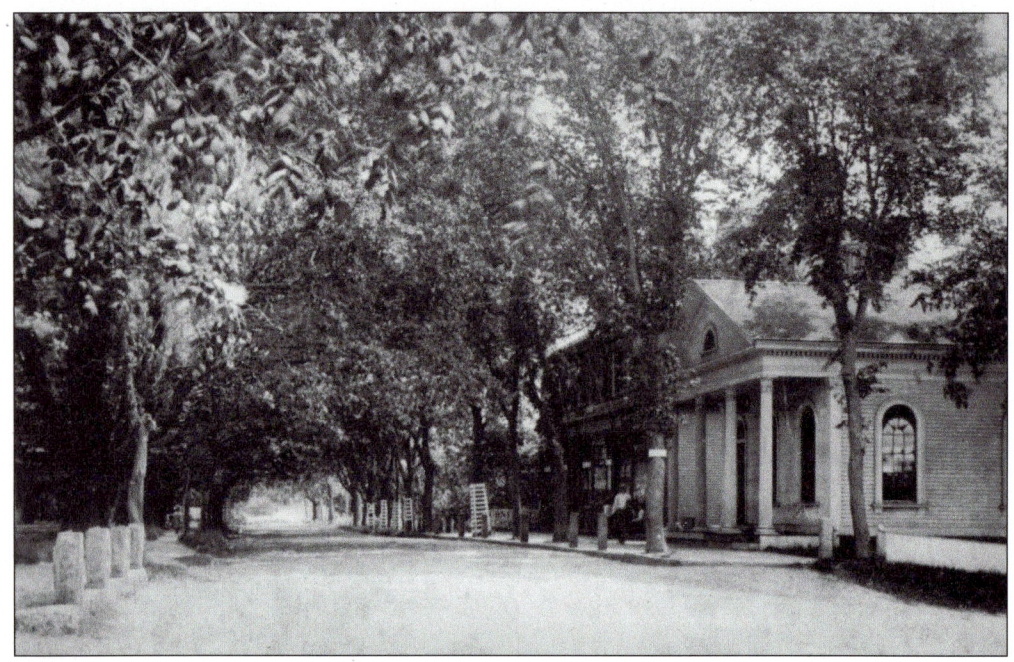

CAPE COD BANK. The building at the intersection of Harwich Center's Main and Banks Streets was erected in 1855. It was also used by the Five Cents Savings Bank for two decades. Later, it housed the town's first telephone exchange.

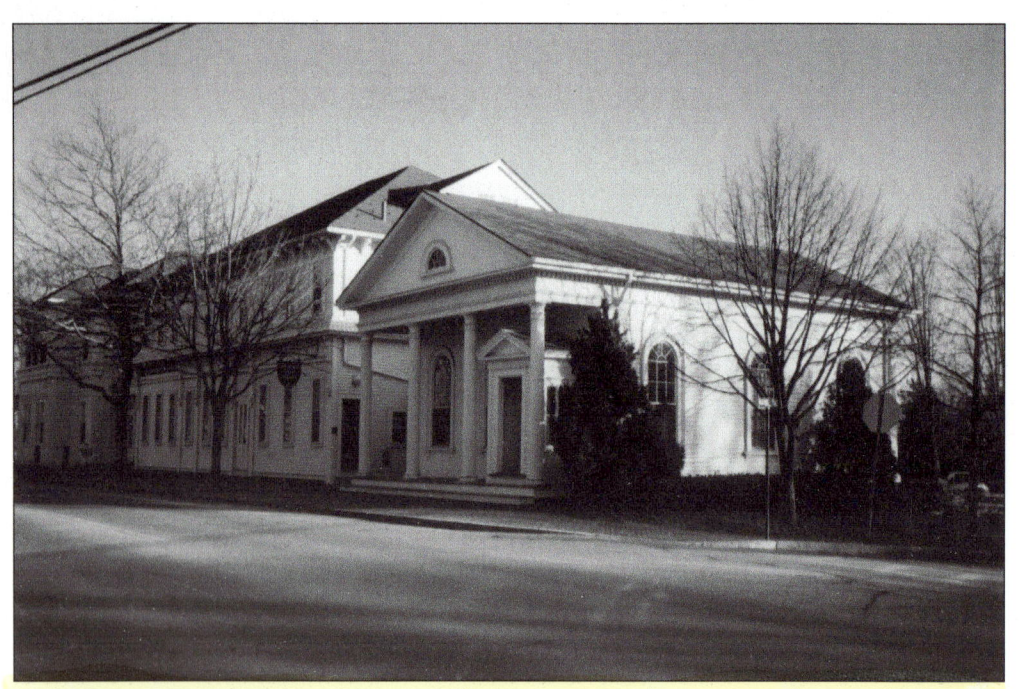

THE BROOKS FREE LIBRARY TODAY. Following an award-winning architectural plan, the original building was preserved and a large wing was added in the late 1990s. The old bank building, now joined to the library, is the children's reading room. (Sr. Aureen Rose Behrend.)

Two

SALVATION BY CRANBERRIES

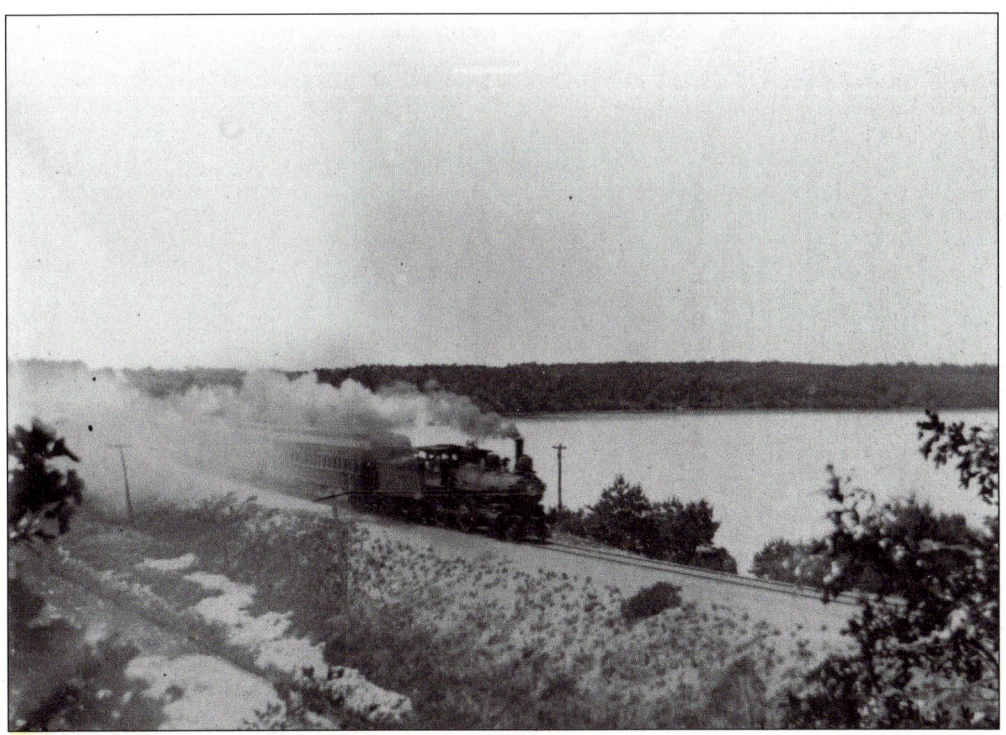

THE COMING OF THE RAILROAD. The beginning of train service from Barnstable to Orleans in 1865 (and later on to Provincetown) forever changed Harwich and other towns of the Lower Cape.

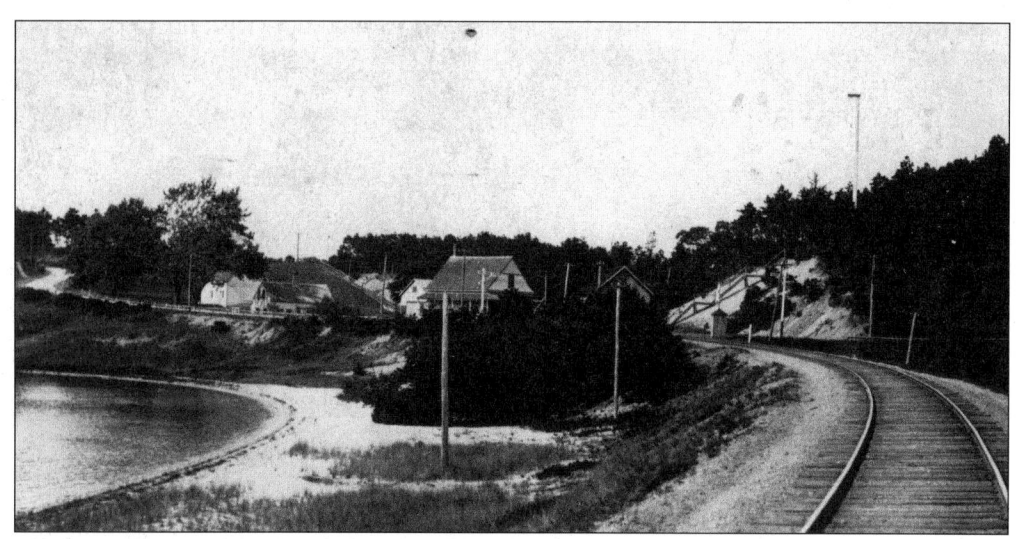

Pleasant Lake. The eastbound train passed along the shores of Hinkley's Pond. It stopped only upon signal from the country store, seen in the background. The store is still in operation.

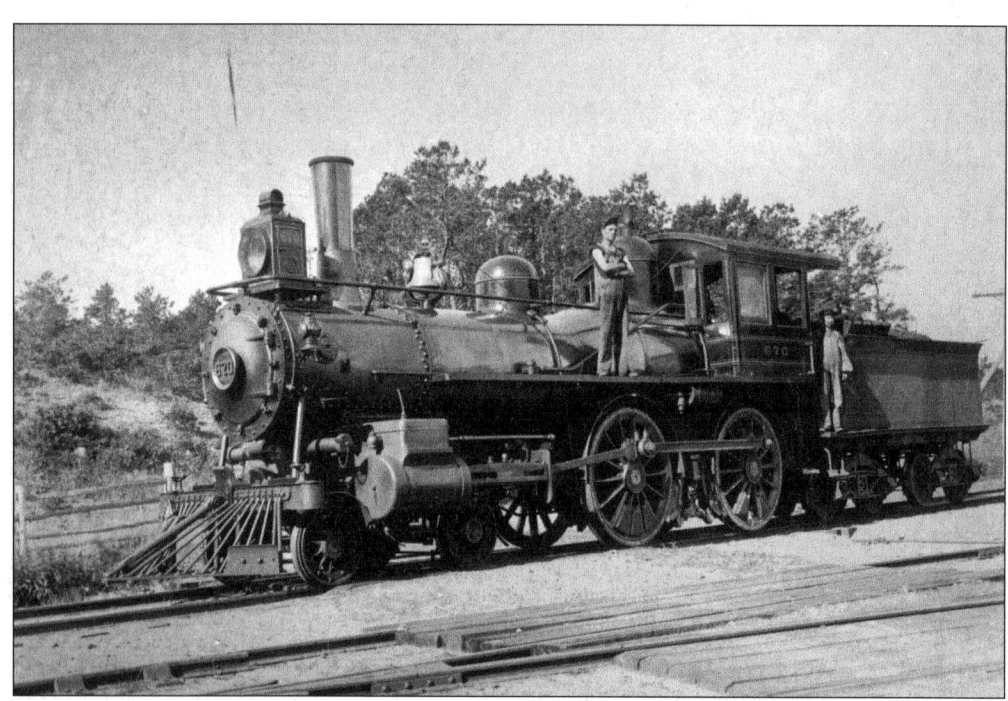

Arriving in Harwich Center. Since Chatham voters delayed approval of funding a spur line until 1887, stagecoaches did a brisk business carrying passengers from the Harwich depot to points east.

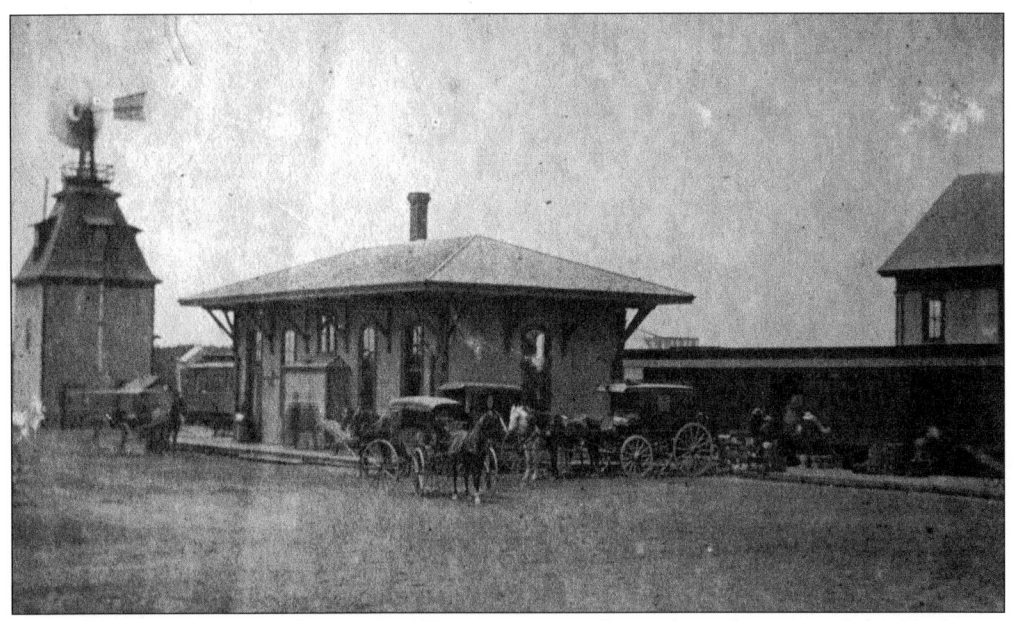

THE HARWICH CENTER STATION. The station was located to the rear of the Exchange Building. Two trains arrived in each direction daily.

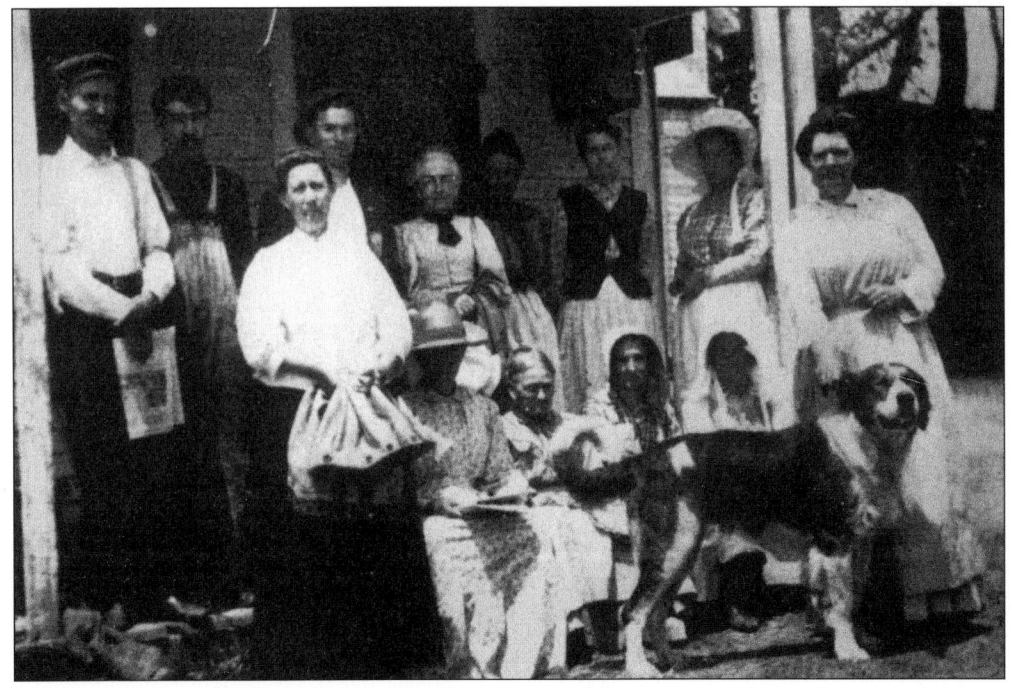

WAITING FOR THE TRAIN. The arrival of the Boston train was awaited eagerly by people, since it brought the mail and major newspapers.

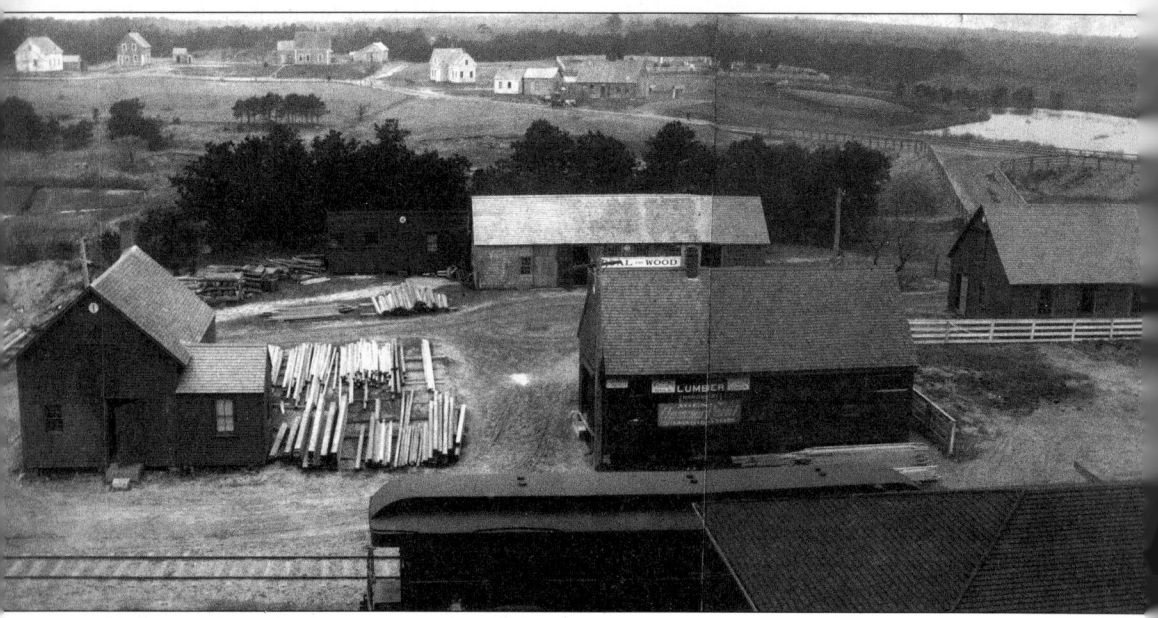

The North Harwich Depot. The construction of a large lumberyard in the shadow of the railway station illustrates how the packet ships had outlived their usefulness.

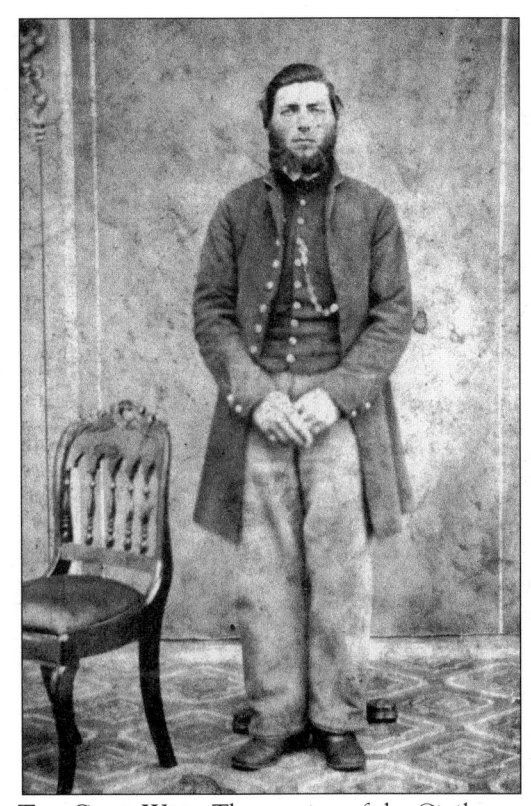

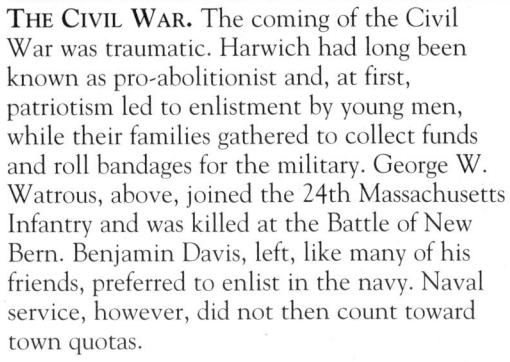

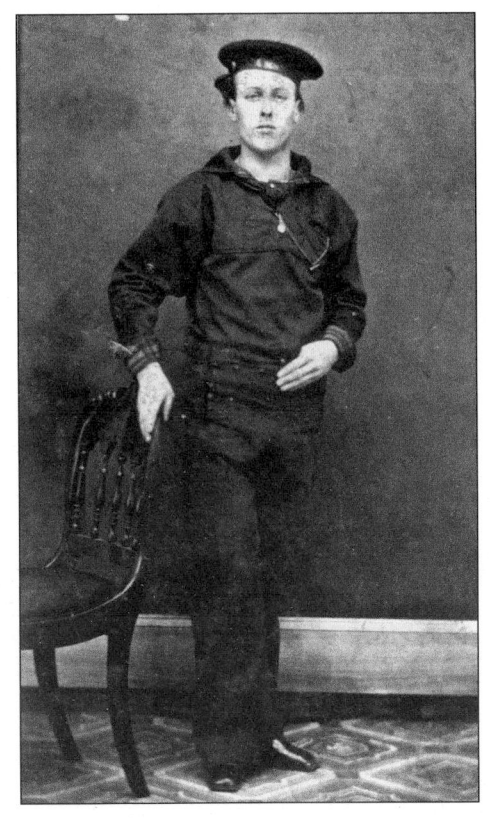

THE CIVIL WAR. The coming of the Civil War was traumatic. Harwich had long been known as pro-abolitionist and, at first, patriotism led to enlistment by young men, while their families gathered to collect funds and roll bandages for the military. George W. Watrous, above, joined the 24th Massachusetts Infantry and was killed at the Battle of New Bern. Benjamin Davis, left, like many of his friends, preferred to enlist in the navy. Naval service, however, did not then count toward town quotas.

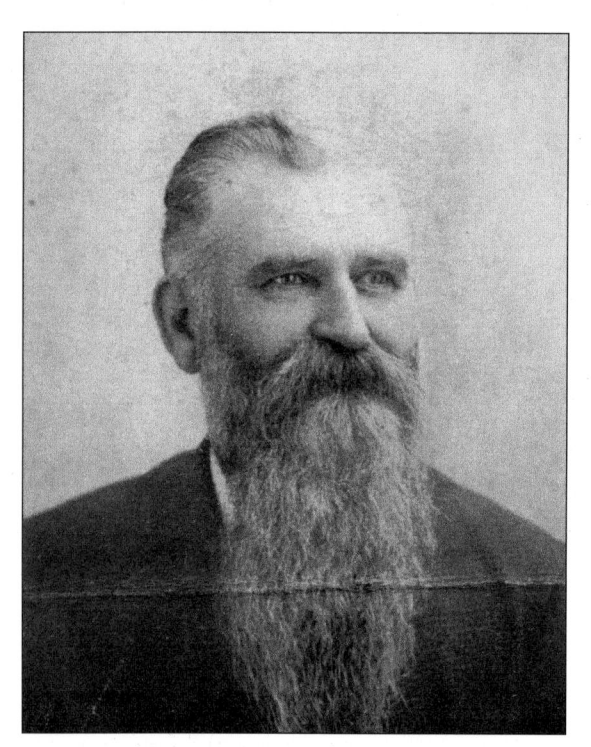

DR. GEORGE MUNSELL. Munsell left his Harwich Center practice to enlist in the army. He was soon wounded and sent home, but he retained his loyalties to the men with whom he had served. He was instrumental in establishing the Hammond Post of the Grand Army of the Republic.

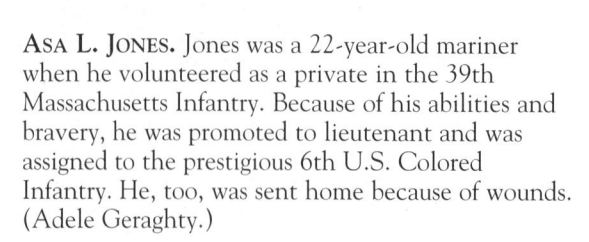

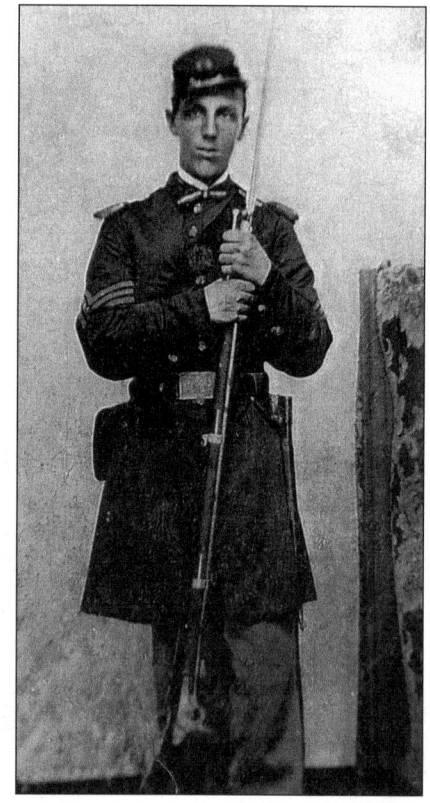

ASA L. JONES. Jones was a 22-year-old mariner when he volunteered as a private in the 39th Massachusetts Infantry. Because of his abilities and bravery, he was promoted to lieutenant and was assigned to the prestigious 6th U.S. Colored Infantry. He, too, was sent home because of wounds. (Adele Geraghty.)

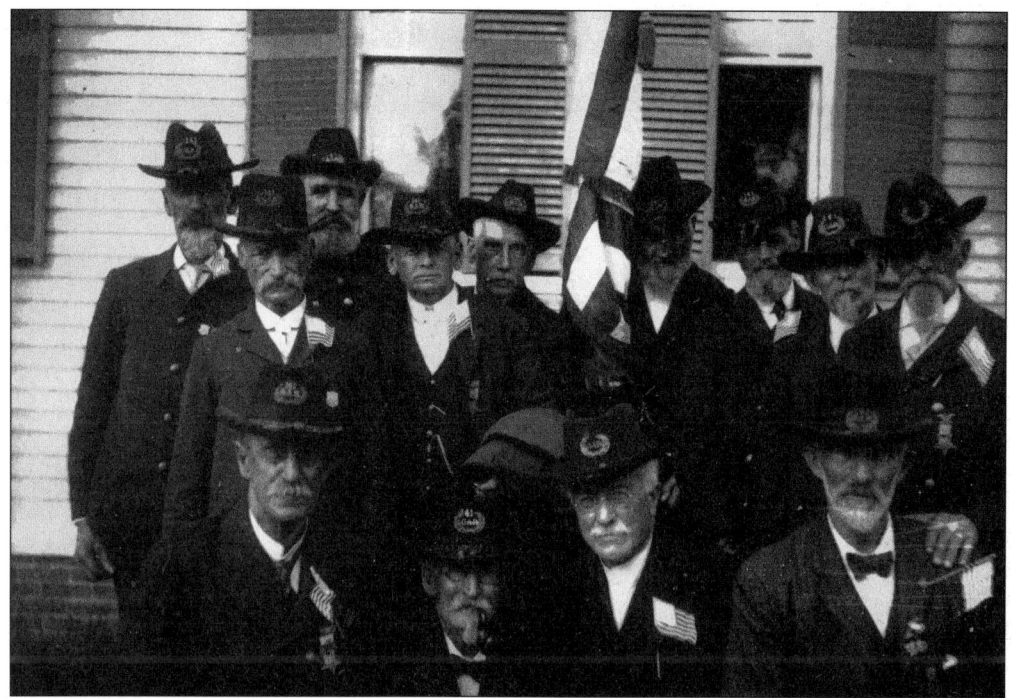

THE GRAND ARMY OF THE REPUBLIC REUNIONS. Harwich is credited with having supplied 341 men for the military. Had all been residents, this would mean nearly two-thirds of those of draft age served. Instead, voters agreed to provide money for substitutes to meet quotas. Although Harwich was fourth in population of the Cape's towns, it had the highest quota. This expenditure drained the town treasury and led to higher taxes. Consequently, feelings ran high between those who had served and those who had stayed home. Veterans gathered frequently at events such as the muster in Orleans in 1887. In World War I, a few elderly veterans, proudly in uniform, provided honor guards for those who died on the battlefields in France.

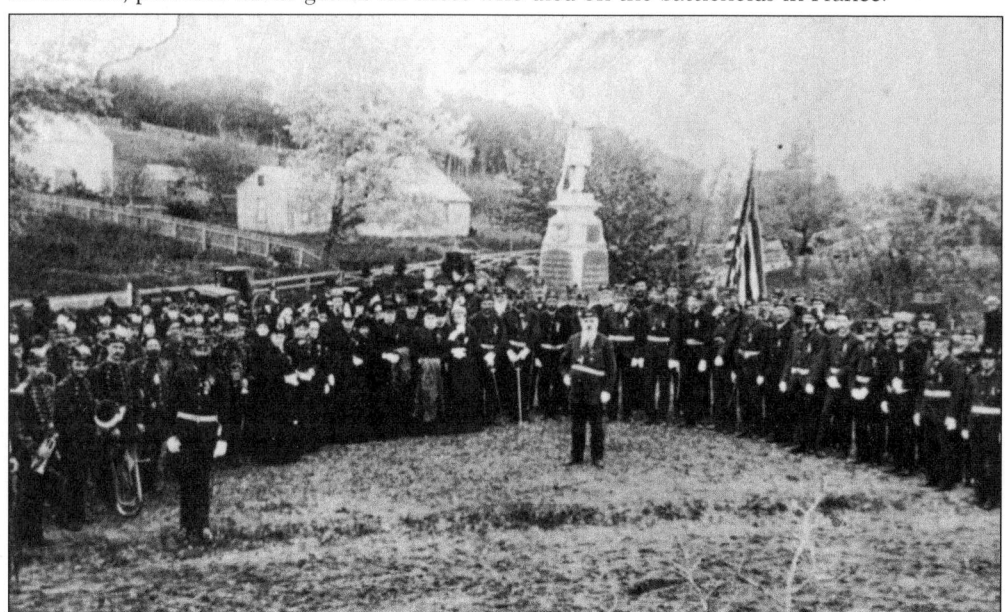

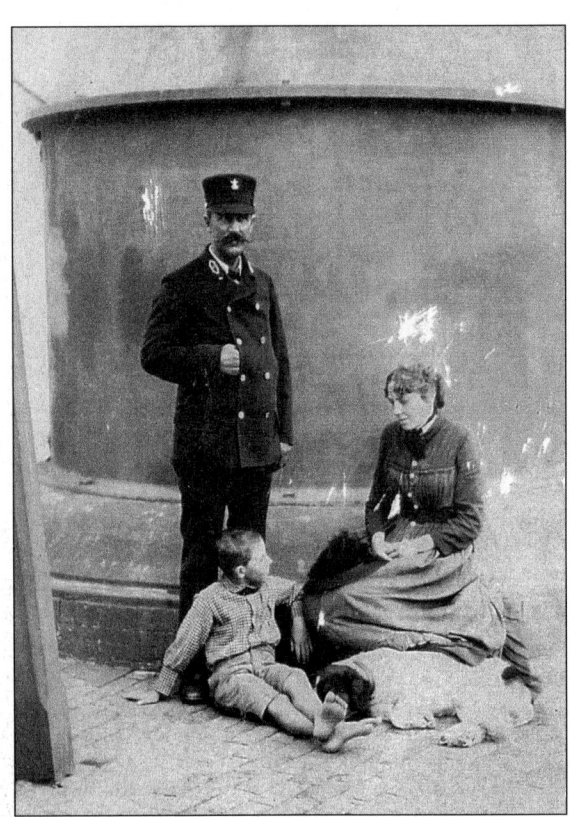

LIGHTHOUSE KEEPER ASA JONES. Jones was one of the more fortunate veterans. He was first appointed as resident lighthouse tender at Monomoy Point in Chatham. Later, he built an impressive home on Harwich Center's Oak Street, from which he operated the town's undertaking establishment. (Adele Geraghty.)

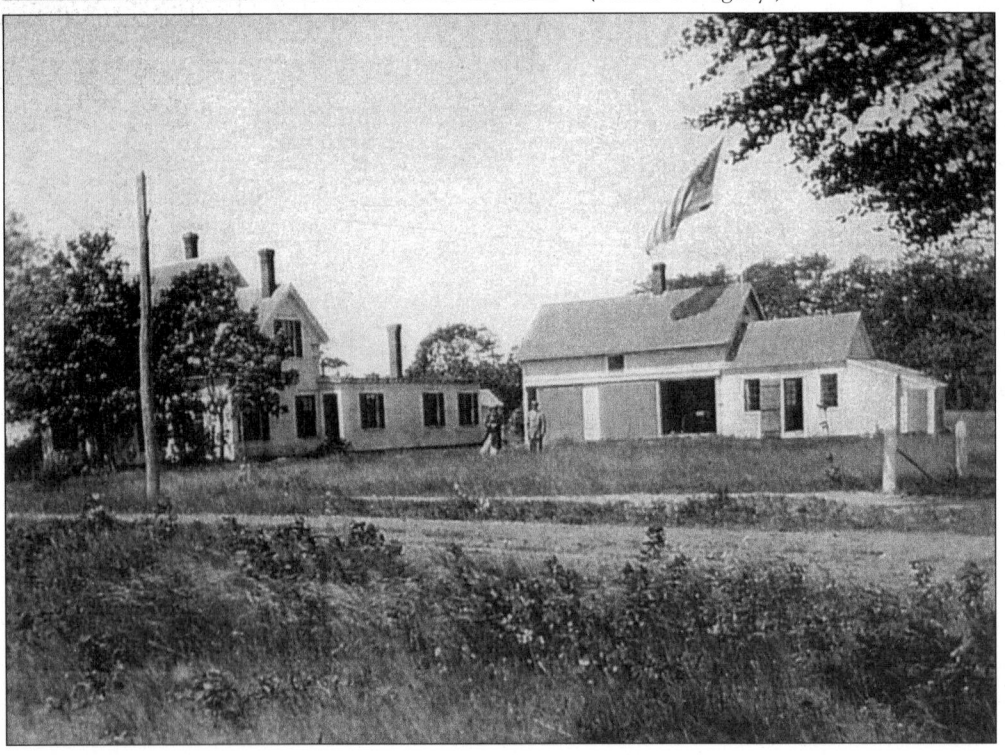

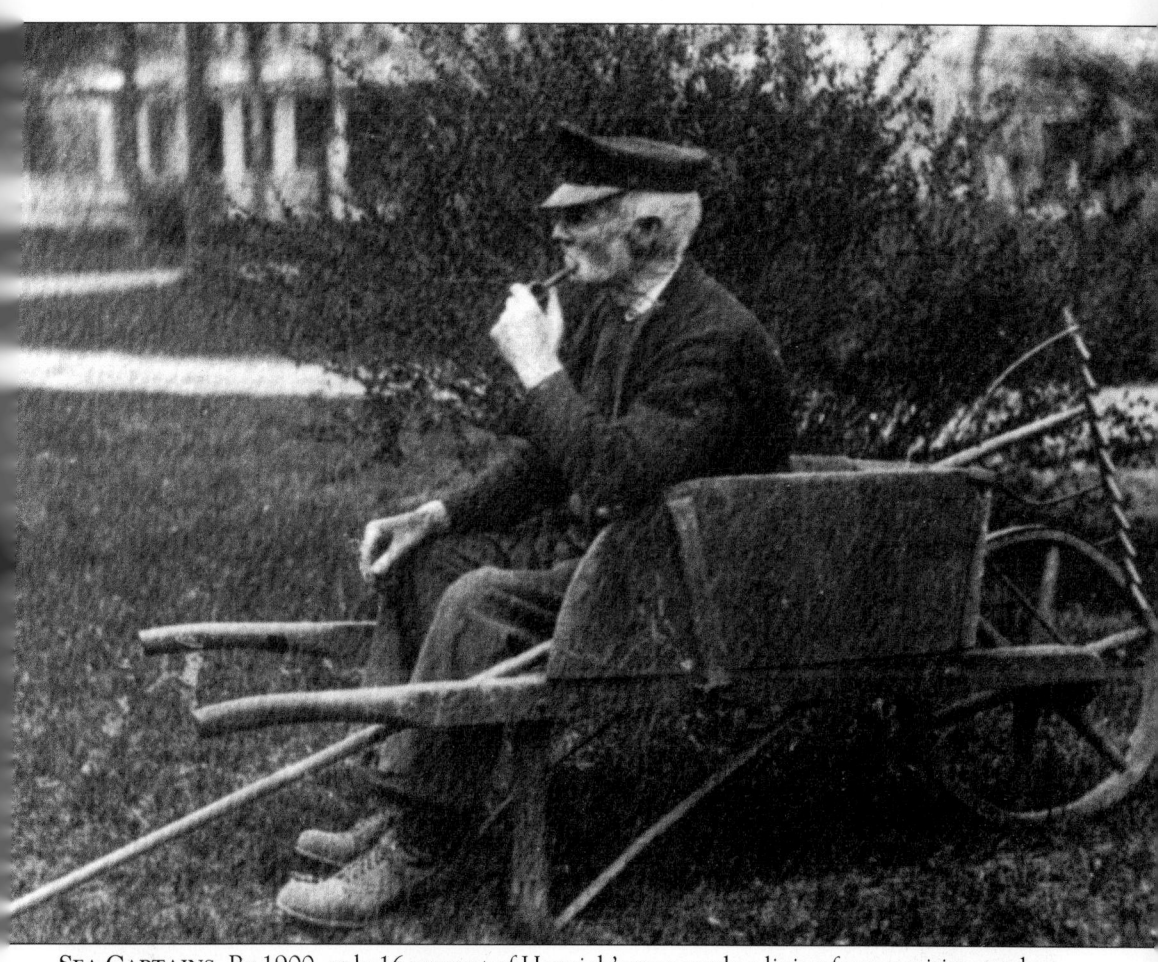

SEA CAPTAINS. By 1900, only 16 percent of Harwich's men made a living from maritime trades. In 1860, the town's 136 captains had been powerful and highly respected. By 1900, however, only 14 captains lingered on, some reduced to commanding tugboats. A retired captain might well muse about loss of his profession.

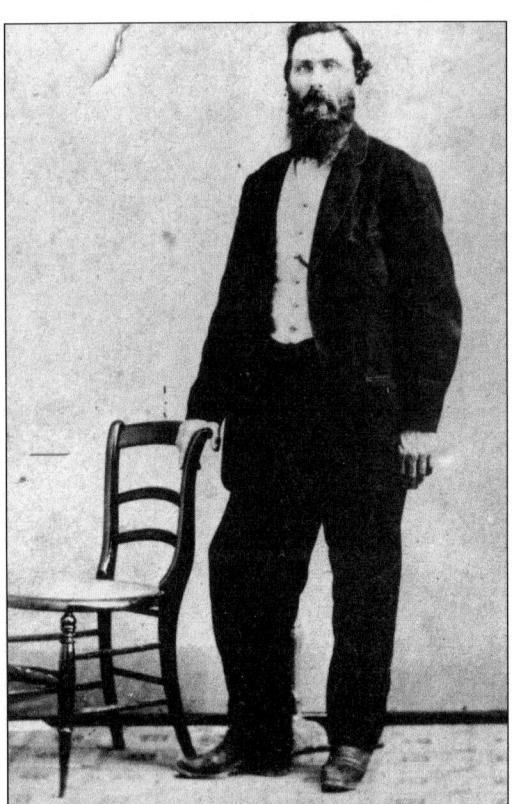

Capt. David Phillips. Command of a ship was often dangerous. A native of West Harwich, David Phillips died of yellow fever while sailing to the West Indies.

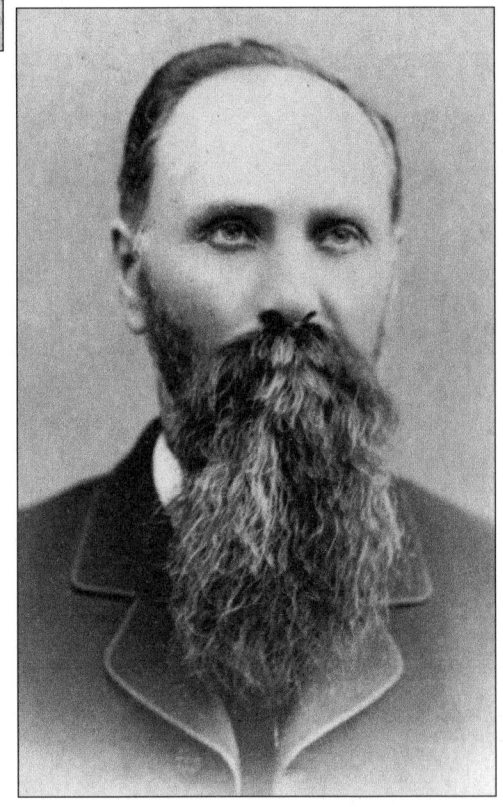

Capt. Theophilus B. Baker Sr. Theophilus B. Baker Sr. went to sea when he was 11 and remained a mariner for 36 years, many of them in command of his own ship. He later invested well in several enterprises, including sales of coal, lumber, and fish.

THEOPHILUS B. BAKER JR. Theophilus B. Baker Jr. eschewed seafaring and, with the help of his father's resources, became a highly successful cranberry grower.

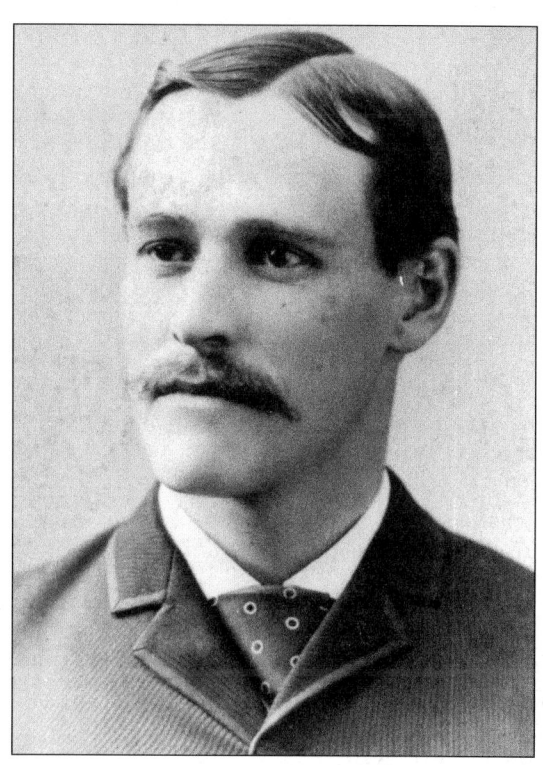

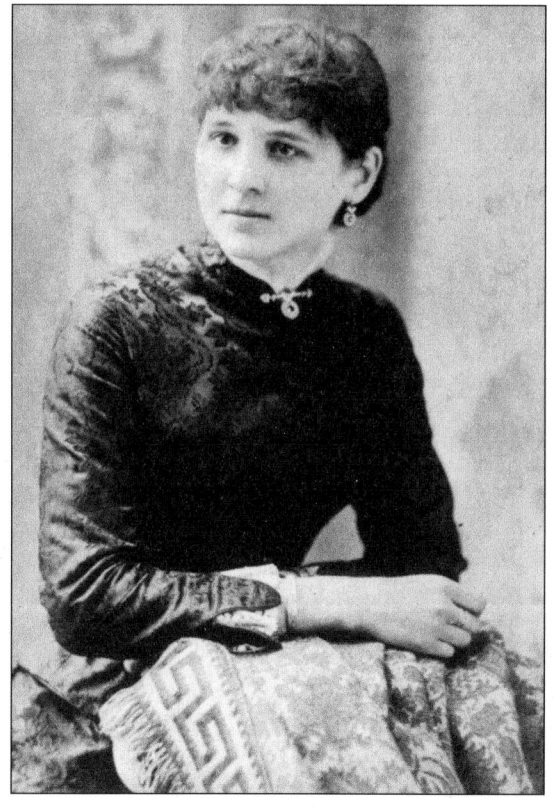

ANNIE PHILLIPS. Born in Dennis, Annie Phillips came to Harwich as the bride of Theophilus B. Baker Jr. She died shortly after giving birth to their child.

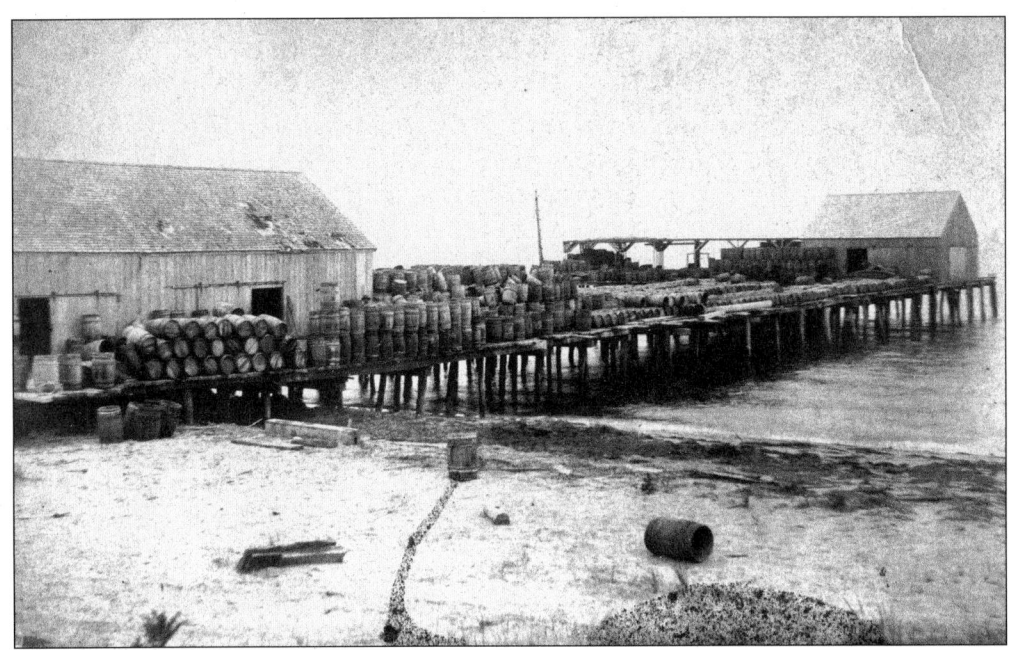

THE BANK STREET FISH MARKET. A few commercial fishing enterprises survived. This market was owned by Theophilus B. Baker Sr.

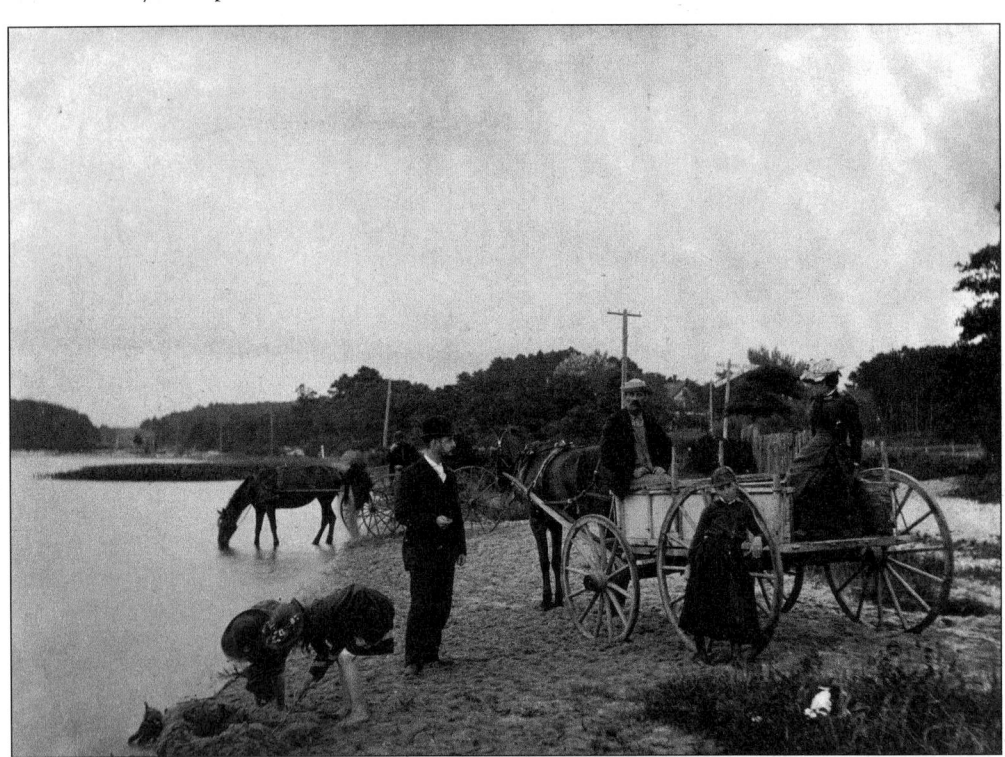

SPORTFISHING. As this scene of Bang's Pond (Seymour Pond) indicates, most men came to regard fishing as a recreation to be shared with family on a picnic rather than as a steady source of income.

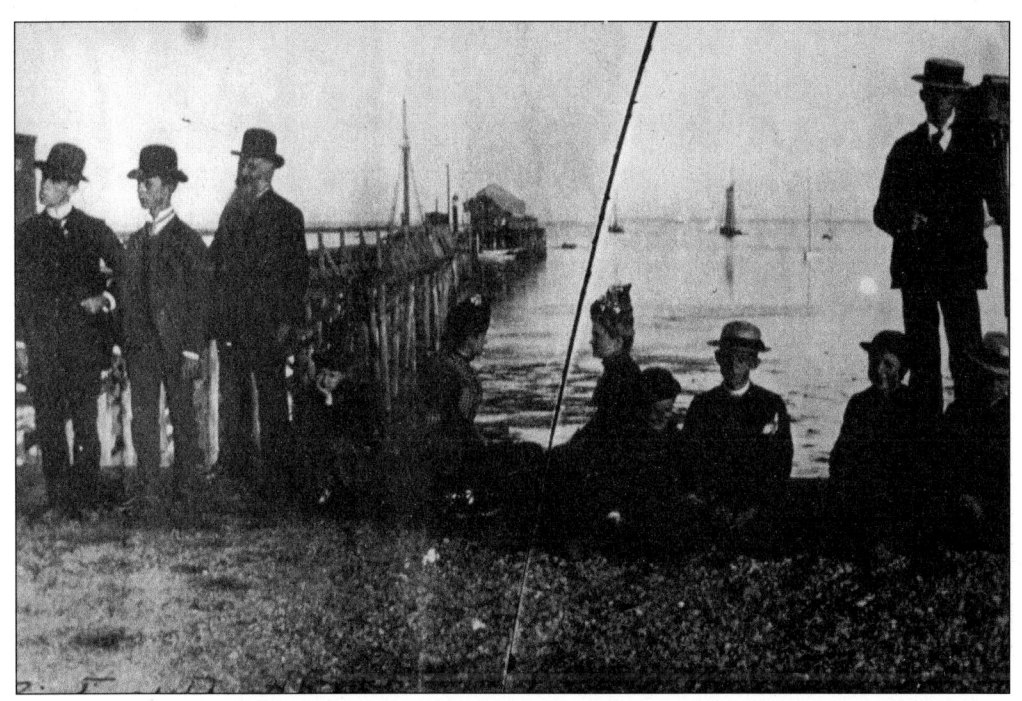

PICNICS BY THE SEA. The surviving wharves were largely abandoned and served merely as a backdrop for picnics. The third person from the left is Dr. George Munsell.

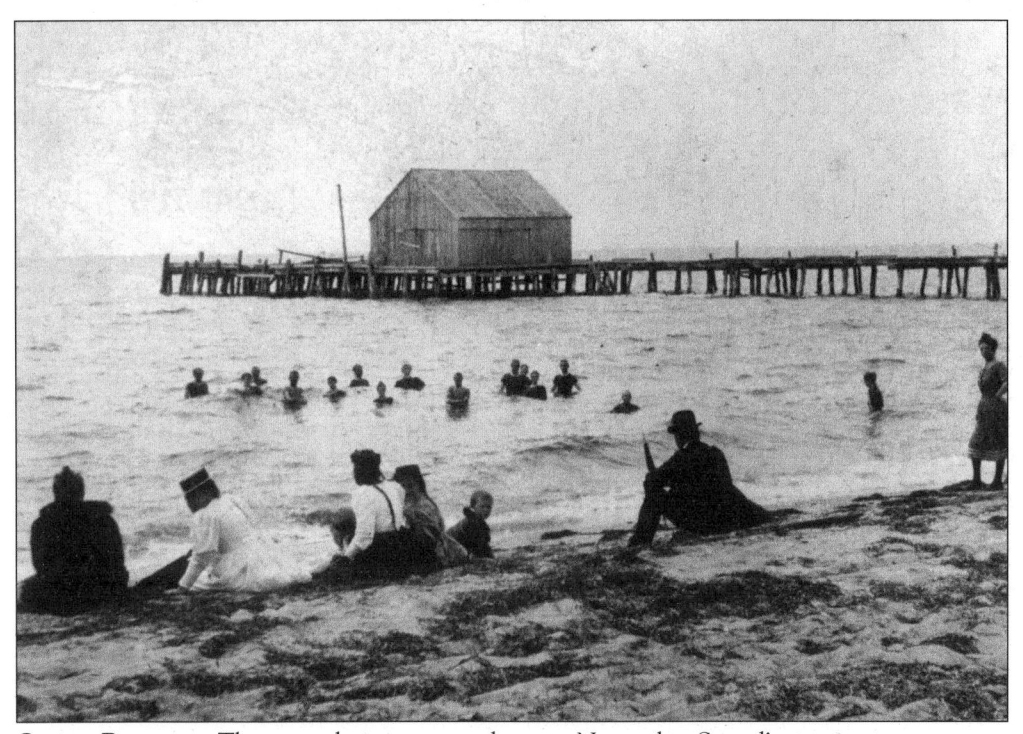

OCEAN BATHING. The more daring ventured to test Nantucket Sound's waters.

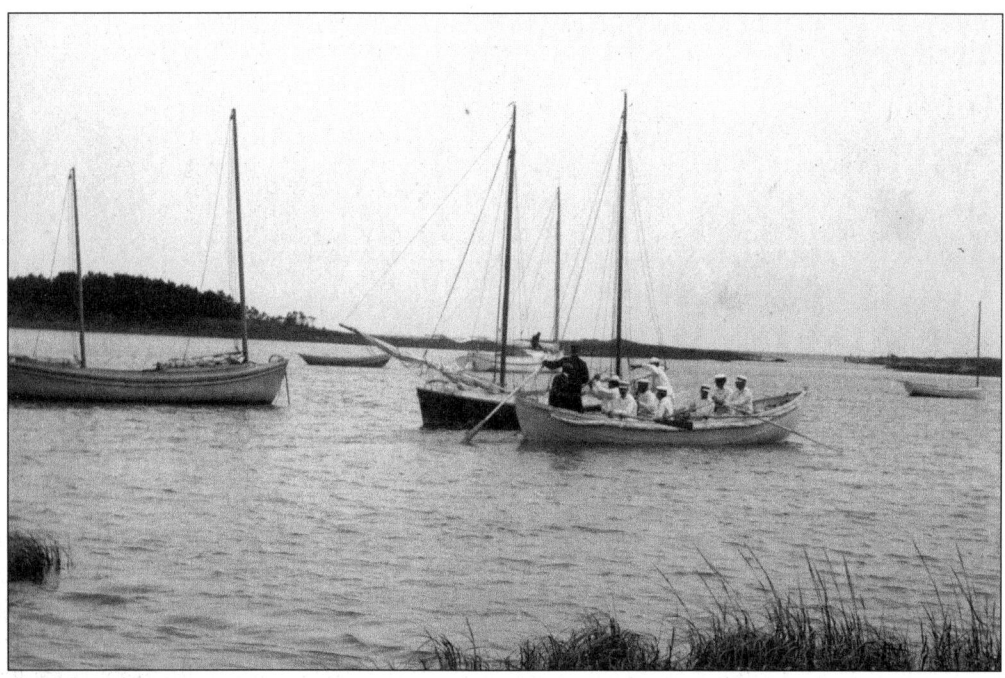

THE LIFESAVING SERVICE. The federal government established nine lifesaving stations for outer Cape Cod in 1872. These stations were absorbed into the U.S. Coast Guard in 1915. The purpose of the stations was primarily to conduct rescues. This crew is practicing in Wychmere Harbor to pick up sailors in distress.

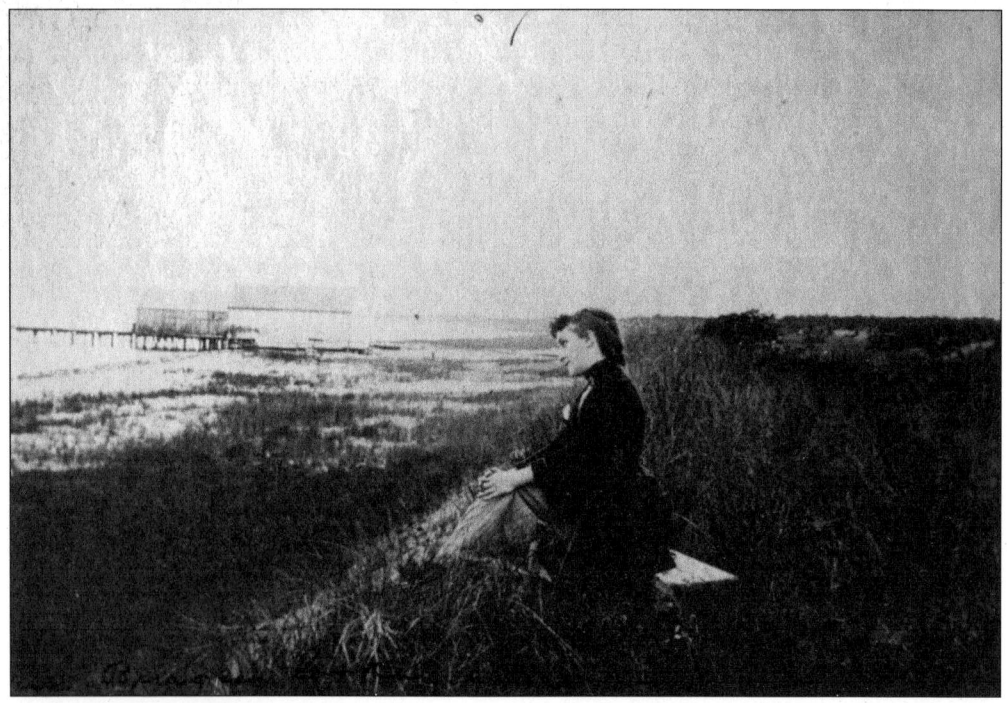

WAITING FOR A SHIP. In timeless fashion, women are often shown waiting by the shore for men to return from sea voyages.

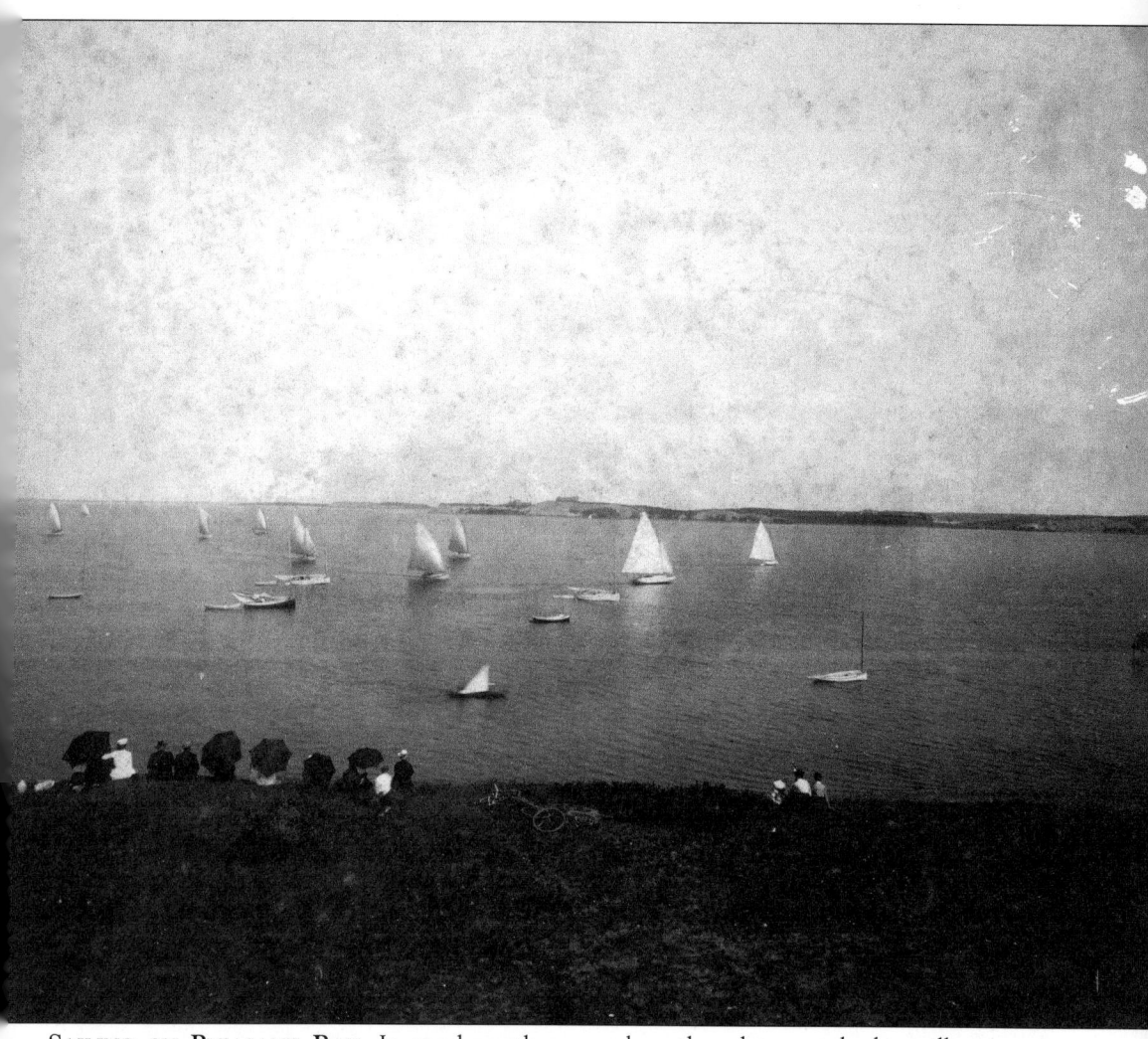

SAILING ON PLEASANT BAY. In good weather, people gathered to watch the sailboats on Pleasant Bay. Women sought the shelter of umbrellas to avoid acquiring a tan.

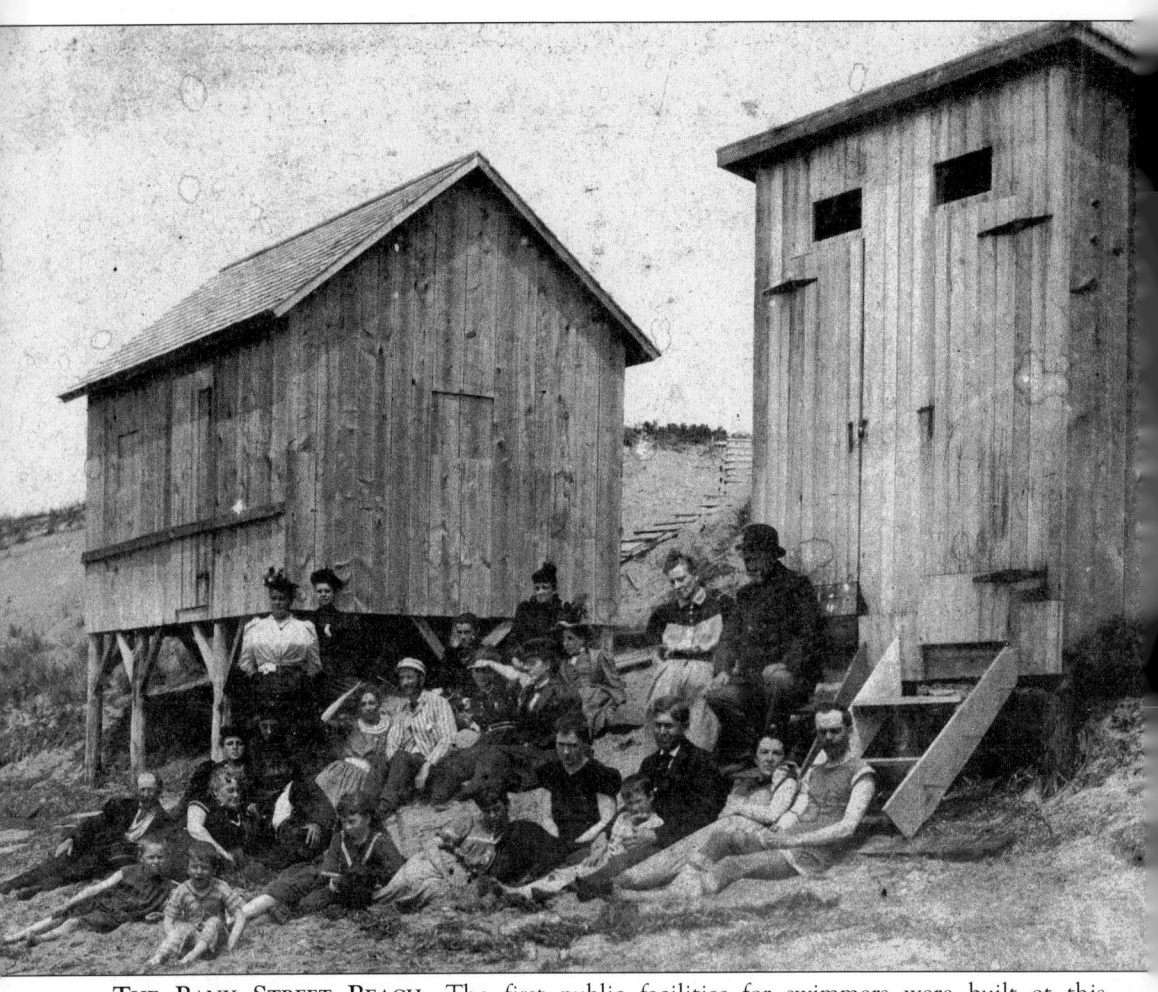

THE BANK STREET BEACH. The first public facilities for swimmers were built at this popular beach.

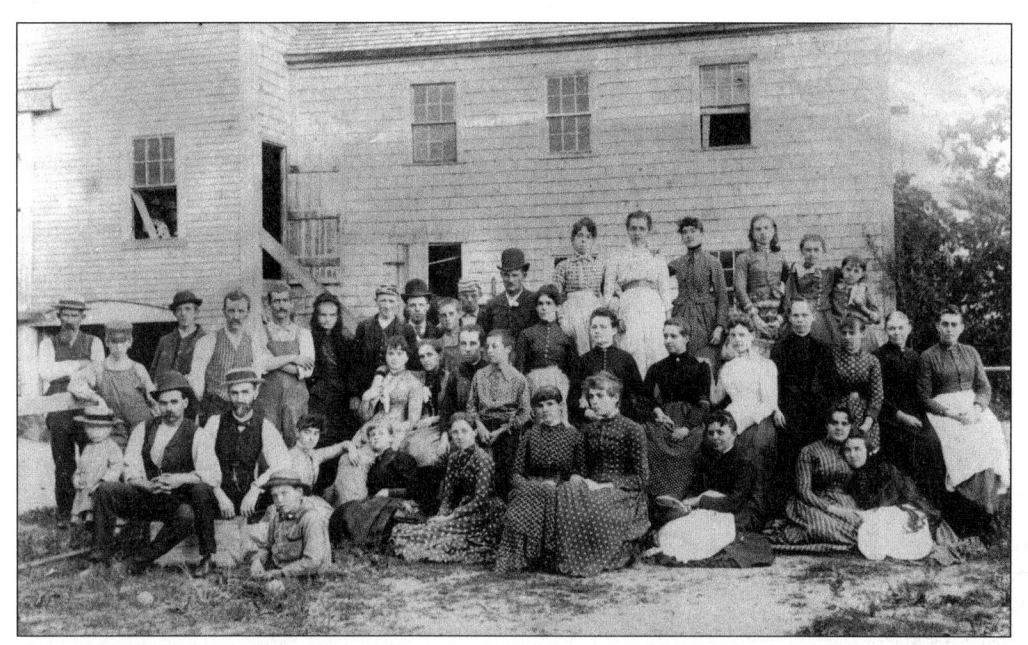

STOKES'S OVERALLS FACTORY. Hannah C. Stokes, a self-supporting widow, opened this factory in 1865 to produce overalls. The business was so successful that she expanded it to produce shirts. It was one of only a handful of industrial enterprises in town. Some 50 people were employed, many of them women.

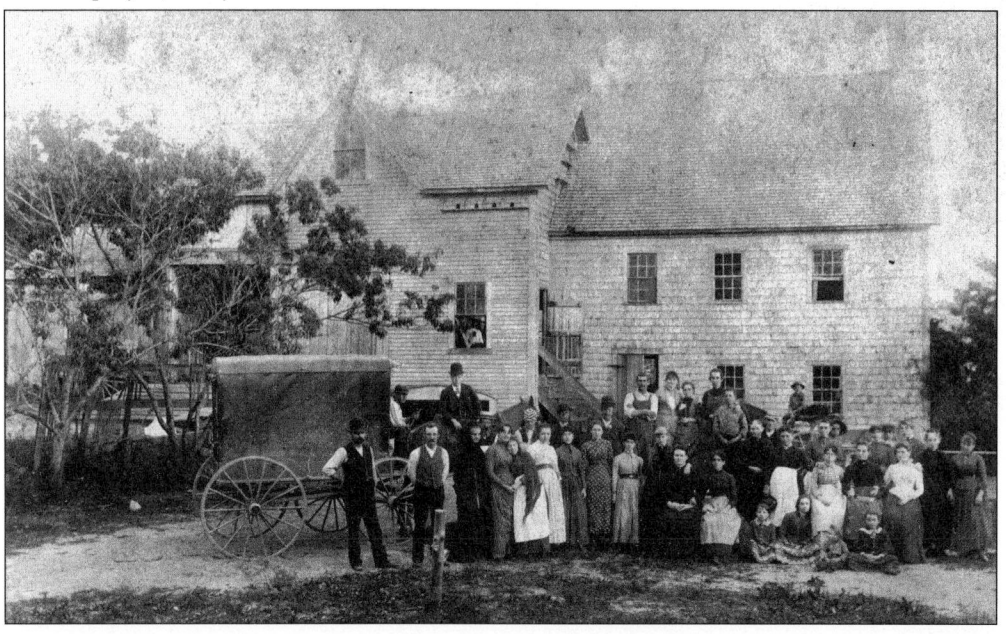

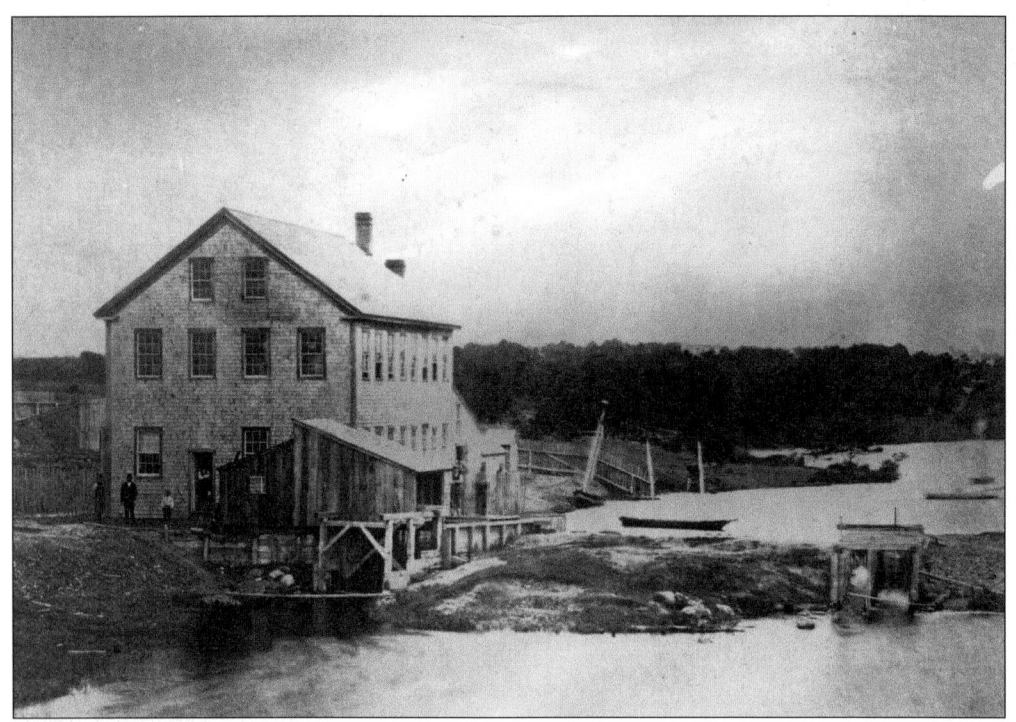

THE TAP AND DIE FACTORY. In 1867, this factory began operations on the west side of the Herring River. It burned two years later and was never rebuilt.

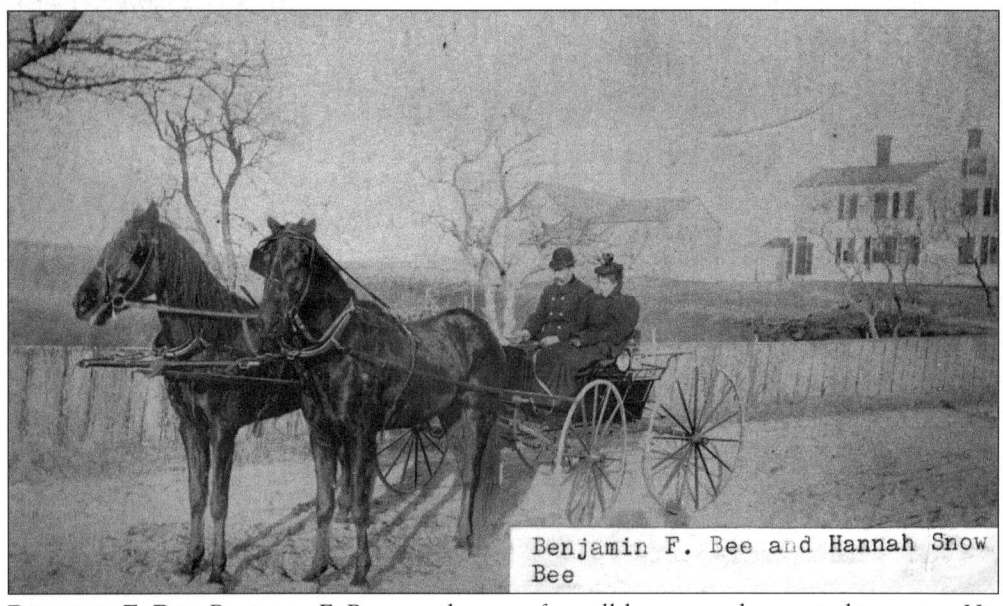

Benjamin F. Bee and Hannah Snow Bee

BENJAMIN F. BEE. Benjamin F. Bee was the son of a well-known and respected inventor. His father, Benjamin Bee, served in the Civil War and then perfected his various patents, from button fasteners to safety boilers, which were manufactured in his factory.

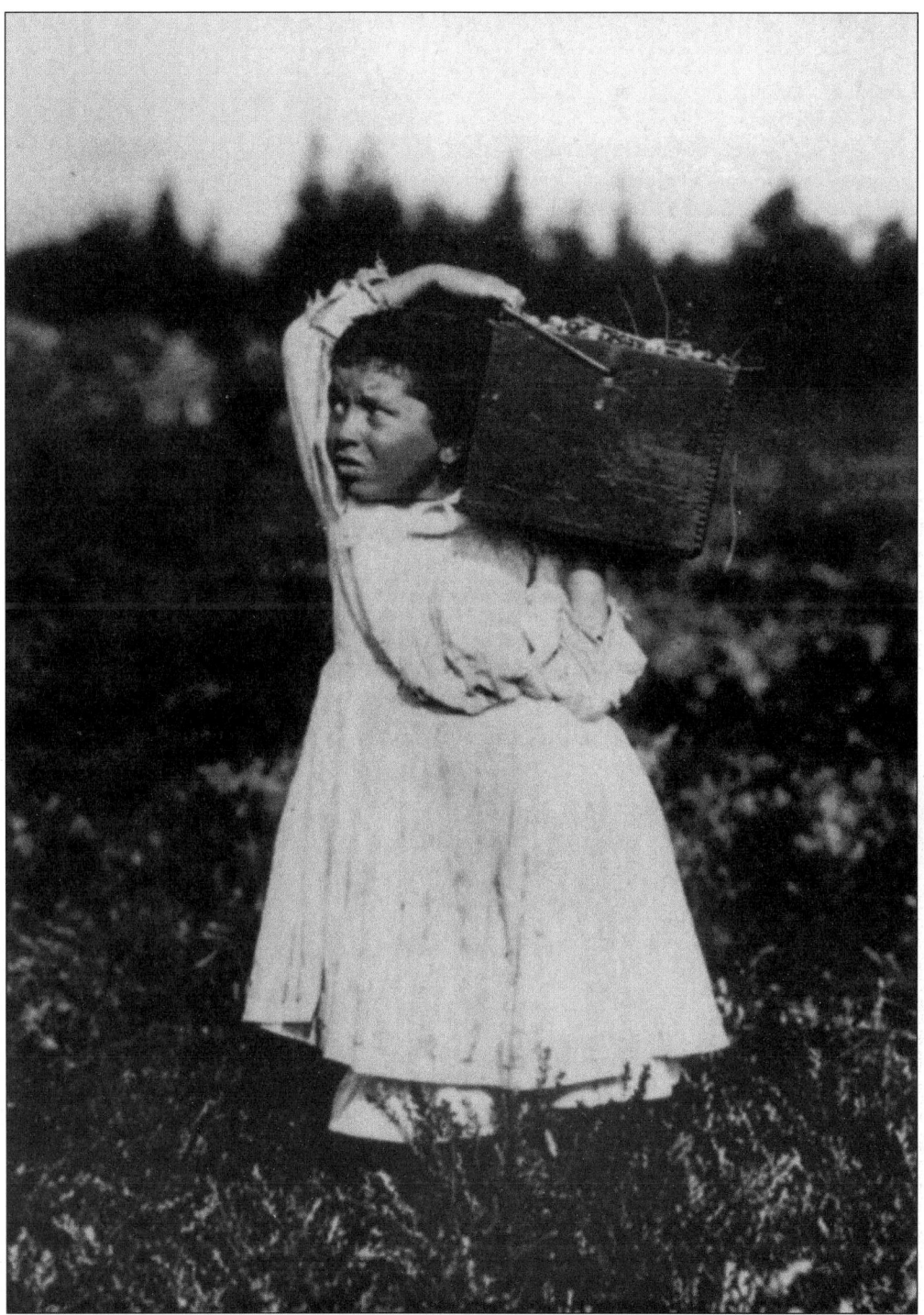

THE CRANBERRY INDUSTRY. Ultimately, Harwich was able to reverse its declining economy by relying on cranberry harvests. The vine, which had been cultivated since the 1840s, flourished in the town's bogs. In the fall, schools were suspended so children could join parents in picking the berries.

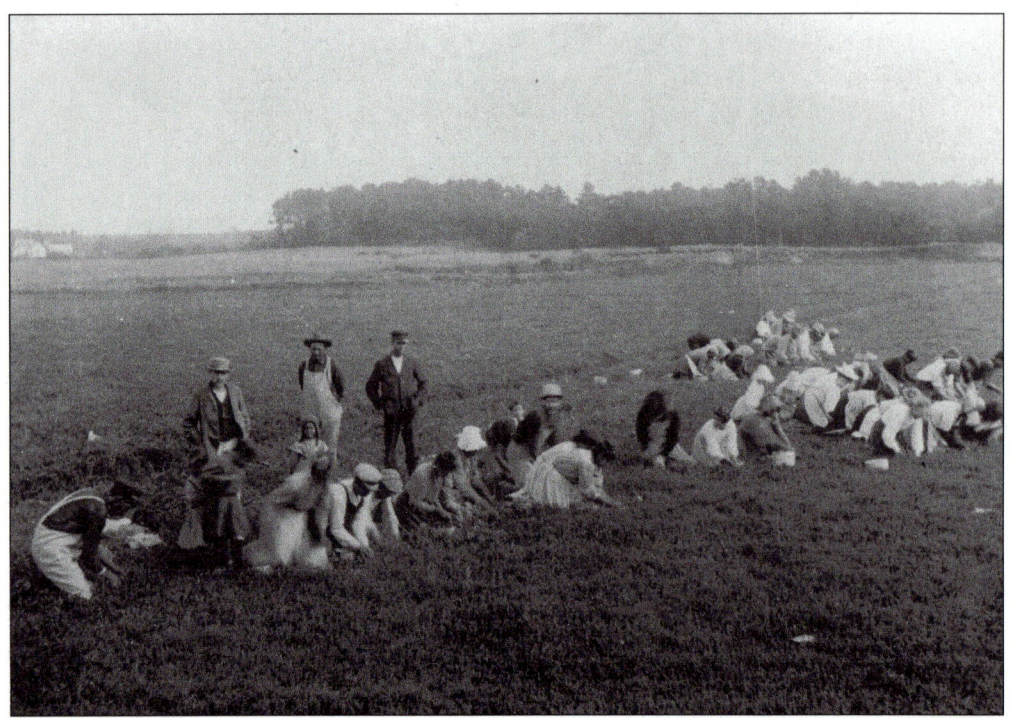

CRANBERRY HARVESTING. Pickers were assigned rows marked off by cords. They used their hands or simple scoops to separate the berries and were paid according to the weight of the buckets picked. The women often wore a type of bonnet and neck protector against the irritation of mosquitoes in the swampy areas. Pickers often protected their legs by wrapping them in burlap.

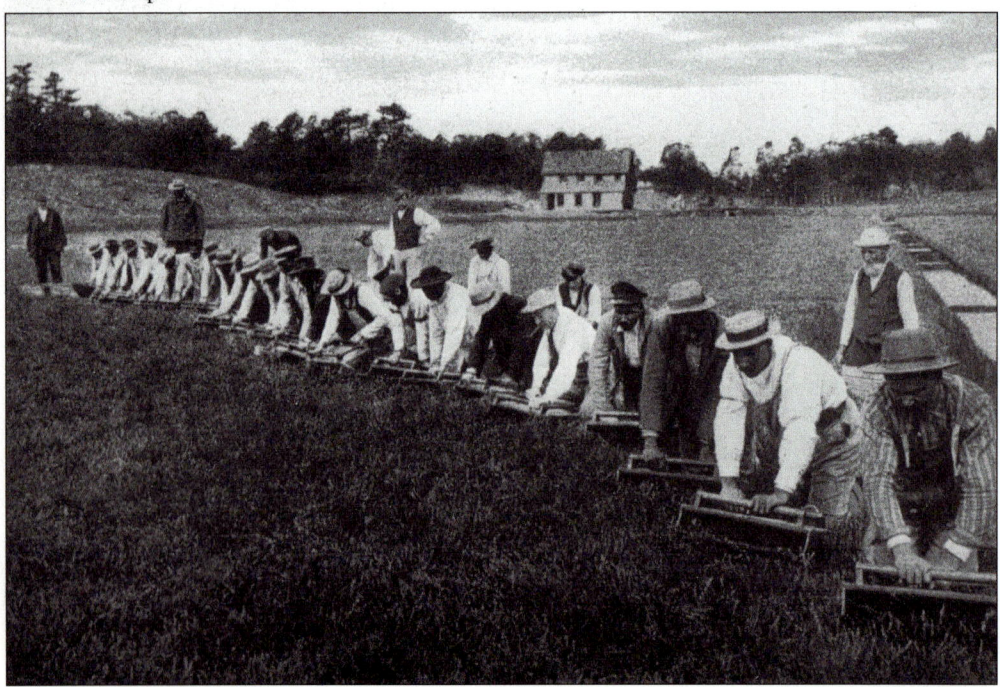

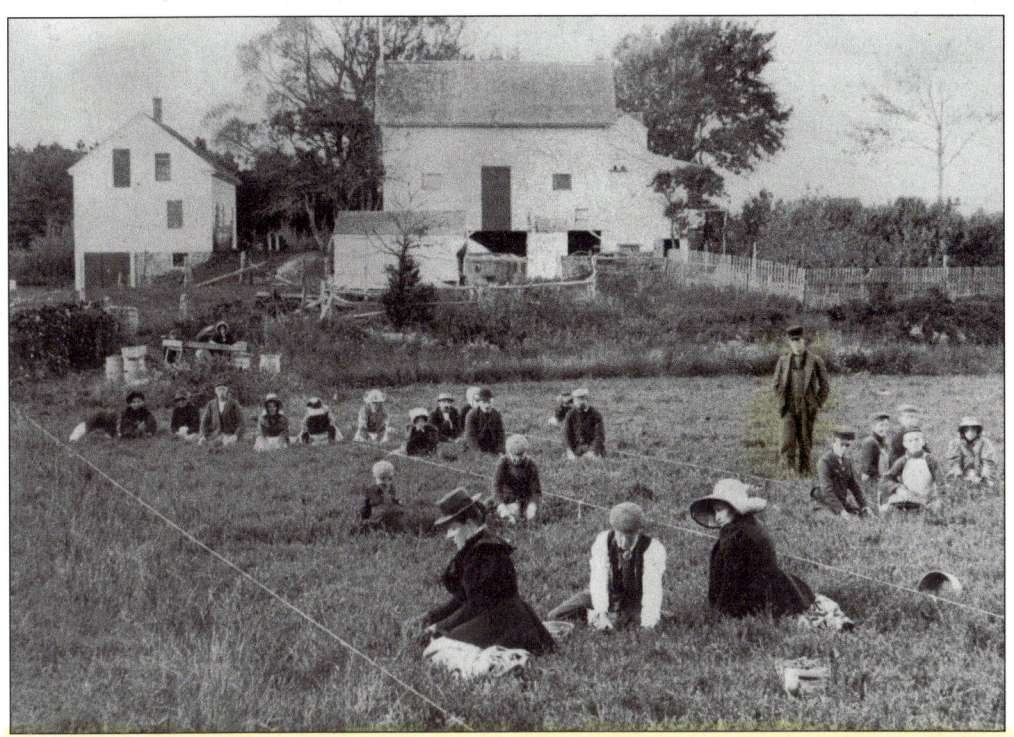

THE HARVEST AT PLEASANT LAKE. Cyrus Cahoon, whose house is in the background, was one of the first local men to see the value of the cranberry trade.

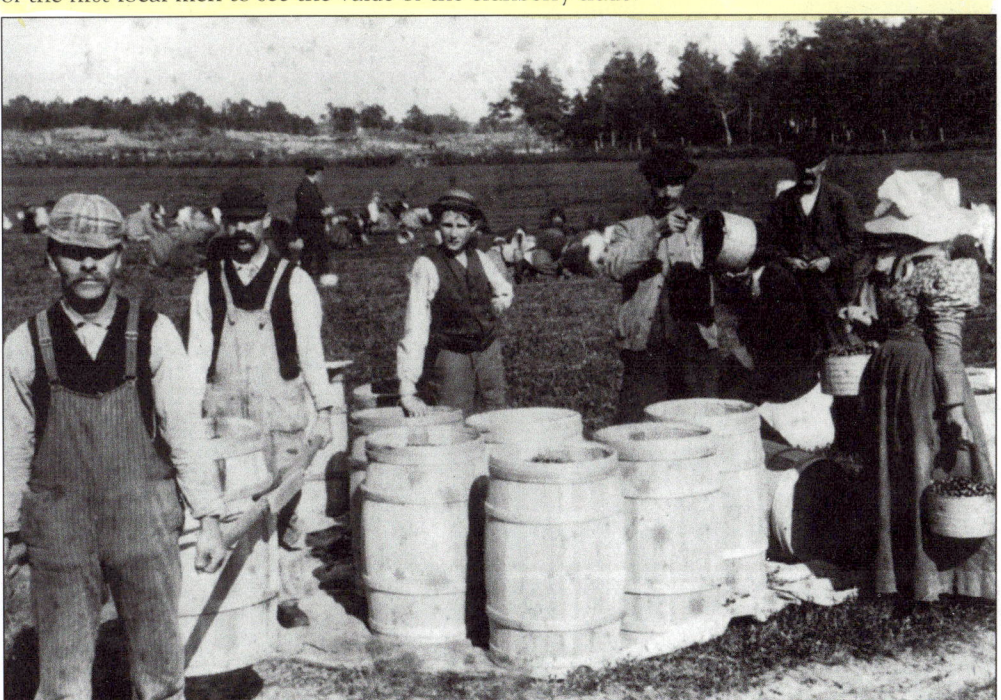

THE FOREMAN. The owner or his designee stood watch to ensure that the pickers stripped the vines of the last berry and did not spoil the fruit in transit.

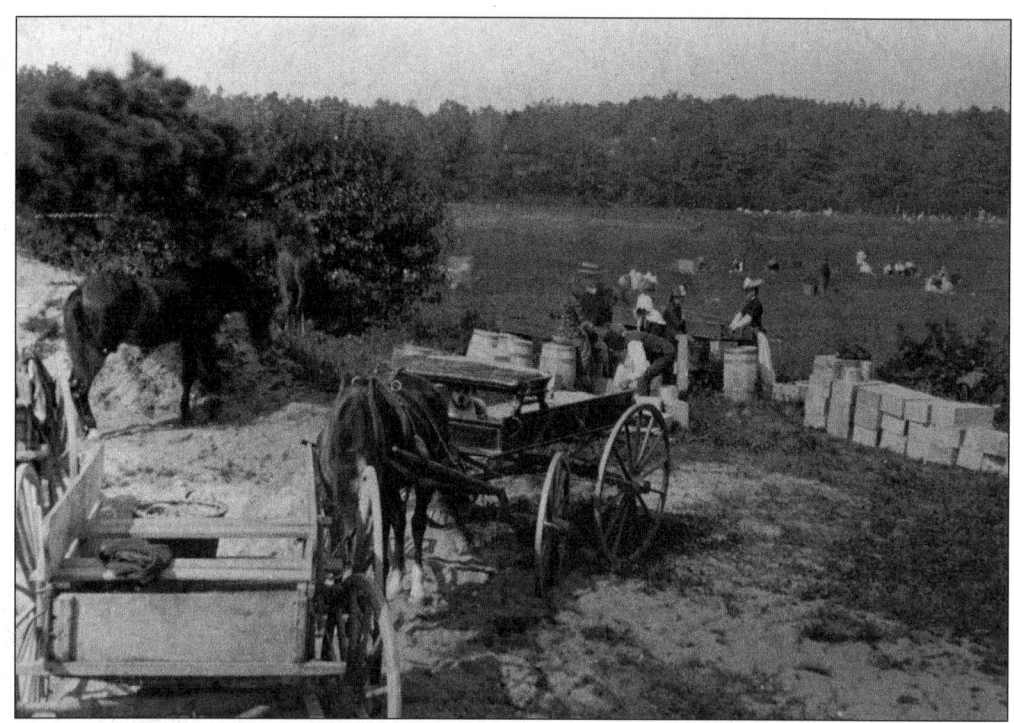

THE SCREENING PROCESS. The berries were carried carefully in 100-pound barrels to the screening sheds. According to the posted rules, harvesters were required to clean their berries. Nevertheless, screeners carefully removed damaged fruit to prevent other berries from being spoiled.

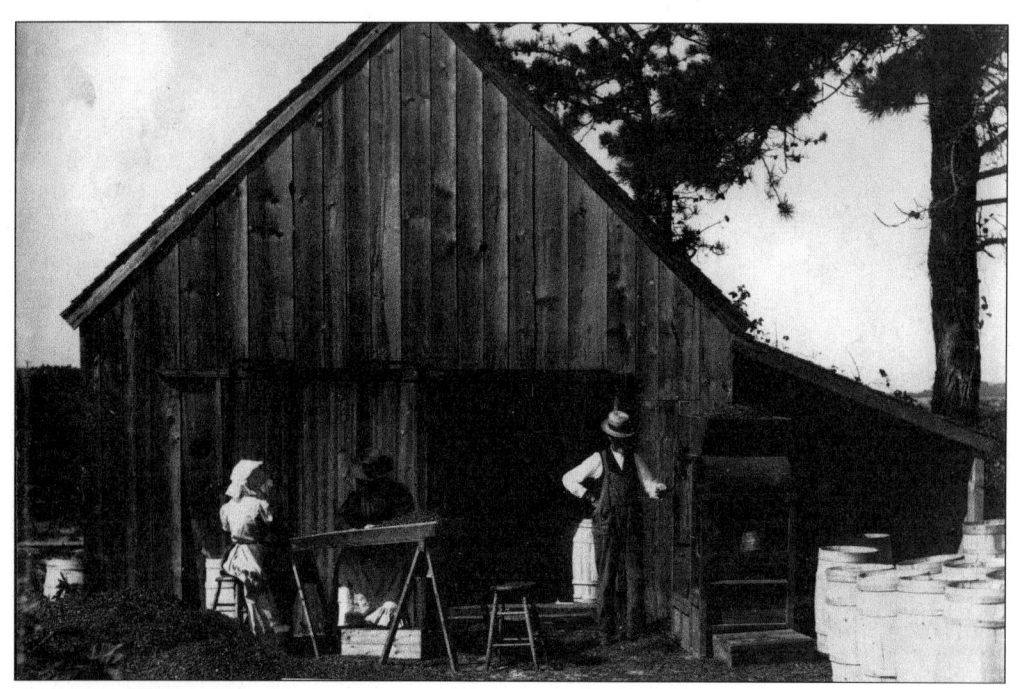

THE COMPLETION. Workers gather to celebrate completion of the arduous task.

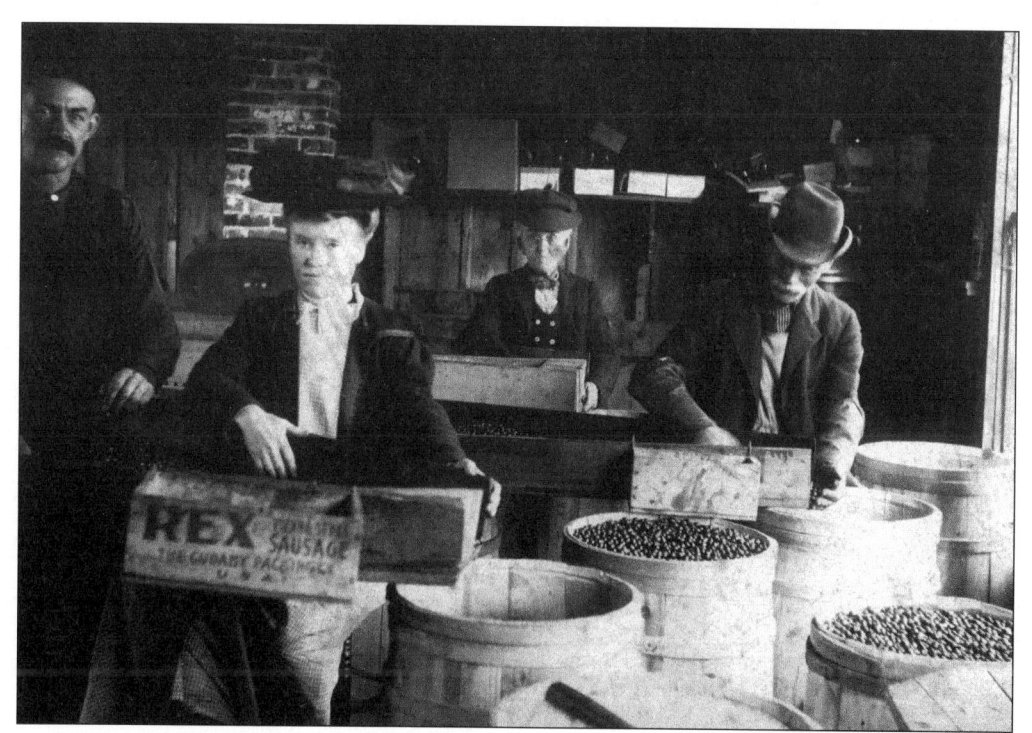

PACKING THE BERRIES FOR MARKET. Older people were usually employed to sort out and remove any spoiled berries.

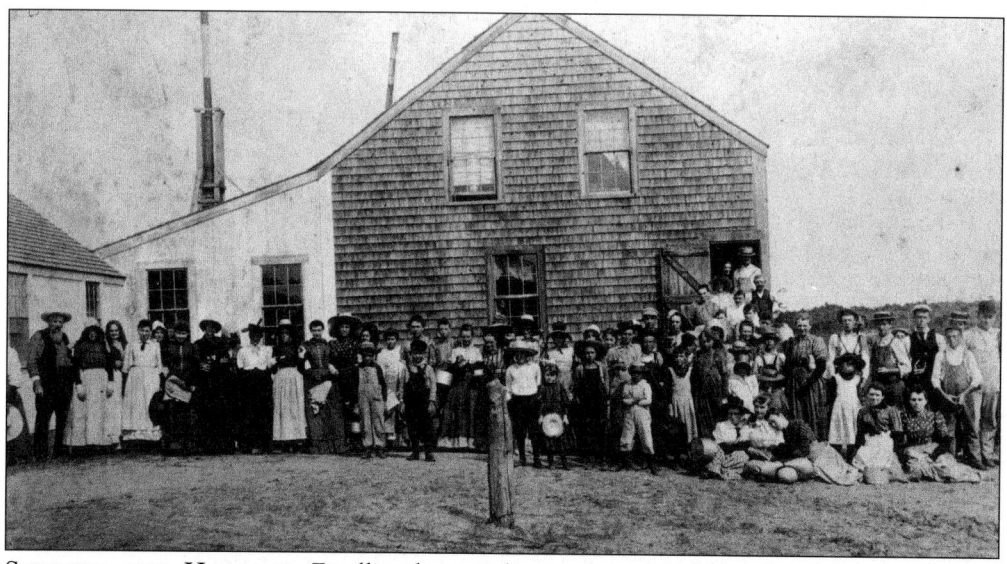

SHIPPING THE HARVEST. Finally, the cranberries were ready to be shipped to major urban markets.

65

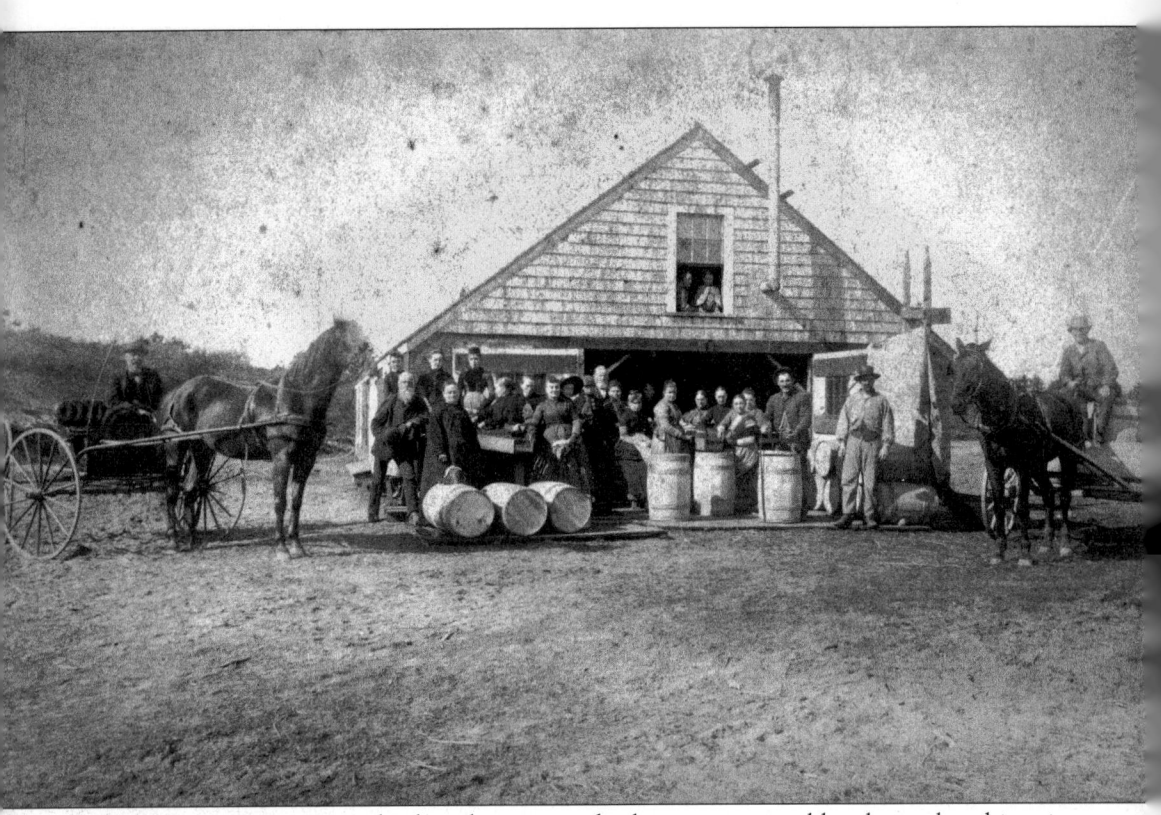

HARVEST'S END. Once the barrels were ready, bog owners could redeem the chits given to the pickers with cash. Some local store owners graciously accepted these chits to tide families over until distribution of the cash. In the 1860s, a harvester received about 40¢ for each bushel picked.

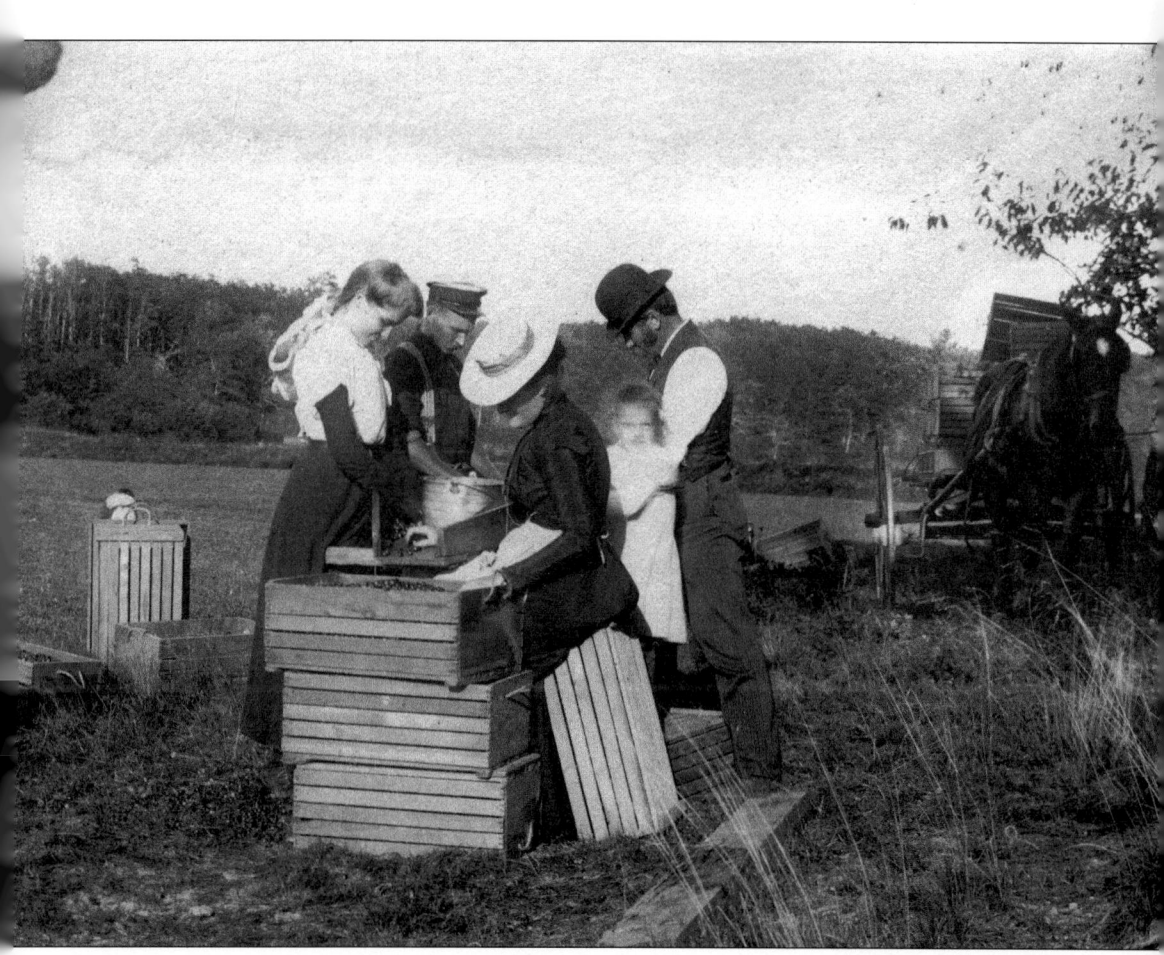

A COMMUNITY SHARES. This photograph appears almost idyllic in depicting how entire families joined in the harvesting process. Without the income earned, local merchants would have failed and more people would have been forced to leave in search of work.

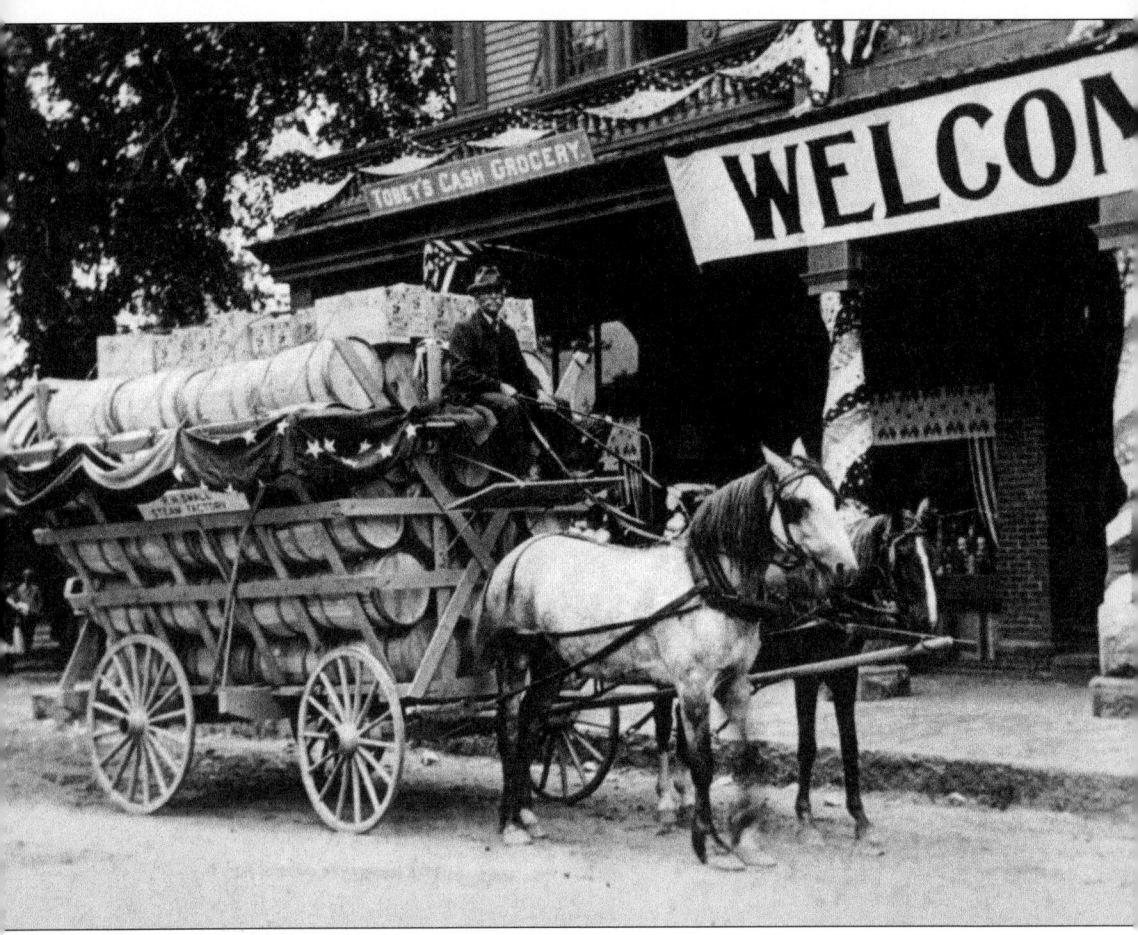

SHIPPING THE HARVEST. Finally, the crop was on its way to be shipped by rail to the major urban markets. The Indians had molded dried cranberries and fatty meat into cakes—an early "energy bar." Urban buyers, however, sought the berries because of their reputed medicinal value, most notably to prevent scurvy.

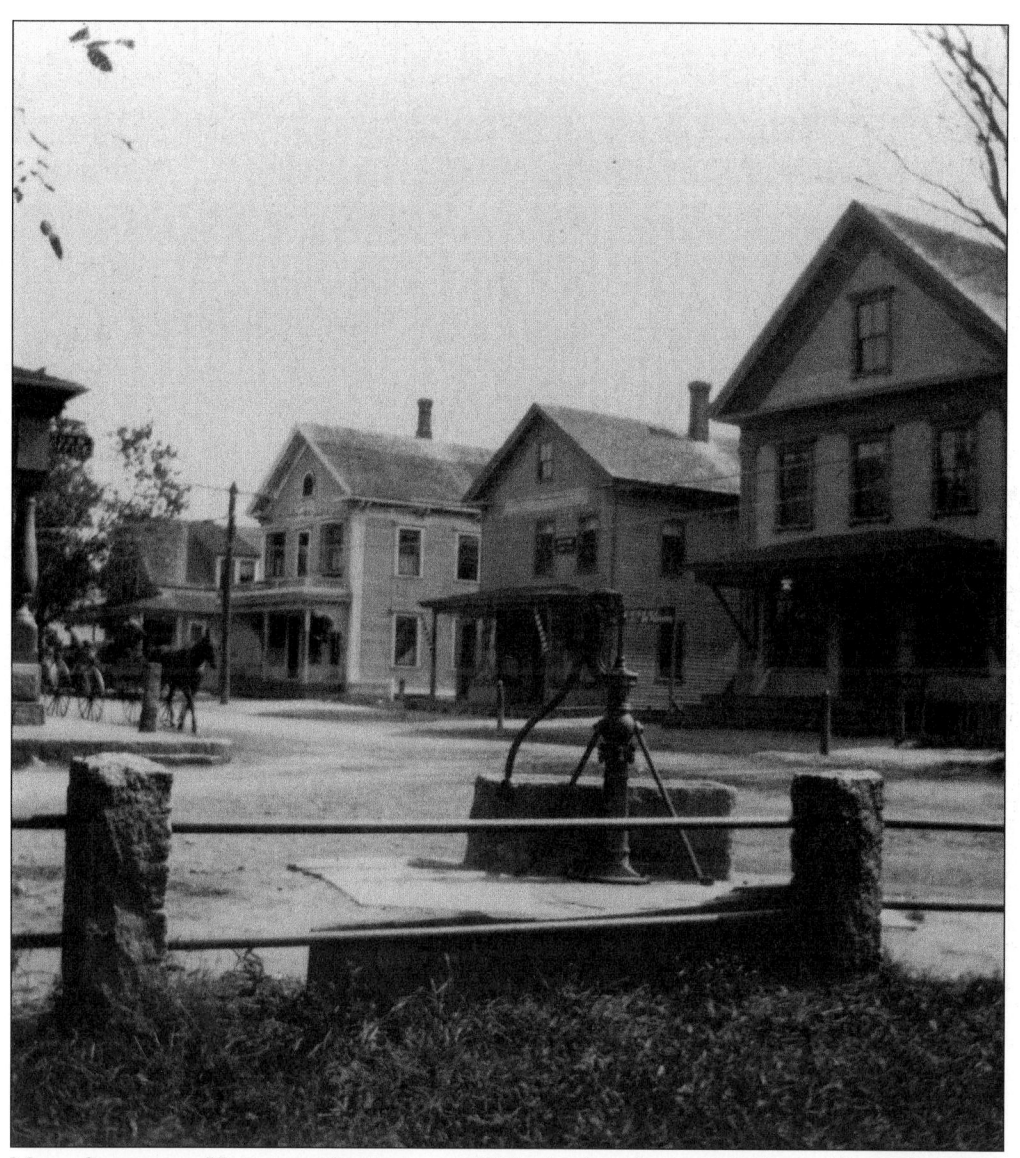

MAIN STREET IN HARWICH CENTER, C. 1905. As this photograph shows, Harwich Center retained most of its shape of the 1870s. From left to right are the Moody residence, the pharmacy and photographic studio, a shoe store, and a general store. One new feature was the town pump, installed with the help of the Society for the Prevention of Cruelty to Animals and maintained by a bequest from Benjamin D. Nickerson to provide relief for horses.

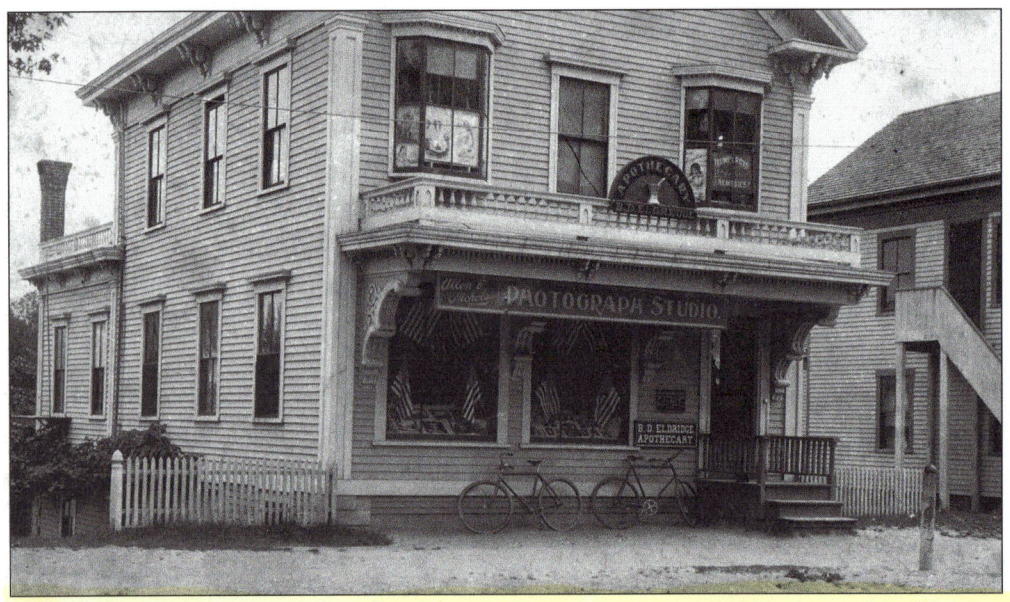

ELDRIDGE'S PHARMACY. This flourishing pharmacy also provided space for Clement Cahoon's studio.

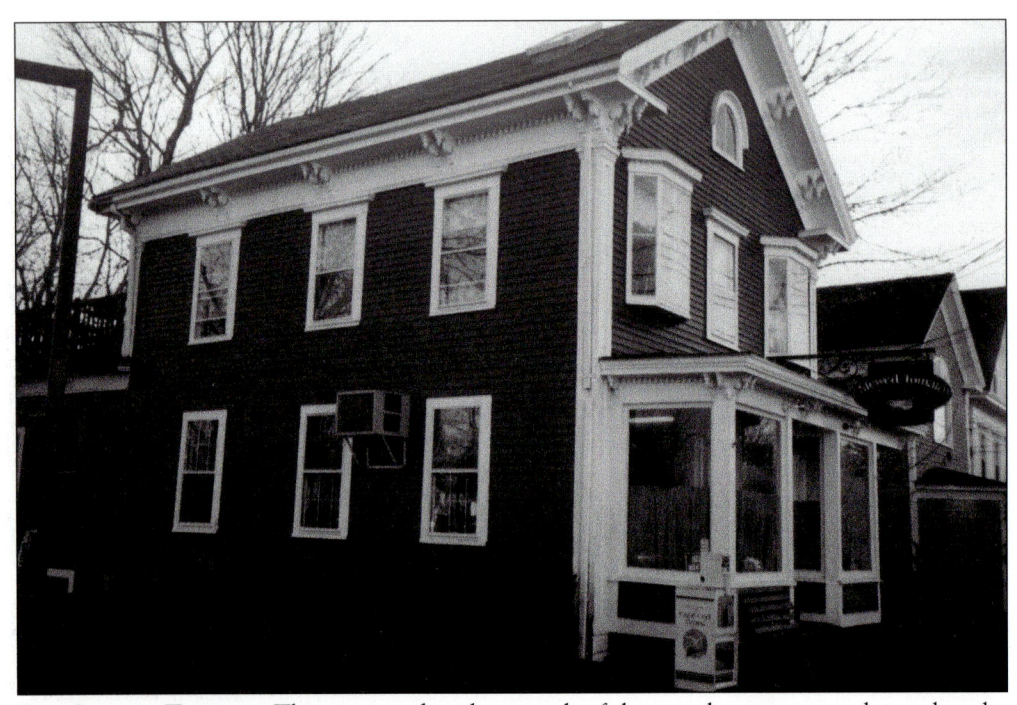

THE STEWED TOMATO. This present-day photograph of the popular restaurant shows that the building retains its historical characteristics. (Sr. Aureen Rose Behrend.)

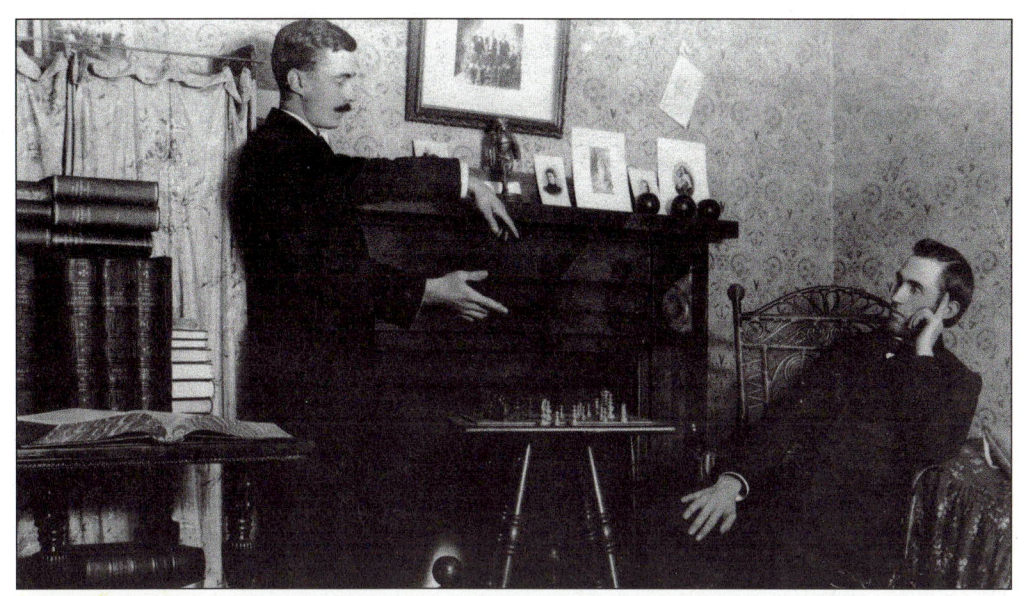

CHARLES DREW CAHOON. Charles Drew Cahoon, left, often visited the studio of his cousin Clement Cahoon. Charles Cahoon is shown here with his friend A.J. Haynes, who was a minister at the Bethel Church for a time. Haynes kept his summer camp on Long Pond after moving to a new assignment and visited it often to indulge his love of fishing. He died in a tragic boating accident on the pond in 1908.

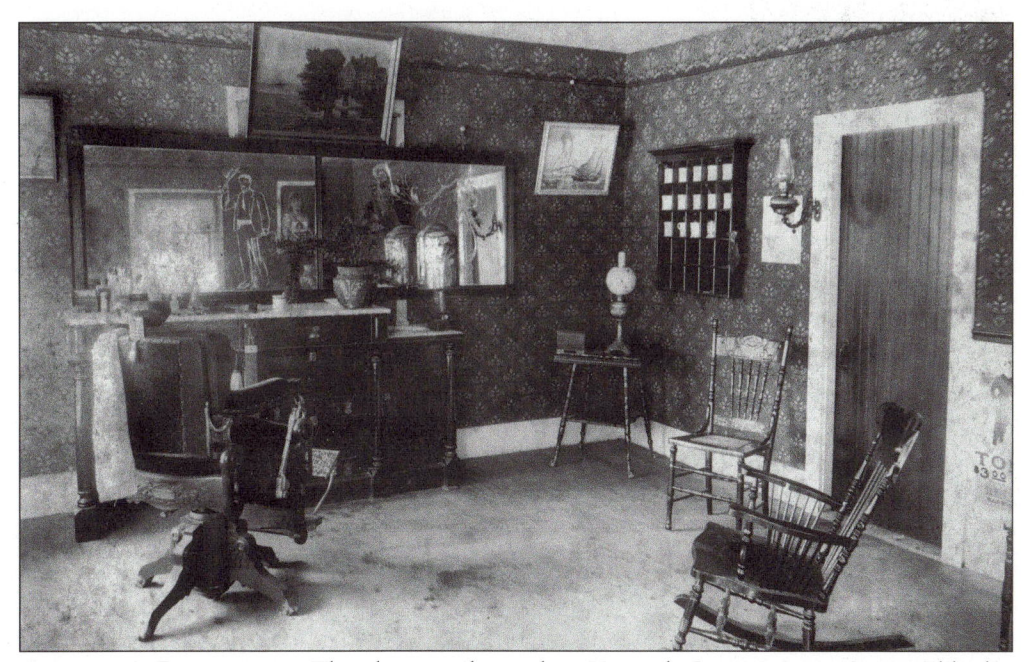

ELDREDGE'S BARBERSHOP. This shop was located on Harwich Center's Main Street. Eldredge required that customers take out a "membership" to avoid serving people he did not care for.

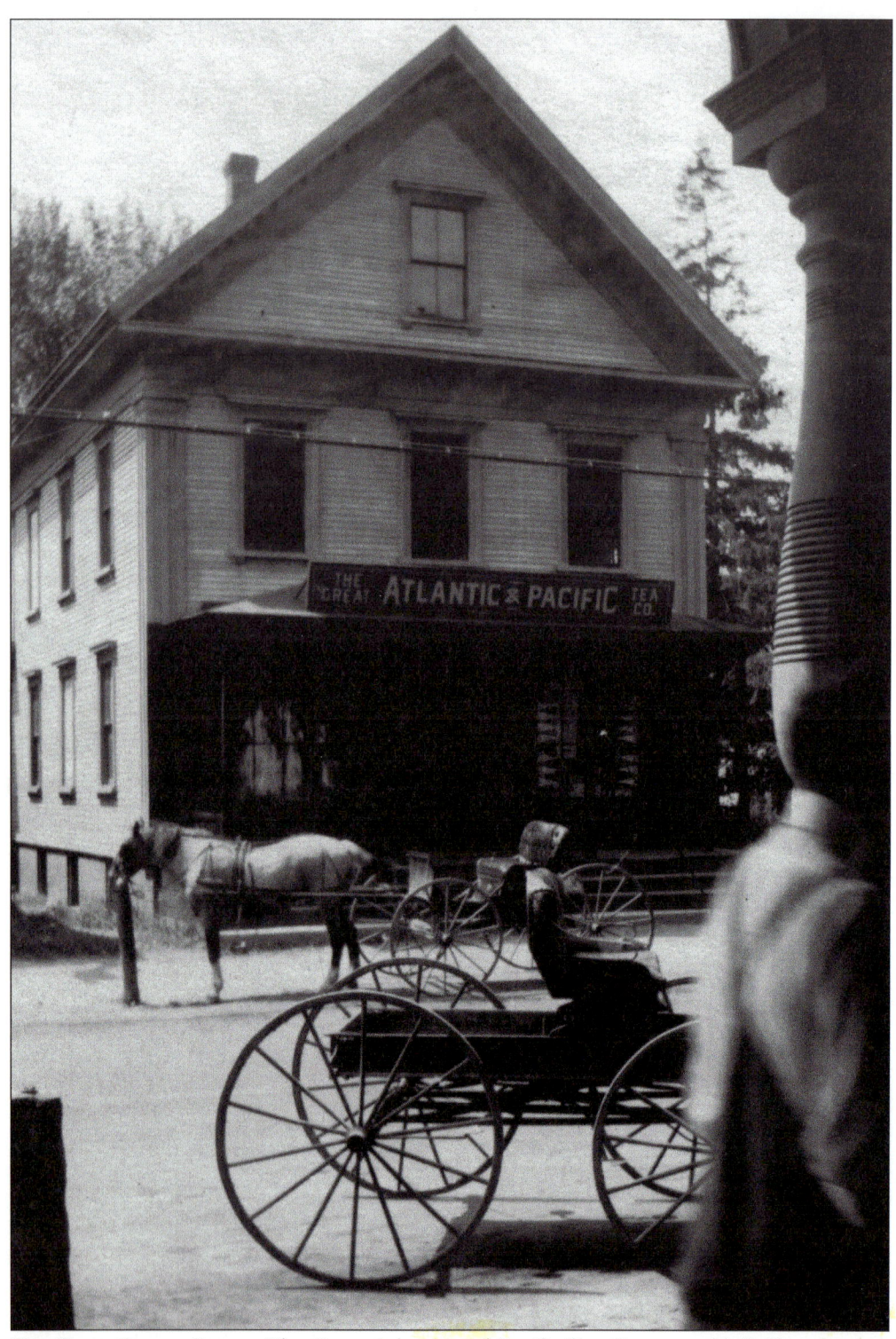

THE FIRST CHAIN STORE. The Great Atlantic and Pacific Tea Company (A & P) opened its first store in Harwich next to the Congregational church's new parsonage.

SARAH BROOKS. The youngest sibling of the family, Sarah Brooks inherited the family homestead and much of her brother Henry Brooks's fortune. She redrew her will to include a provision that $2,000 be provided for construction of a new parsonage on the lot earlier given by her father to the church.

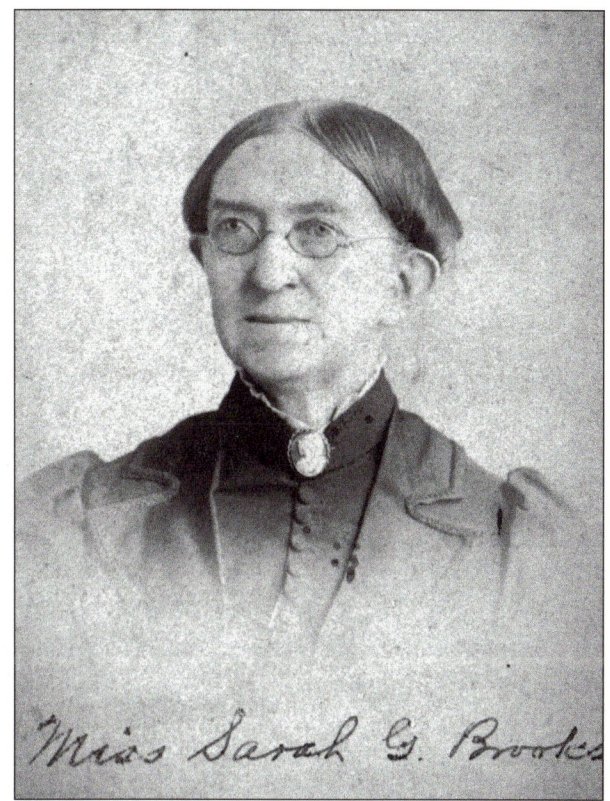

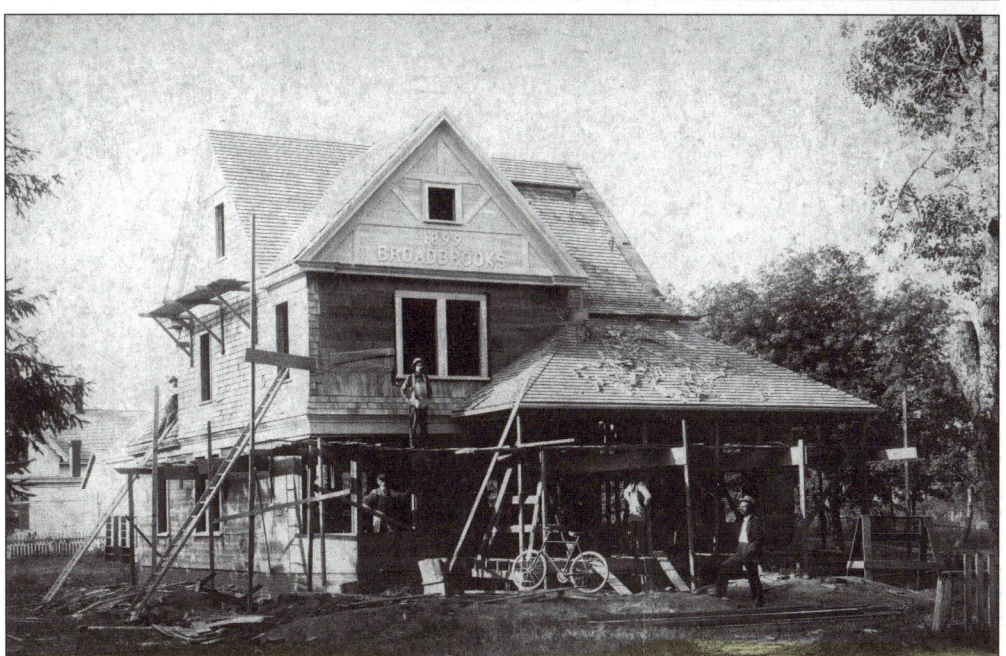

Miss Sarah G. Brooks

THE NEW PARSONAGE. In 1899, Sarah Brooks decided to build the parsonage in her lifetime. The original spelling of the family name, Broadbrooks, was used on the quarterboard to honor all her ancestors.

73

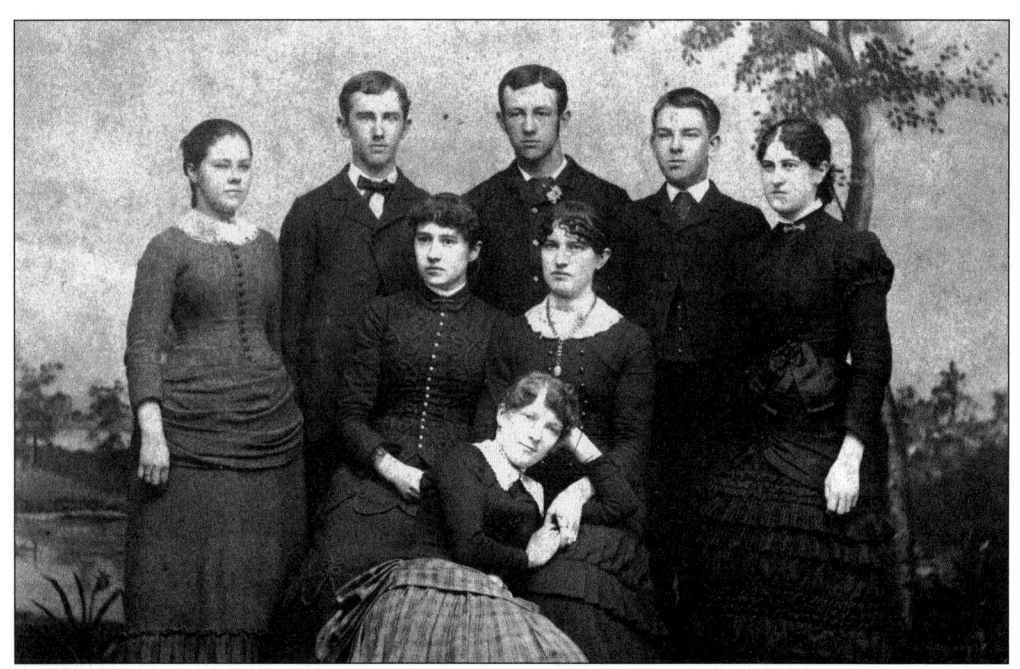

THE FIRST HARWICH HIGH SCHOOL GRADUATING CLASS. The camera captured these young scholars in 1884. The town had taken over Sidney Brooks's academy and offered both classical and commercial tracks to secondary students.

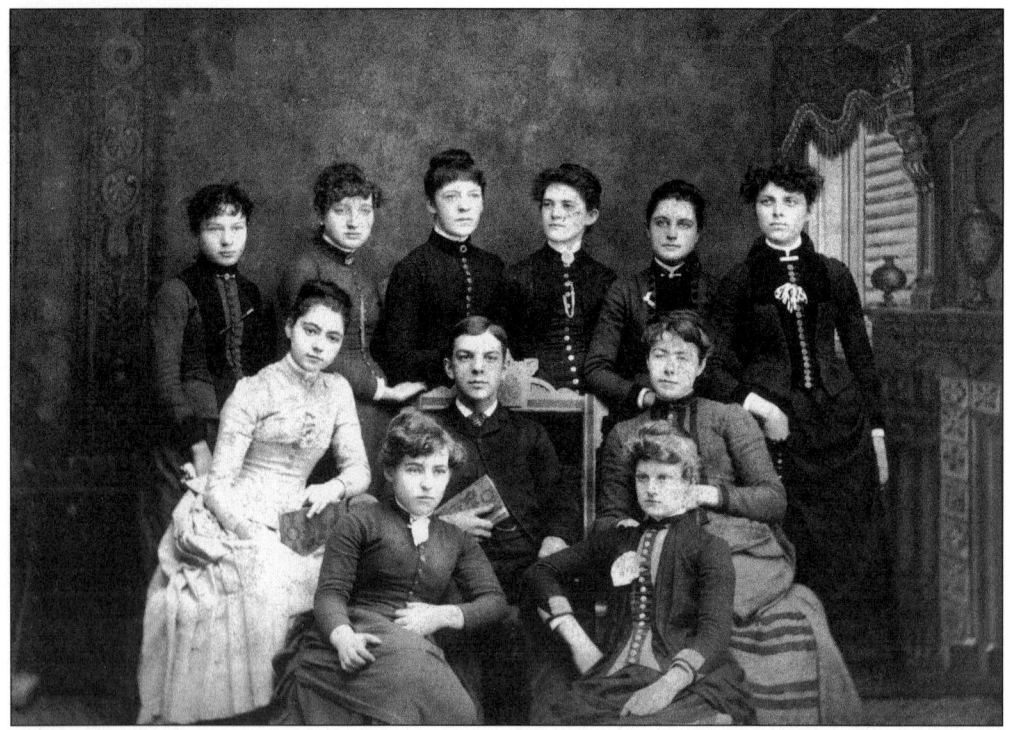

THE CLASS OF 1887. As this photograph shows, few young men could afford to stay in school. An agricultural program was later introduced in hopes of retaining more male students.

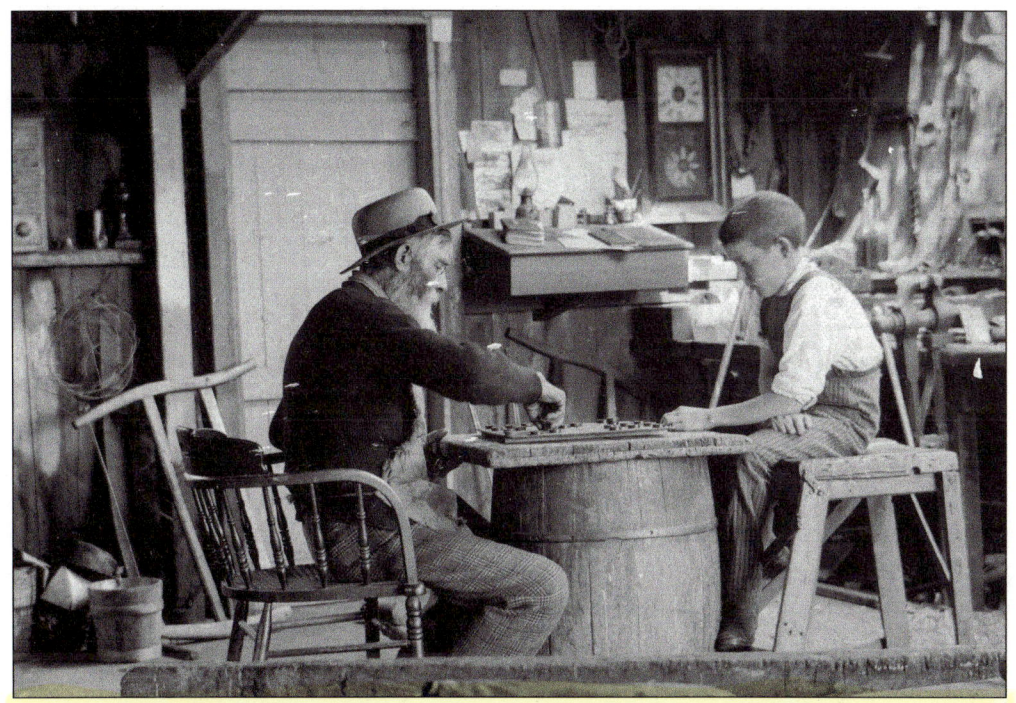

PLAYING CHECKERS. Some things did not change at all. Benjamin F. Robbins could take time from his wheelwright business to play checkers with a very intent boy.

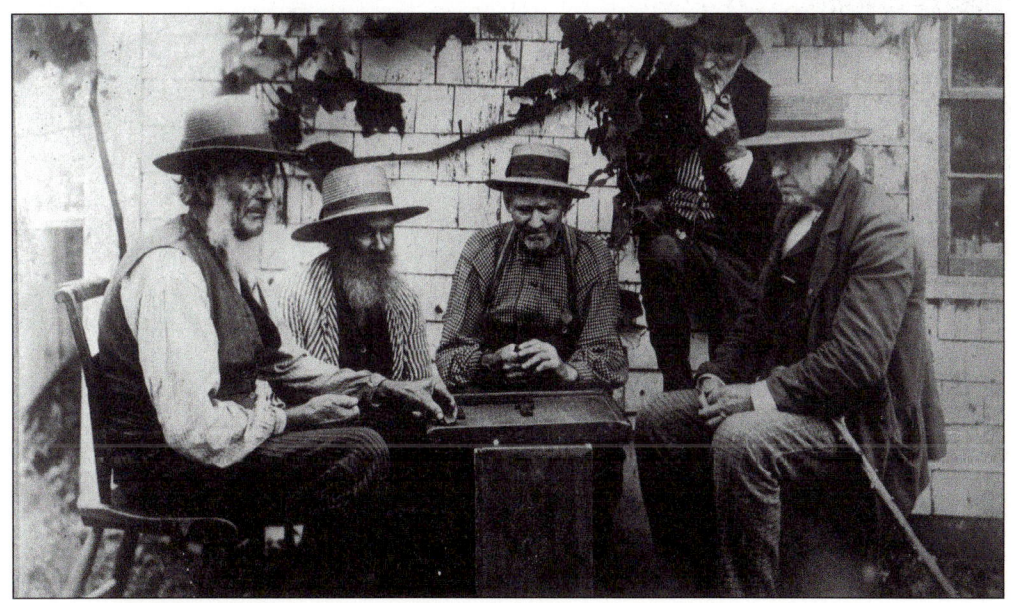

PLAYING DOMINOES. Older men still gathered in the sun outside of Small's shoe store to enjoy a game of dominoes.

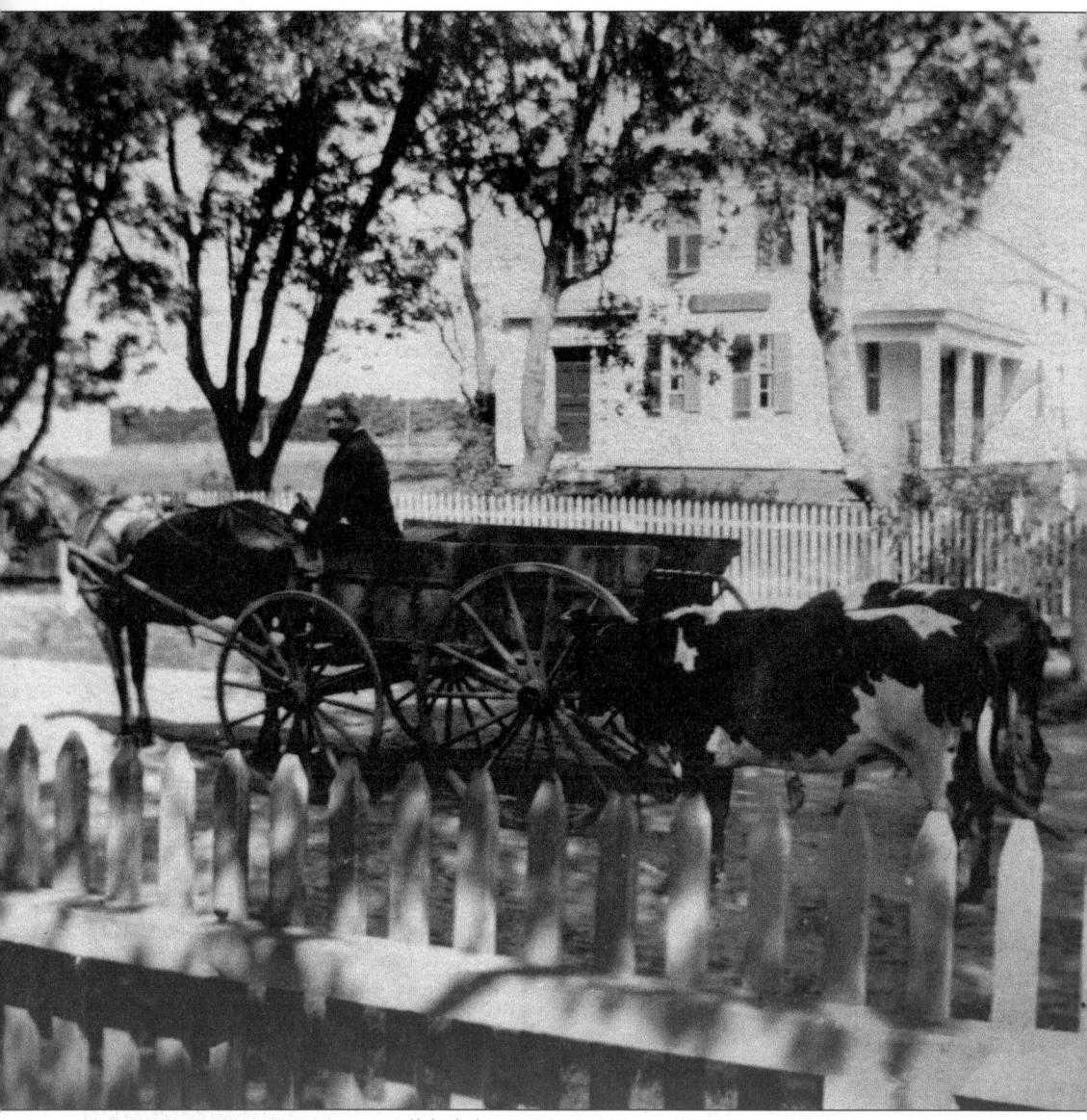

John H. Drum. Cows were still led down Main Street to pastures. John H. Drum, the son of Irish immigrants, maintained a popular livery stable in Harwich Center for more than four decades. He died in 1913, after having served for 12 years as a selectman.

Three

A Vacation Mecca

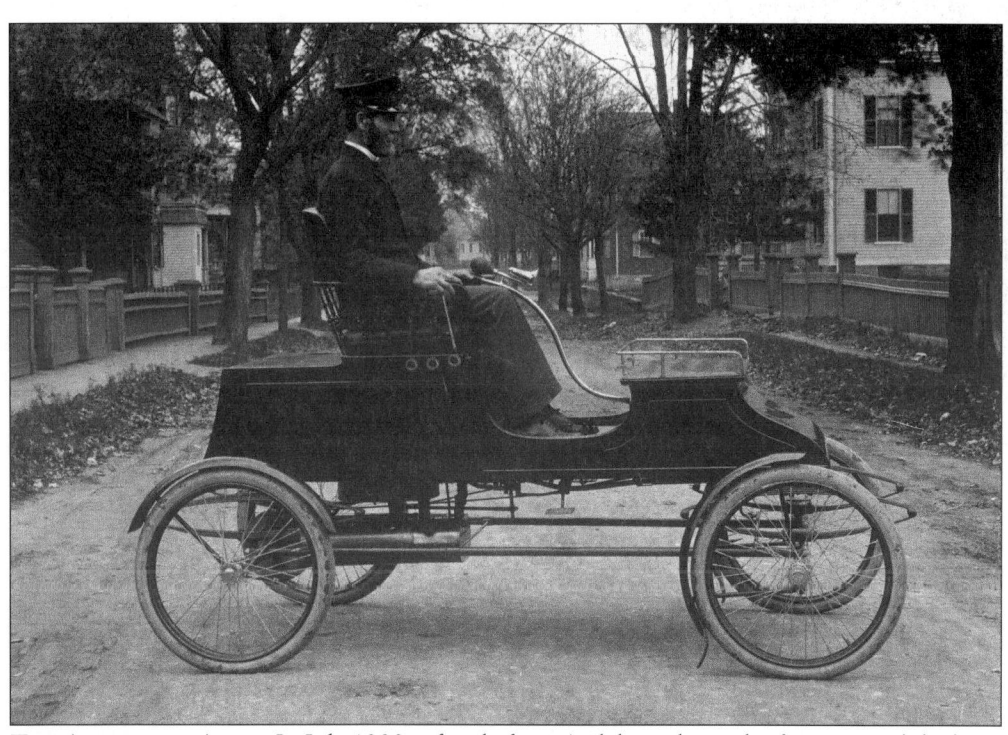

THE AGE OF THE AUTO. In July 1900, a family from Attleboro drove the first automobile down Harwich's Main Street to garage it at the livery stable.

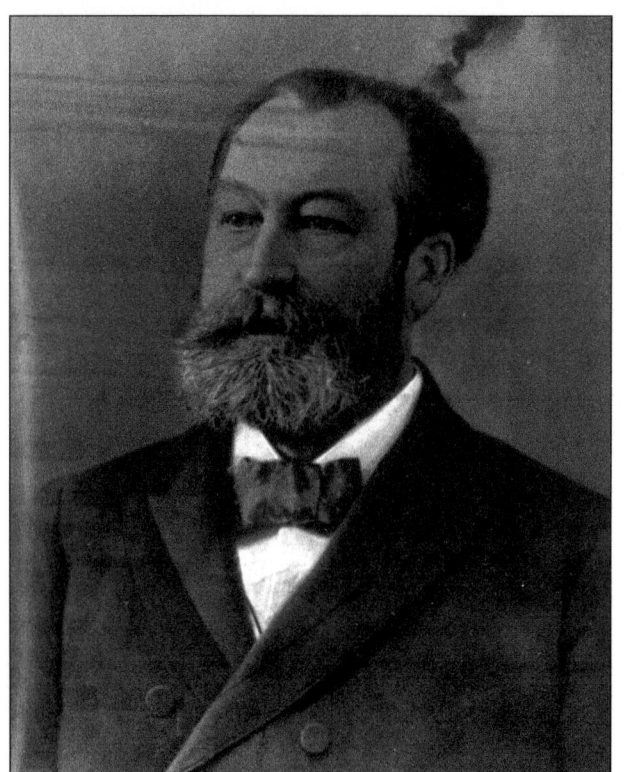

CALEB CHASE. The youngest of 15 children, Caleb Chase left his home town to find fortune in Boston. Later, when he had become a very successful coffee merchant, Chase delighted in bringing visitors to Harwich. He realized that the financial stability of Harwich depended on making the area known for its vacation attractions. After Chase offered matching funds, town voters began a road-building spree. The era of the automobile was launched.

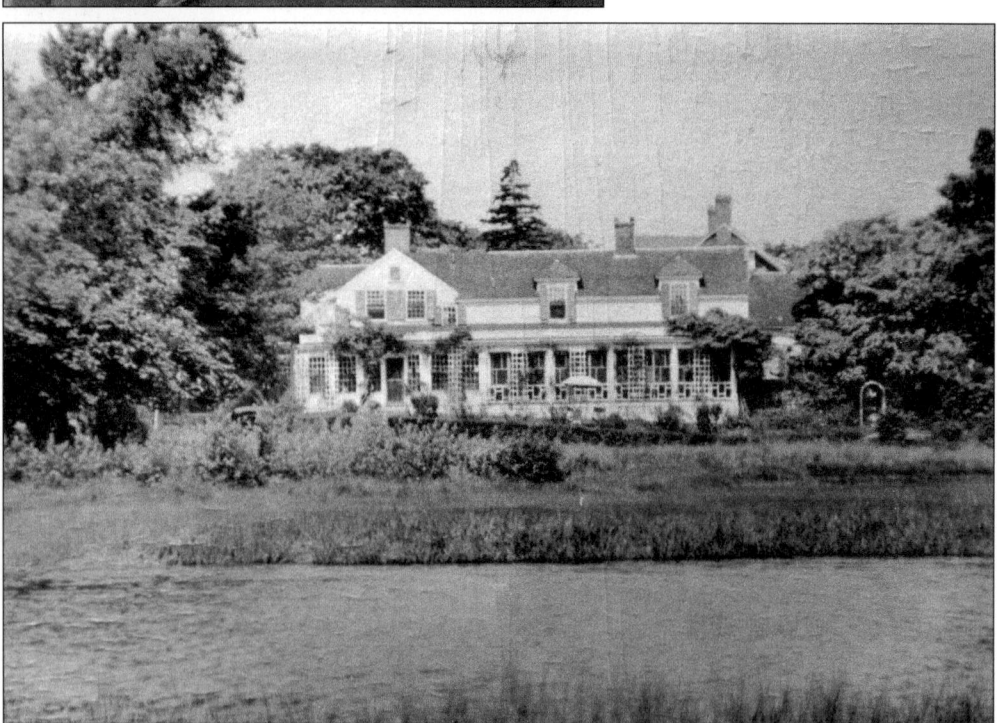

CALEB CHASE'S HOME. This lovely residence on the banks of the Herring River was frequently used by the Chases and their guests. It is now the Irish Pub.

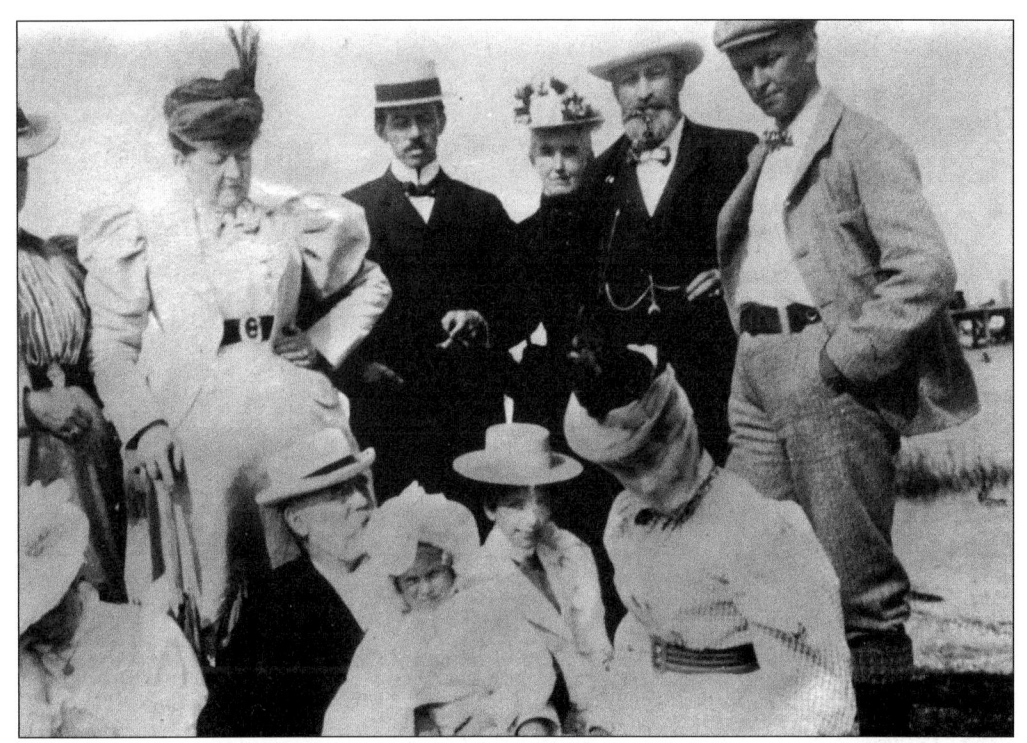

A Chase Family Gathering. Standing are Caleb Chase, second from the right, and his wife, Salome, with her hand on her hip. The Chases had no children. Chase left a considerable part of his fortune to his wife, who died suddenly in 1909.

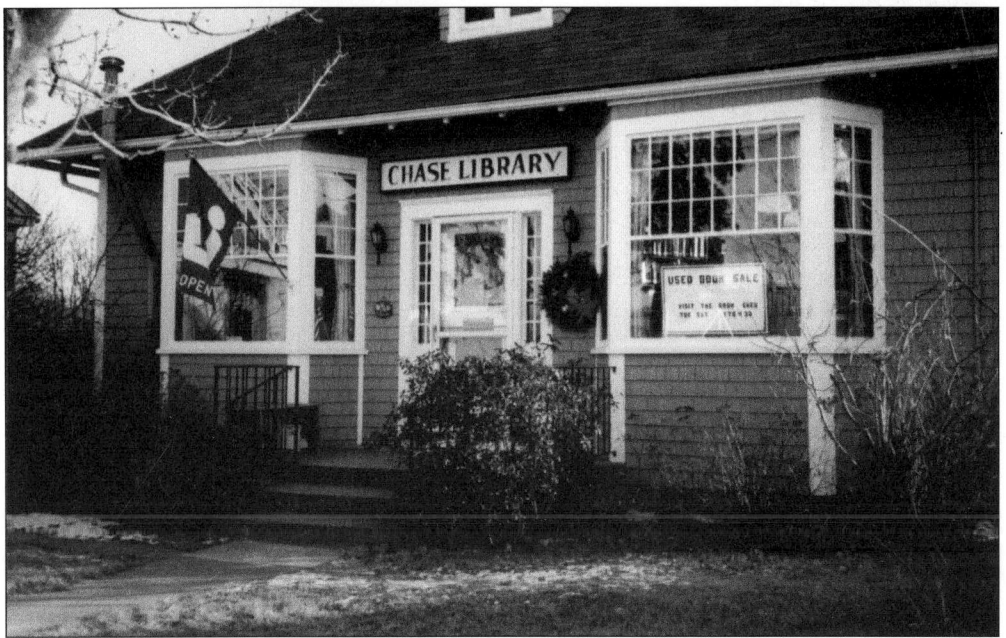

Chase Library, West Harwich. Some of Caleb Chase's many gifts to the people of Harwich included this library, the title to the Exchange Building, and a large fund that still provides for needy residents. (Sr. Aureen Rose Behrend.)

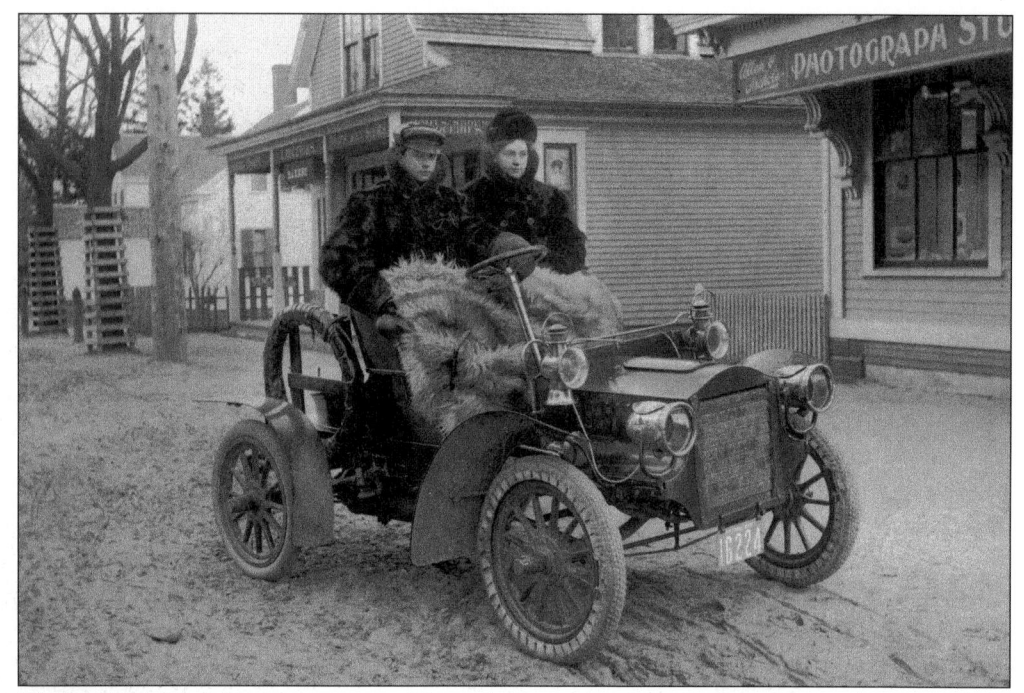

HORSES BEWARE! Visitors traverse Harwich Center's Main Street in an early automobile, complete with fur lap robes. Dr. Harrie Handy was the first in town to purchase a car. In 1900, he paid $1,000 for an eight-cylinder two-seater.

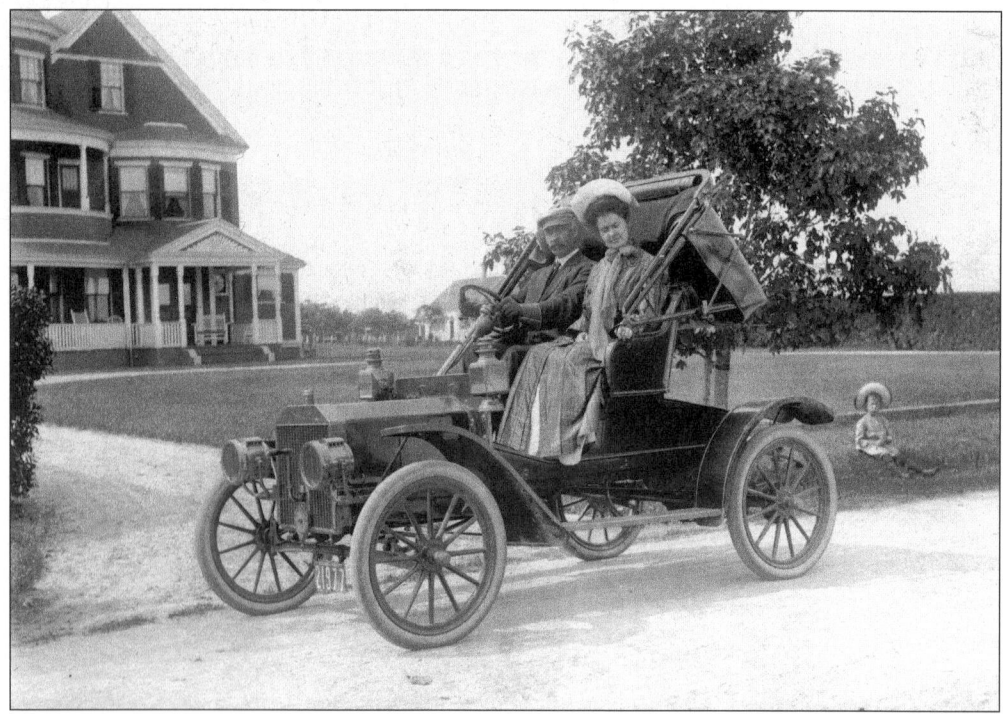

MR. AND MRS. BENJAMIN F. BEE GO TOURING. This photograph was taken in 1911. Benjamin Bee had swapped his horse and buggy (shown on page 50) for this splendid car.

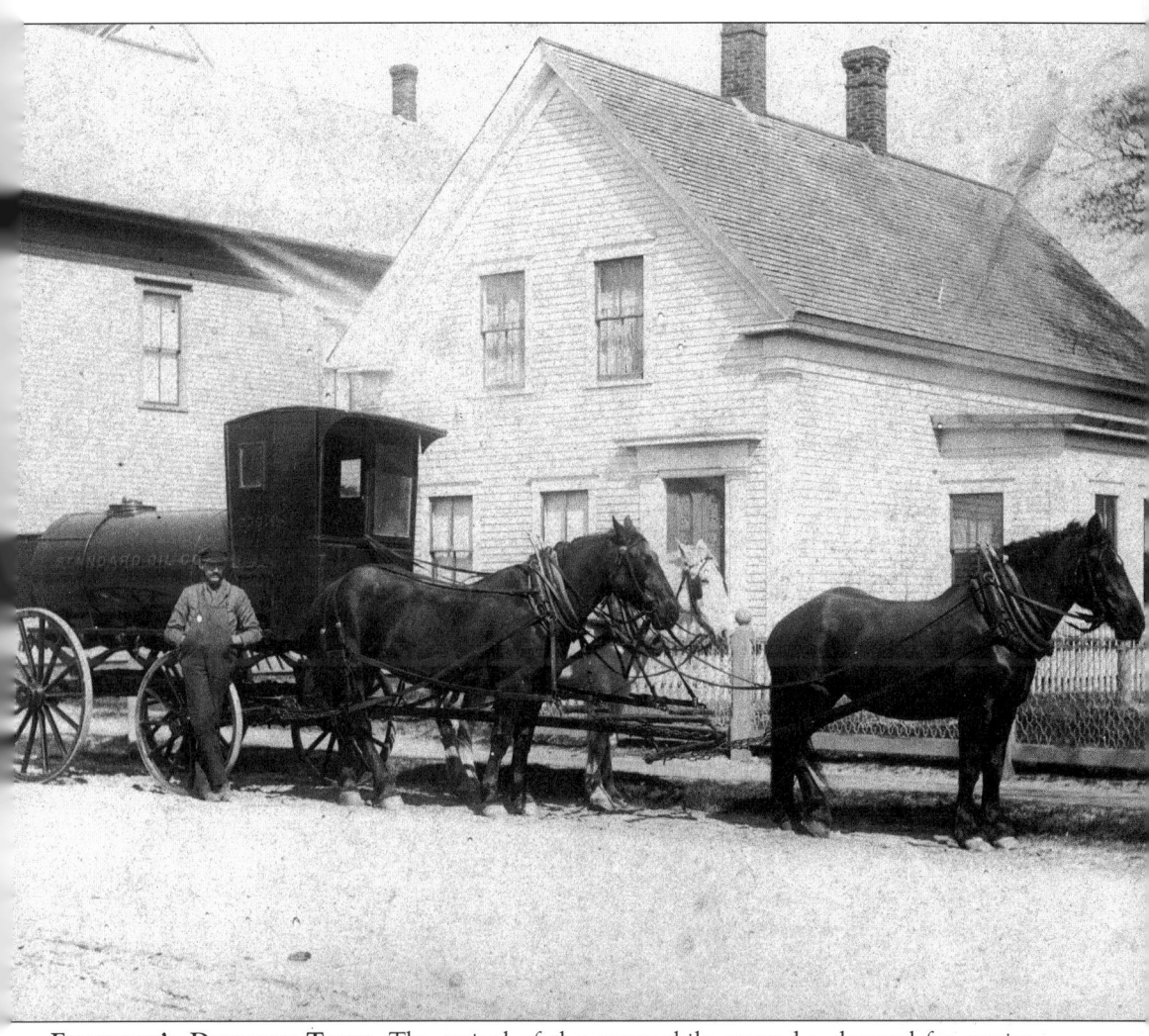

Eldredge's Delivery Tank. The arrival of the automobile created a demand for service stations and fuel. Ralph W. Eldredge began his service delivering for Socony in 1903.

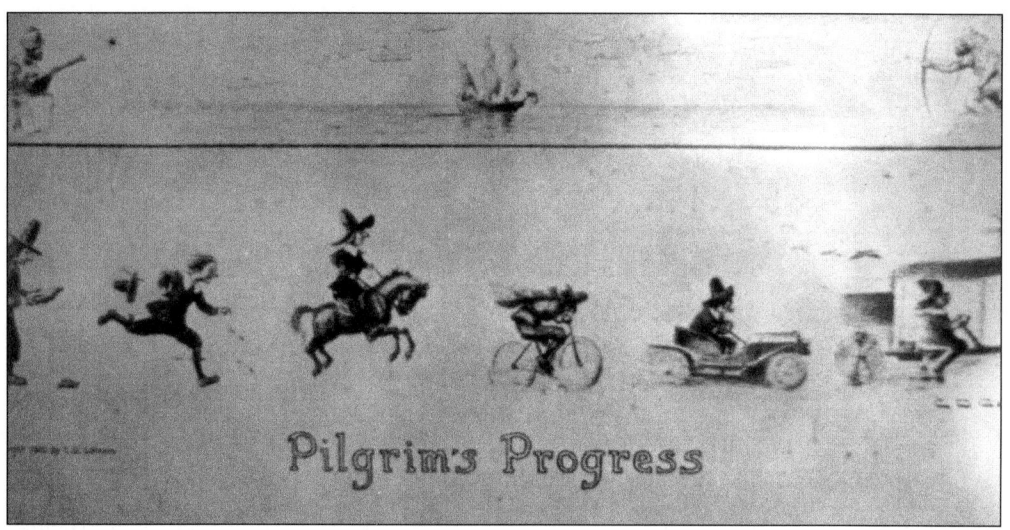

THE SIX STAGES OF MAN. Local artist Charles Cahoon whimsically depicted man's progress in transportation from walking erect to gasoline powered racers.

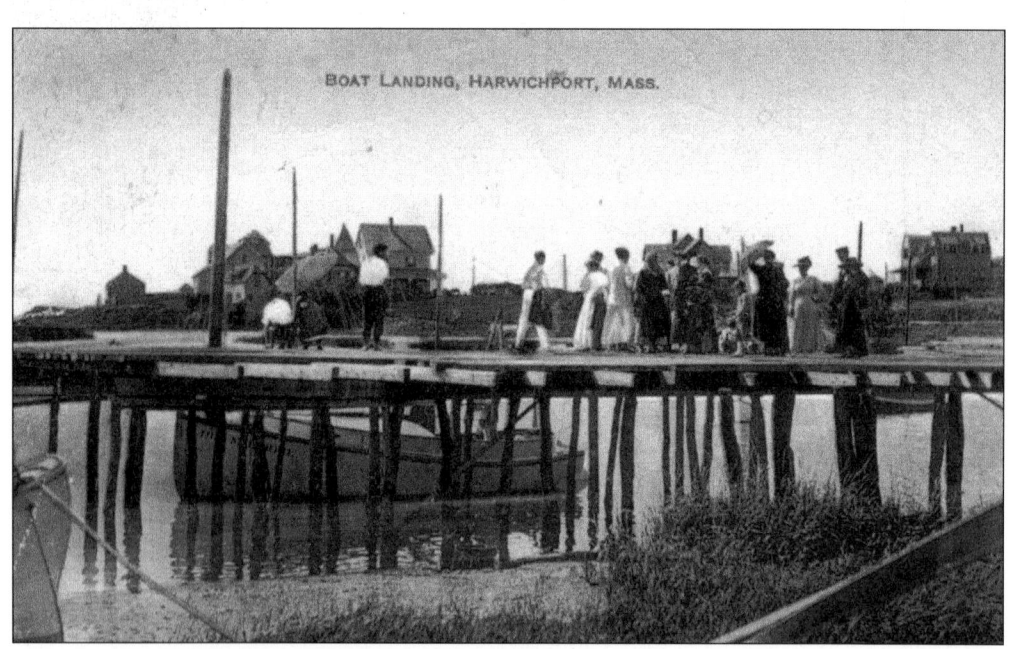

BOAT LANDING. As this scene illustrates, better roads and automobiles meant an influx of visitors, which contributed to Harwich's economic well-being.

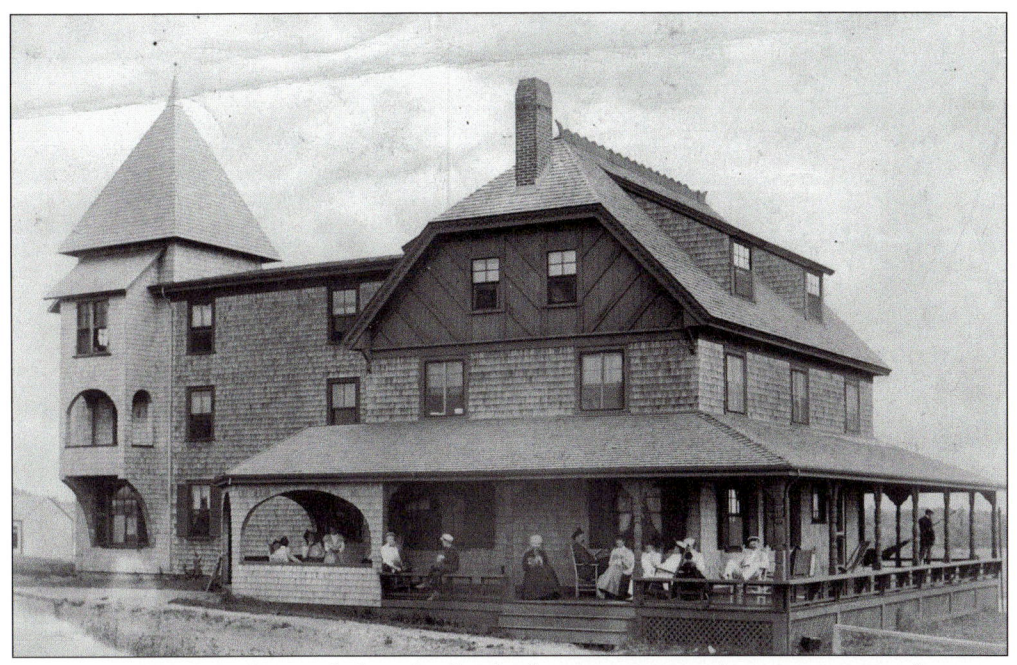

THE SNOW INN. Levi Snow is believed to be the first native to see the opportunities of catering to the tourist trade. After years of entertaining summering relatives, Snow built a 20-room addition onto his home and welcomed relatives as *paying* guests.

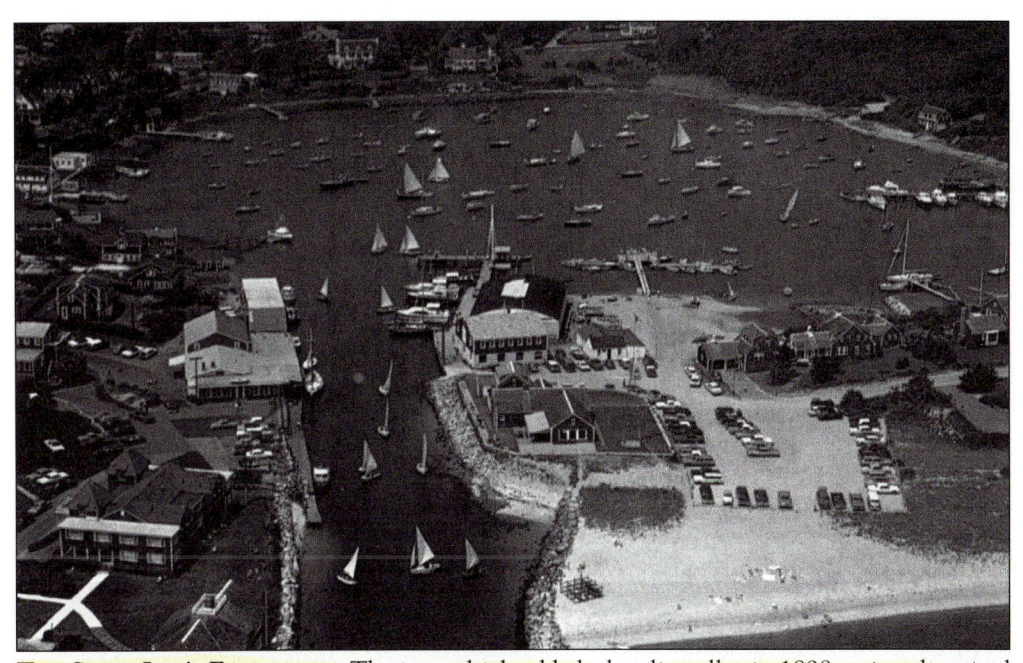

THE SNOW INN'S EVOLUTION. The inn, which added a bowling alley in 1898, enjoyed a prized location on this inlet from Wychmere Harbor. It was the eventual site of the well-known tourist attraction Thompson's Clam Bar. Most of the buildings were razed in the 1990s to make room for condominiums.

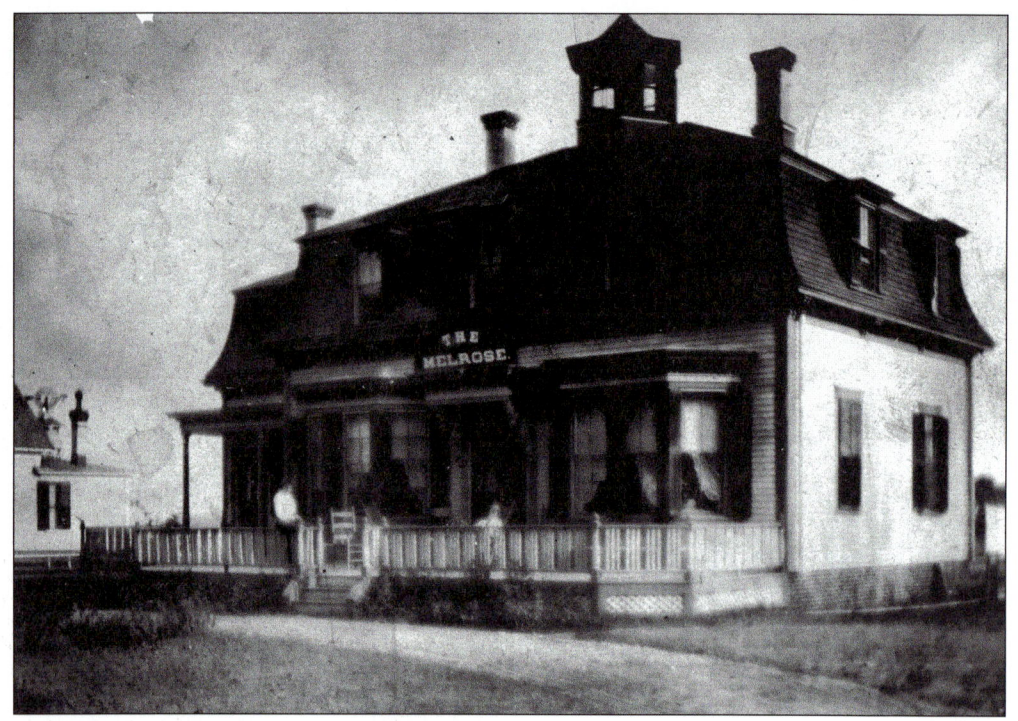

THE MELROSE INN. This inn in Harwich Port entertained generations of summer guests. In 1935, rates were $4 a day. The facility eventually became a boardinghouse and suffered physical deterioration.

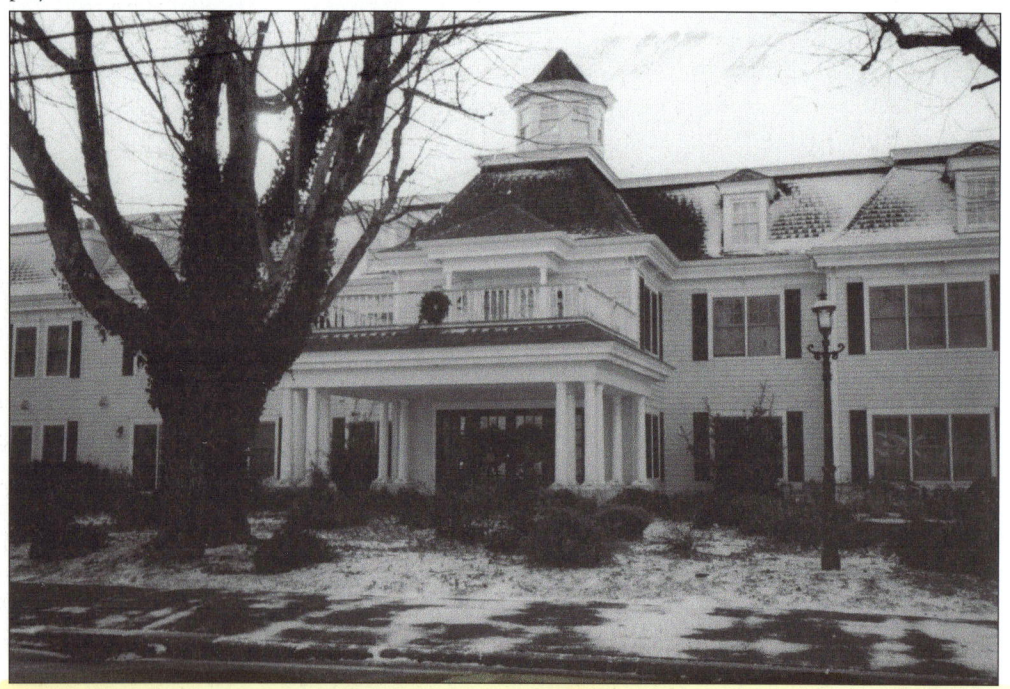

THE MELROSE TODAY. Proudly restored to its former stateliness, the Melrose today is a condominium for retired people. (Sr. Aureen Rose Behrend.)

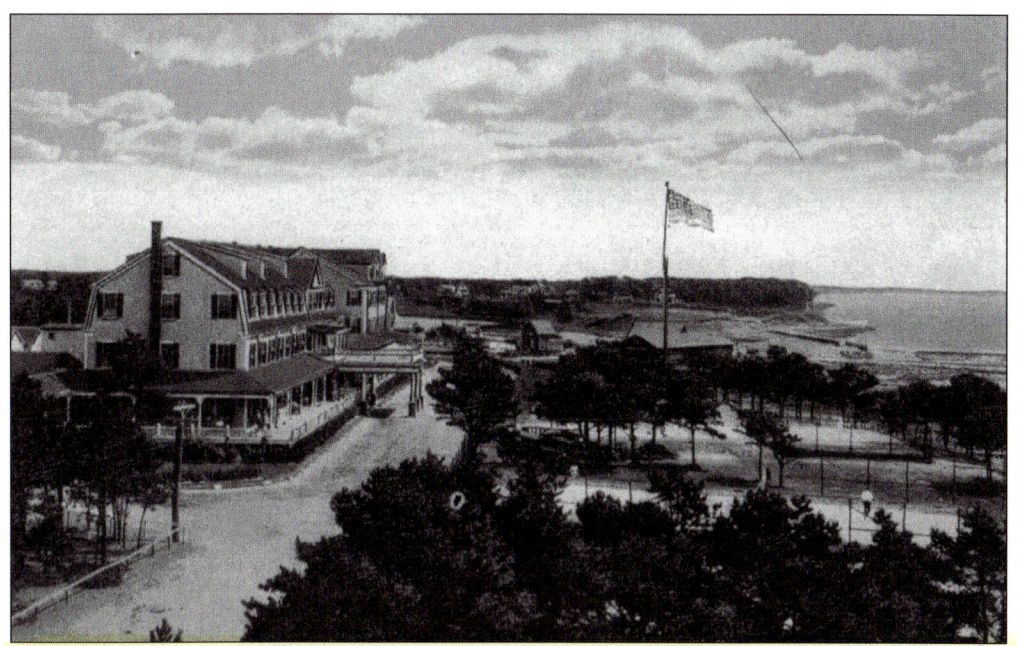

THE BELMONT. Considered the queen of Harwich's resort facilities, the Belmont was built in 1894 on a 22-acre oceanfront tract, which had previously belonged to Caleb Chase. With its casino and private cabanas, the hotel attracted the rich and famous. After a Dow Jones ticker was installed in the lobby for the convenience of guests, the Belmont was often called "the summer Wall Street."

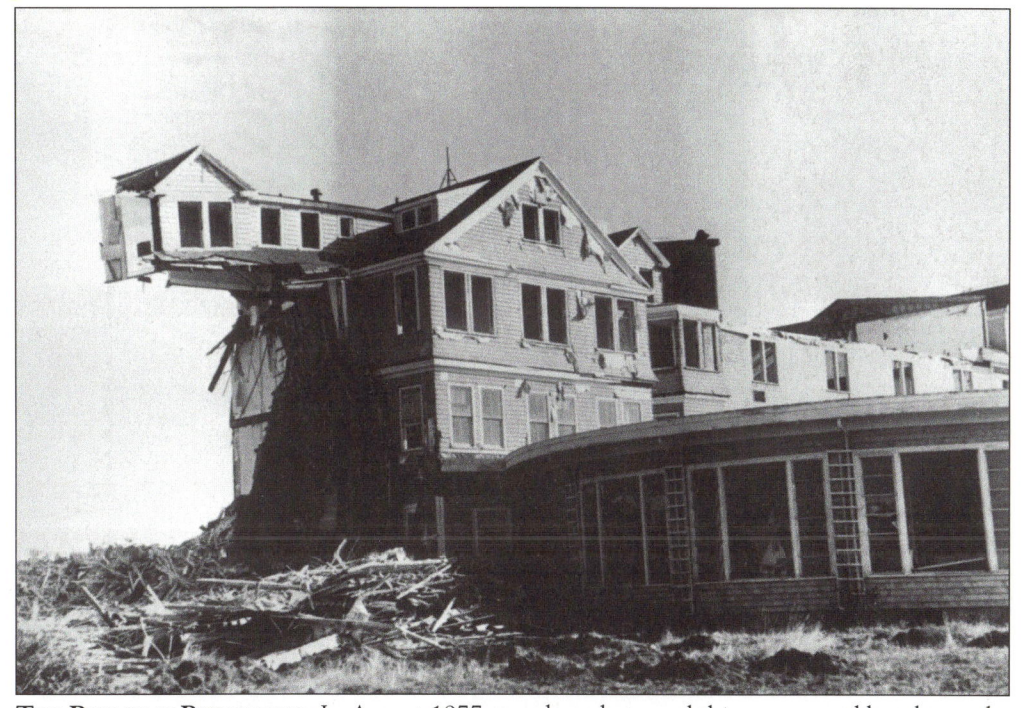

THE BELMONT BULLDOZED. In August 1977, wreckers destroyed this once proud hotel to make room for condominiums.

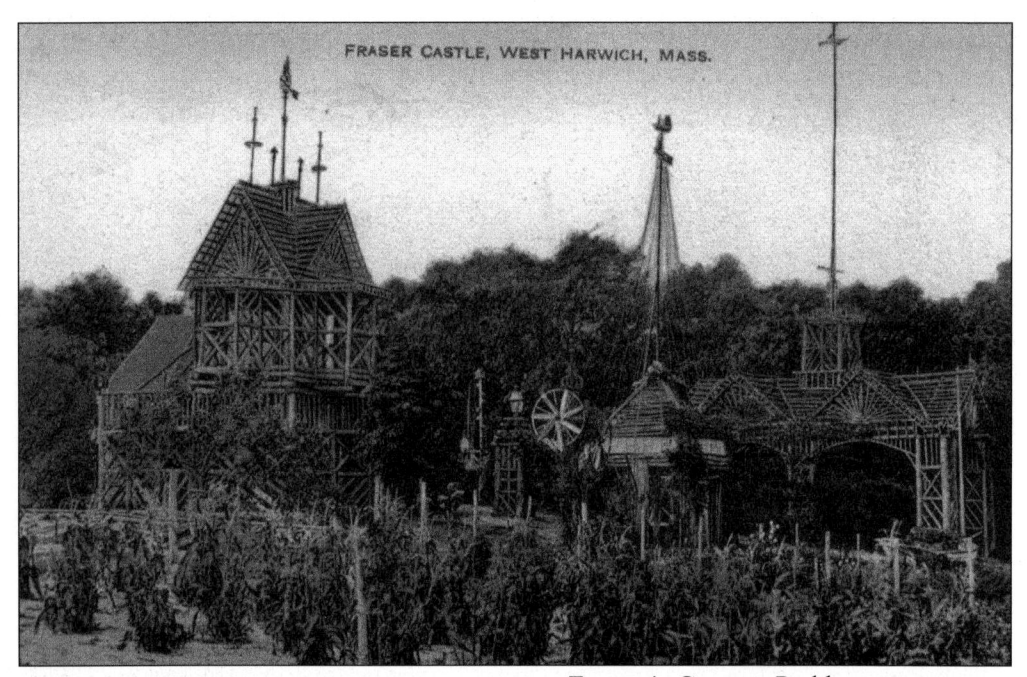

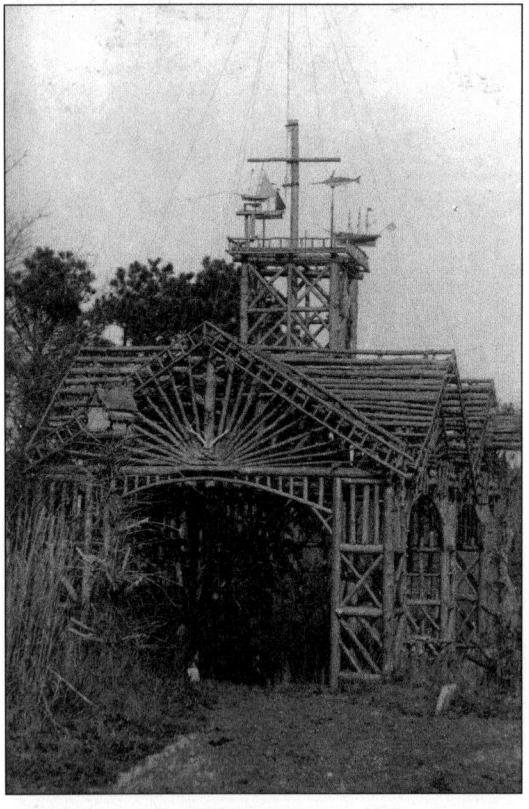

FRASER'S CASTLE. Building was not limited to overnight facilities for guests. Simon Fraser, a gardener, built these odd structures on his property in West Harwich. Did he have delusions of grandeur, or did he hope to attract vacationers' dollars?

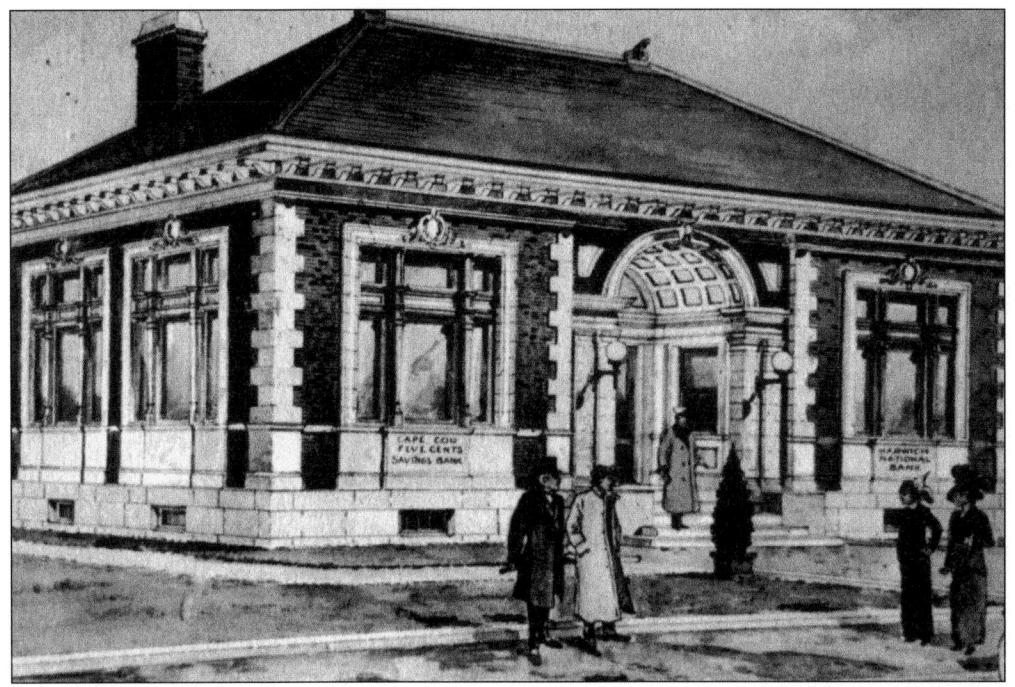

THE NEW BANK BUILDING. The boom created by the resort trade, as well as a disastrous fire that destroyed the Five Cents Savings Bank, led to the construction of this impressive building in 1912 to house both town banks in proper splendor. Located in Harwich Center, the building now houses the Harwich Town Hall.

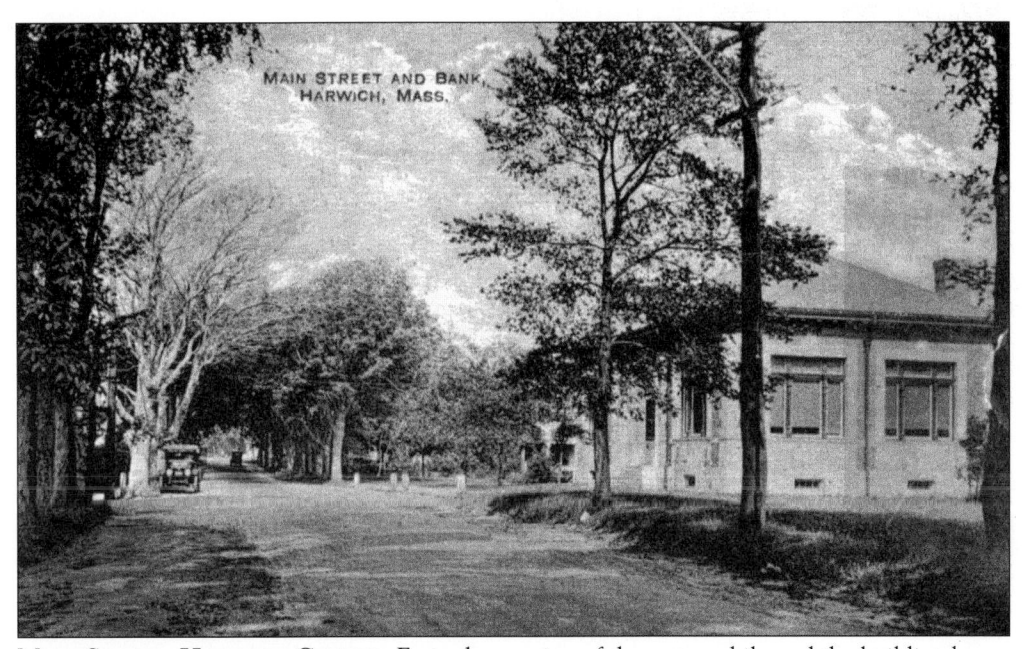

MAIN STREET, HARWICH CENTER. Even the coming of the automobile and the building boom had little effect on the serenity of Main Street.

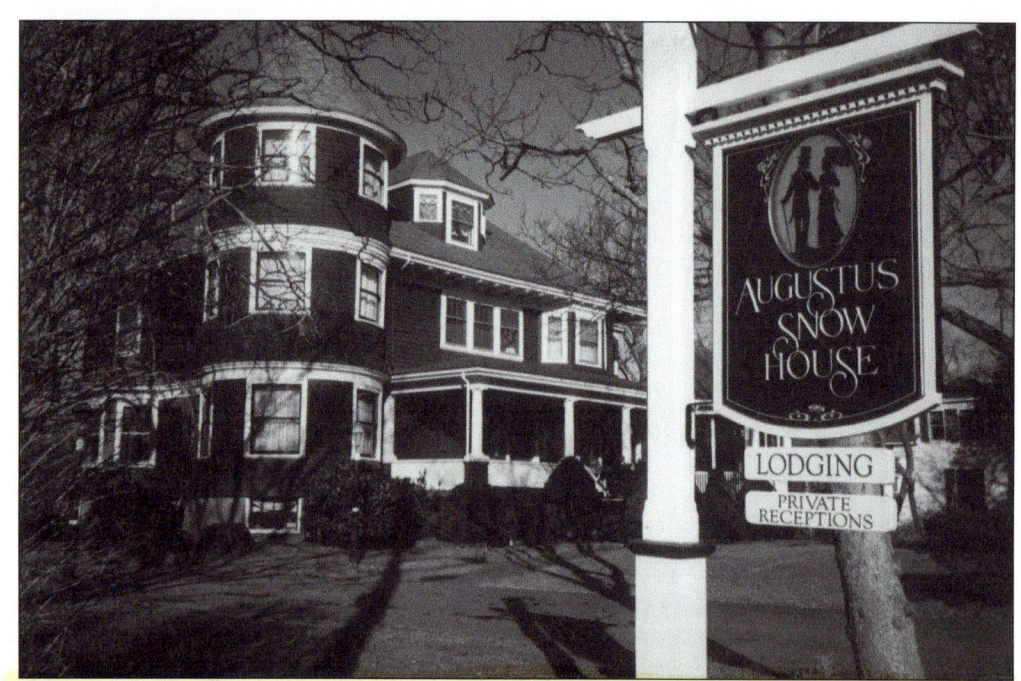

THE AUGUSTUS C. SNOW HOUSE. As the number of visitors has steadily risen, several stately old homes have been carefully converted into bed-and-breakfast facilities. The Snow House in Harwich Port was the residence of three bank presidents. (Sr. Aureen Rose Behrend.)

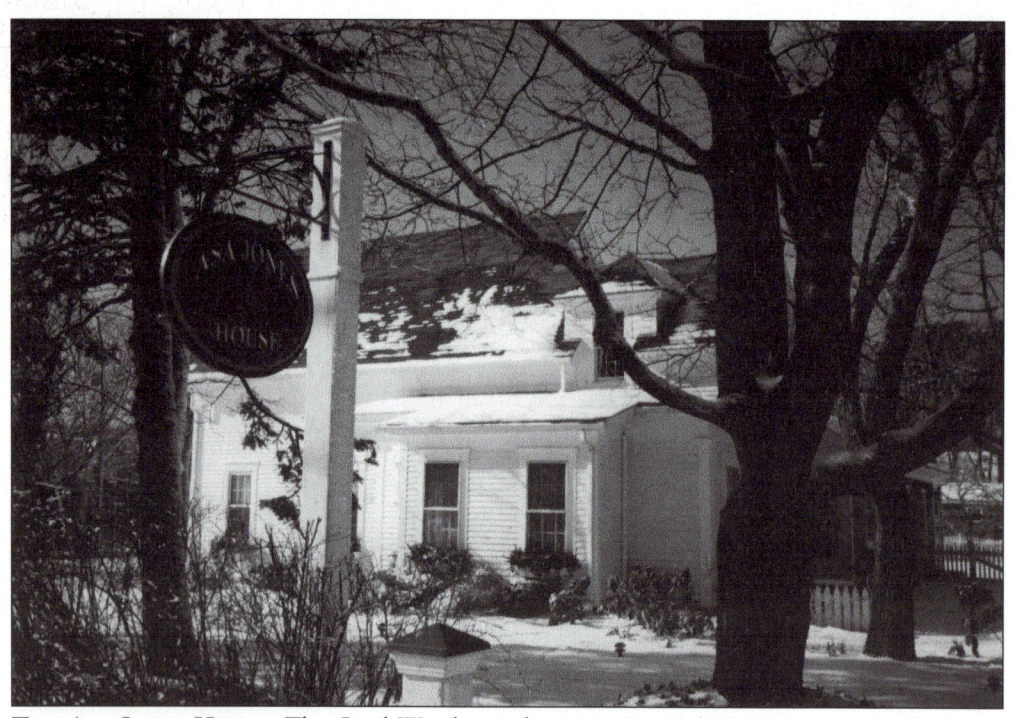

THE ASA JONES HOUSE. The Civil War hero's home in Harwich Center is among the more recent conversions of historic homes into facilities for guests.

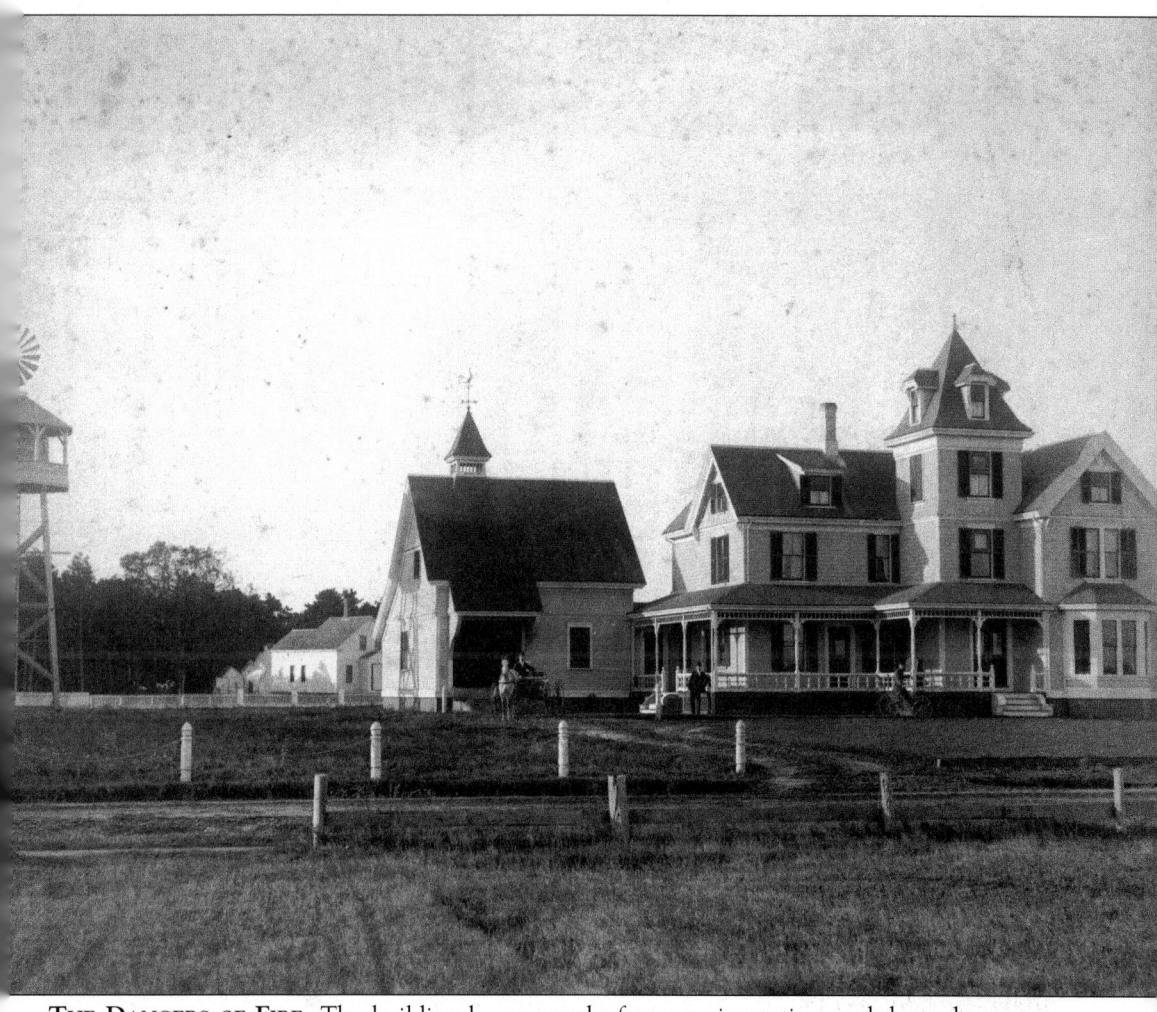

THE DANGERS OF FIRE. The building boom, sparks from passing trains, and dependence on water from wells and ponds all added to the danger of fire. This impressive home, built by Augustus M. Nickerson in 1890, burned to the ground in 1897. It was later rebuilt by Benjamin F. Bee and then became the Village Inn.

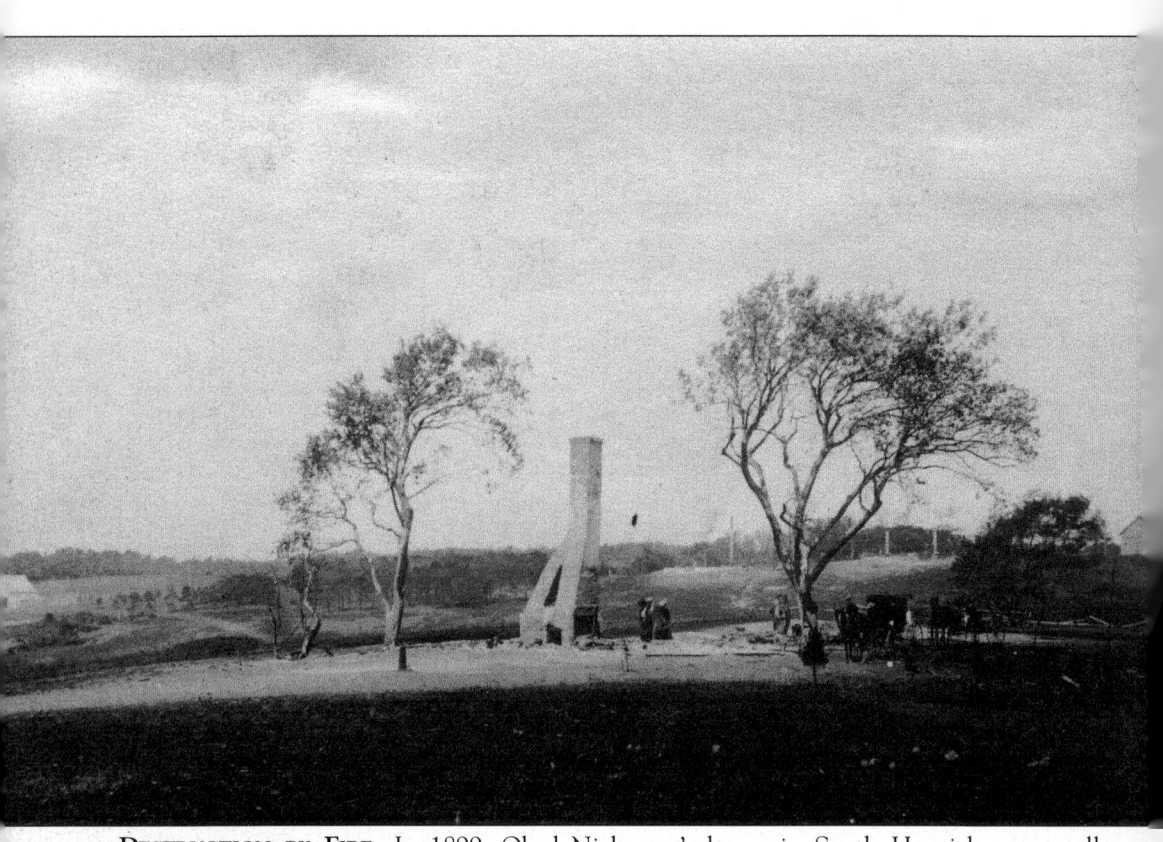

DESTRUCTION BY FIRE. In 1899, Obed Nickerson's home in South Harwich was totally destroyed by fire.

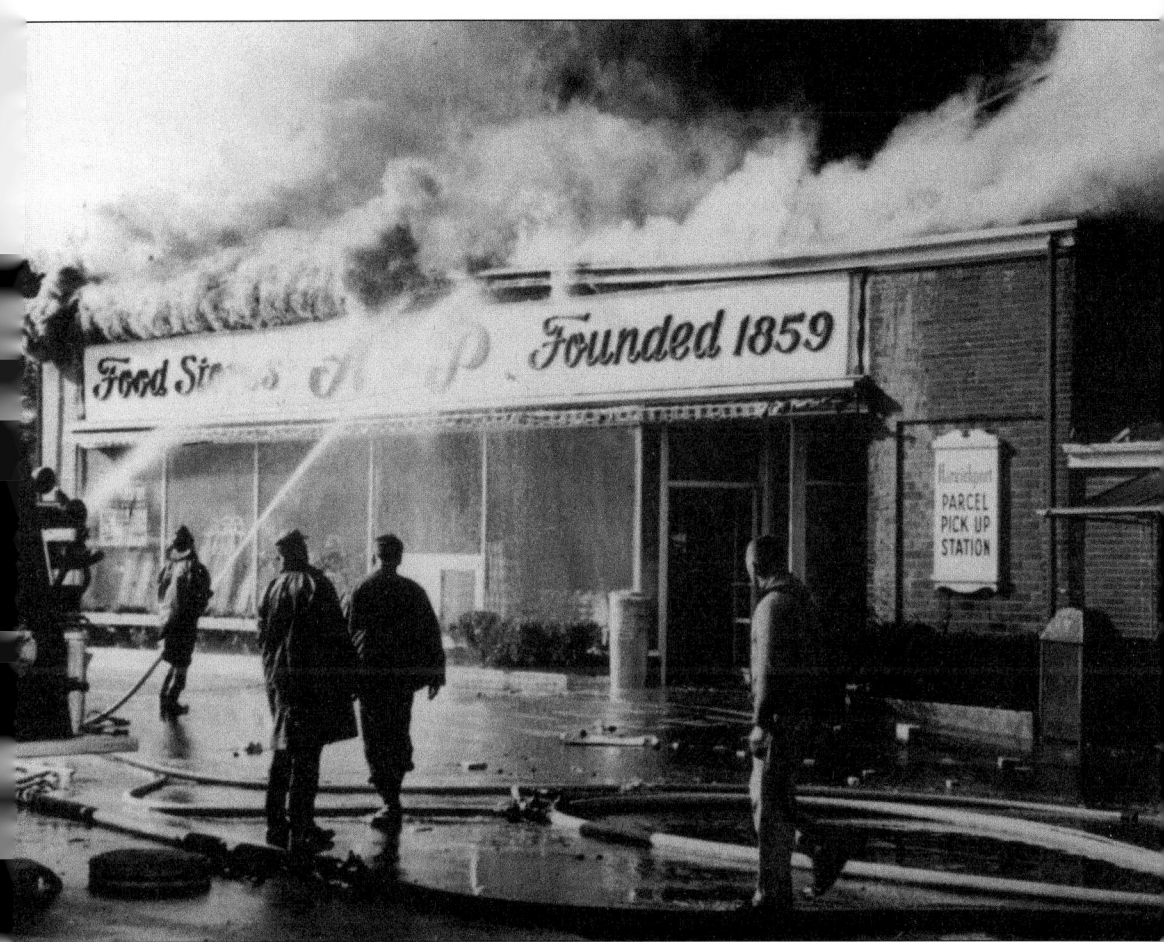

THE A & P FIRE IN HARWICH PORT. Perhaps the most dramatic fire occurred in the 1950s, when the A & P and several adjacent stores were destroyed. The area is now the site of the Harwich Port Post Office and a small shopping center.

Old Fire Engine

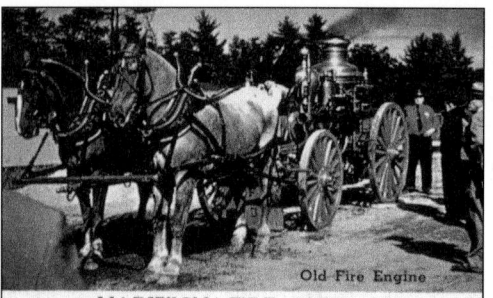

HARWICH FIRE SIGNALS

SECTION	FIRST ALARM	SECOND ALARM	GENERAL ALARM
NORTH HARWICH	12 (Two rounds)	12 (Four rounds)	12 (Four rounds repeated)
EAST HARWICH	13 "	13 "	13 "
SOUTH HARWICH	14 "	14 "	14 "
WEST HARWICH	15 "	15 "	15 "
HARWICHPORT	21 "	21 "	21 "
HARWICH CENTER	31 "	31 "	31 "
PLEASANT LAKE	41 "	41 "	41 "

SPECIAL SIGNALS
NO SCHOOL   1 (Four rounds) Blown on air horn only at 7:30 A.M.
TEST   1 (One round)   Sounded at noon except Sundays and Holidays.
RESCUE SQUAD   1 (Two rounds)   Not sounded between the hours of 6:00 P.M. & 8:00 A.M.
OUT OF TOWN   33 (Four rounds)
AIR RAID   Red -- Wailing of sirens or short blasts of horn for a 3 min. period.
               Yellow -- Steady blast of 3.5 mins. duration on all warning devices.

Emergency Telephone   Harwich 430

Fire Permit Regulations:

Permits are required for all open air fires - including incinerators.

Written permits are mandatory for all fires not on property owned or occupied by permittee. This applies to all fires including cook-out fires in charcoal grills.

For Information on legal burning hours and other fire regulations call the fire station - 286.

FIREFIGHTING. From Colonial bucket brigades to horse-drawn tankers, the community's firefighting capabilities progressed bit by bit to the establishment of a fire department. In 1918, the first gasoline-powered engine was acquired for $5,000. With pneumatic tires and a self-starter, it was considered to be a state-of-the-art vehicle. At the same time, a volunteer department was organized. Another big step was taken in 1935, when voters agreed to provide materials, with labor provided by the Works Projects Administration, to construct a municipal water system.

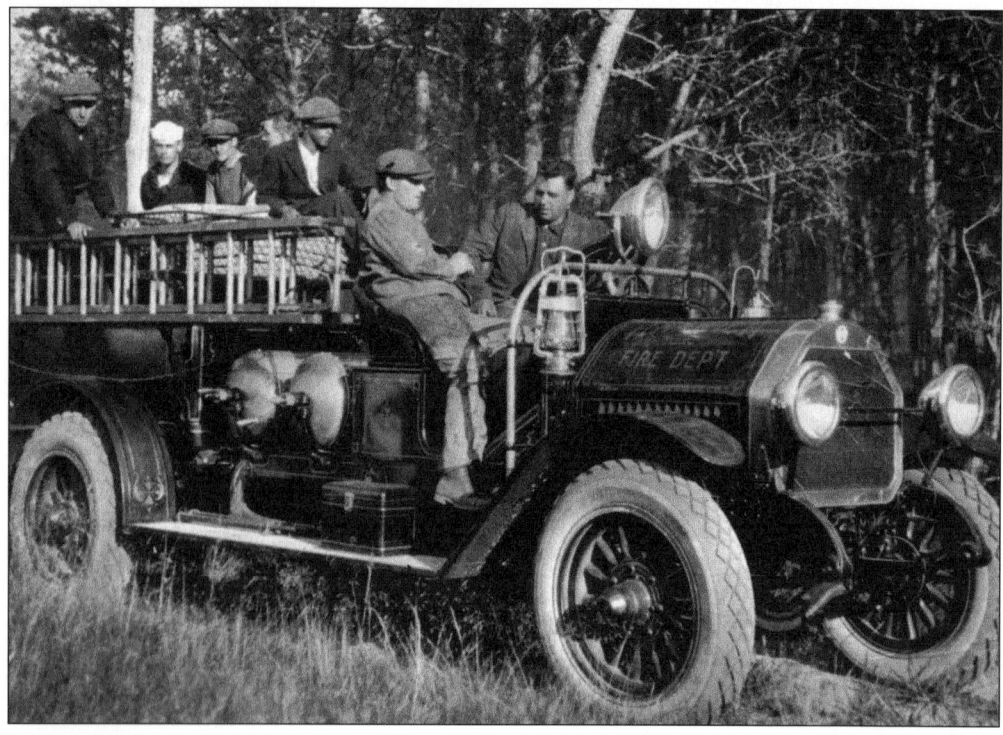

92

I would also like at this time to take the opportunity to thank Dr. Harold F. Rowley of Harwich, for his splendid co-operation in the instructions he gave this Department in the First Aid to the injured.

Since this Department was established February 15, 1933, the night patrol has, in my opinion prevented a lot of crime, as the records of previous years will show, and when this department is fully equipped, it will give to the public more efficient service.

Following is the list of cases brought before the 2nd. District Court:

Automobile violations	16
Assault and Battery	16
Arson	1
Disturbing the Peace	2
Drunk	39
Keeping and Exposing Liquor	1
Larceny	5
Larceny by check	5
Vagrants	1
Non-support	5
Neglected children	10
Total	**101**
Sentenced to House of Correction	5
Sentenced to State Farm	4
Sentenced to Westboro	1

Arrested by State Police

Kidnaping	1
Extortion	1
Drunk	2
Automobile Violations	7
Total	**11**

POLICE PROTECTION. For years, Harwich maintained order primarily by public censure and the aid of a sheriff or two. In 1932, voters approved the establishment of a police force and the construction of a single traffic light. These crime statistics, taken from the town's annual report, represent the first year of operation.

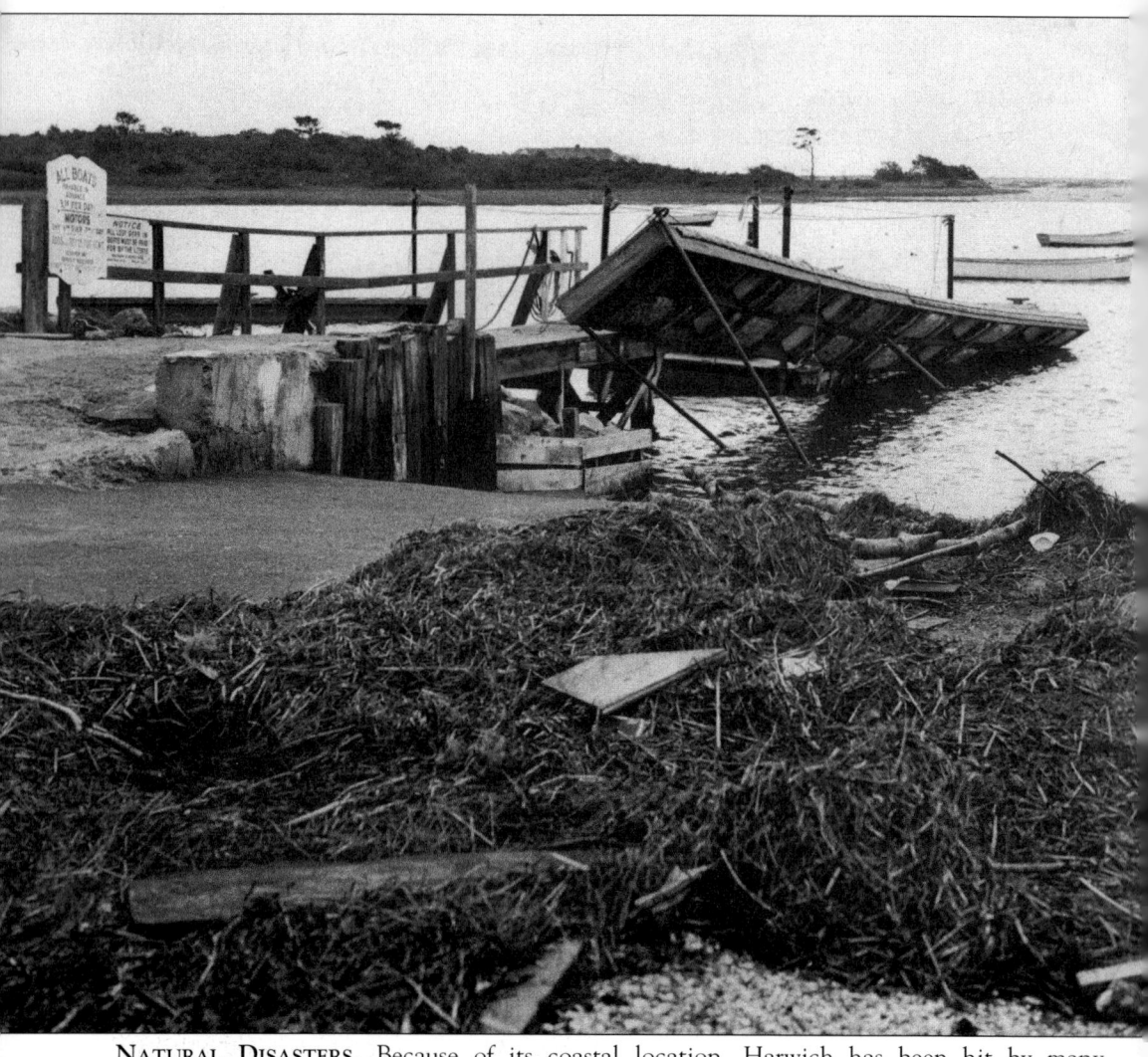

NATURAL DISASTERS. Because of its coastal location, Harwich has been hit by many nor'easters and tropical hurricanes over the years. The most destructive was the hurricane of 1944, when German prisoners were brought from Camp Edwards to repair damage.

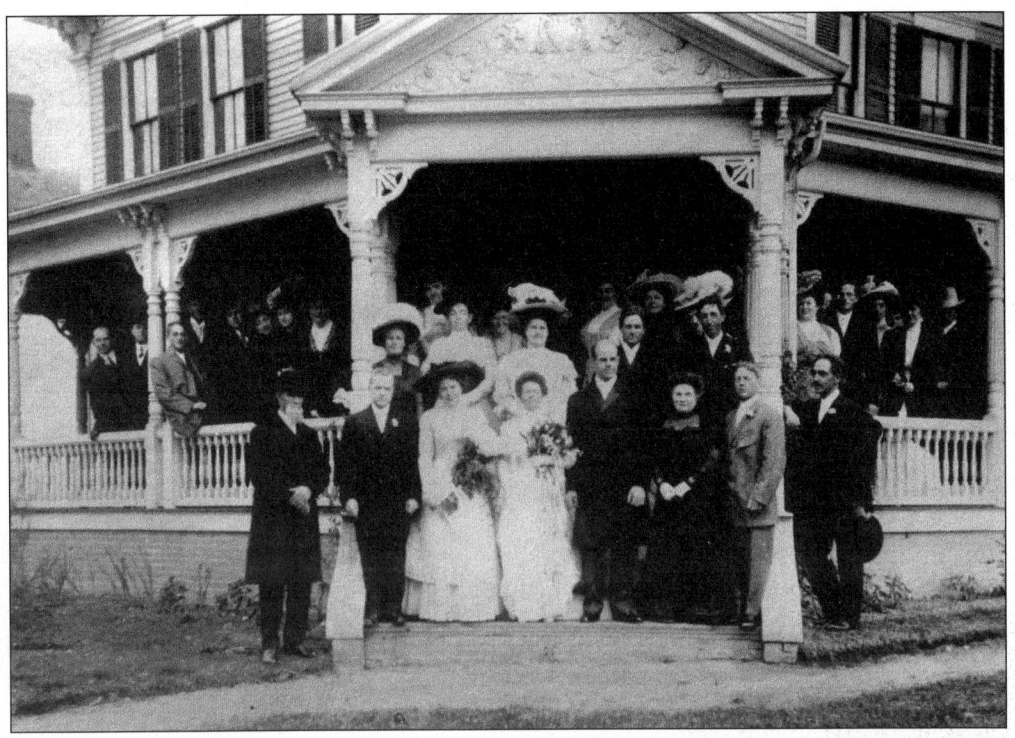

OLD CUSTOMS AND VALUES SURVIVE. Despite the many changes, the community remained family centered. This wedding took place on Bank Street.

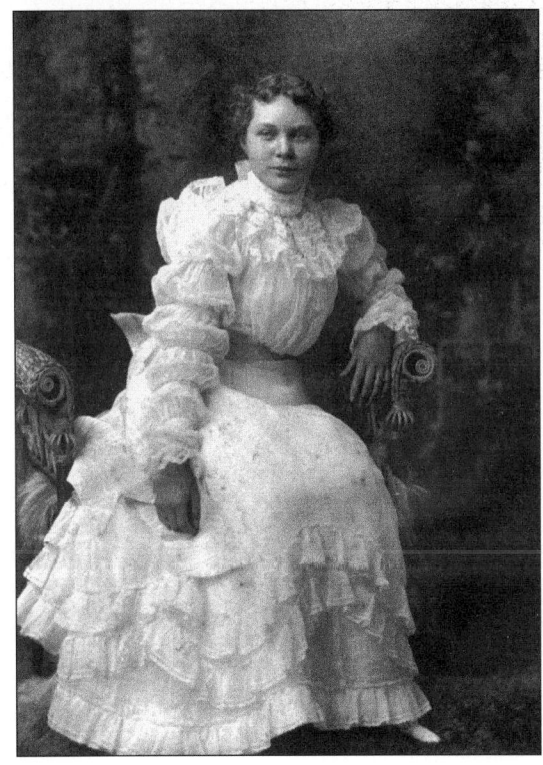

THE BRIDE. Josephine Baker, daughter of a sea captain, poses in her finery.

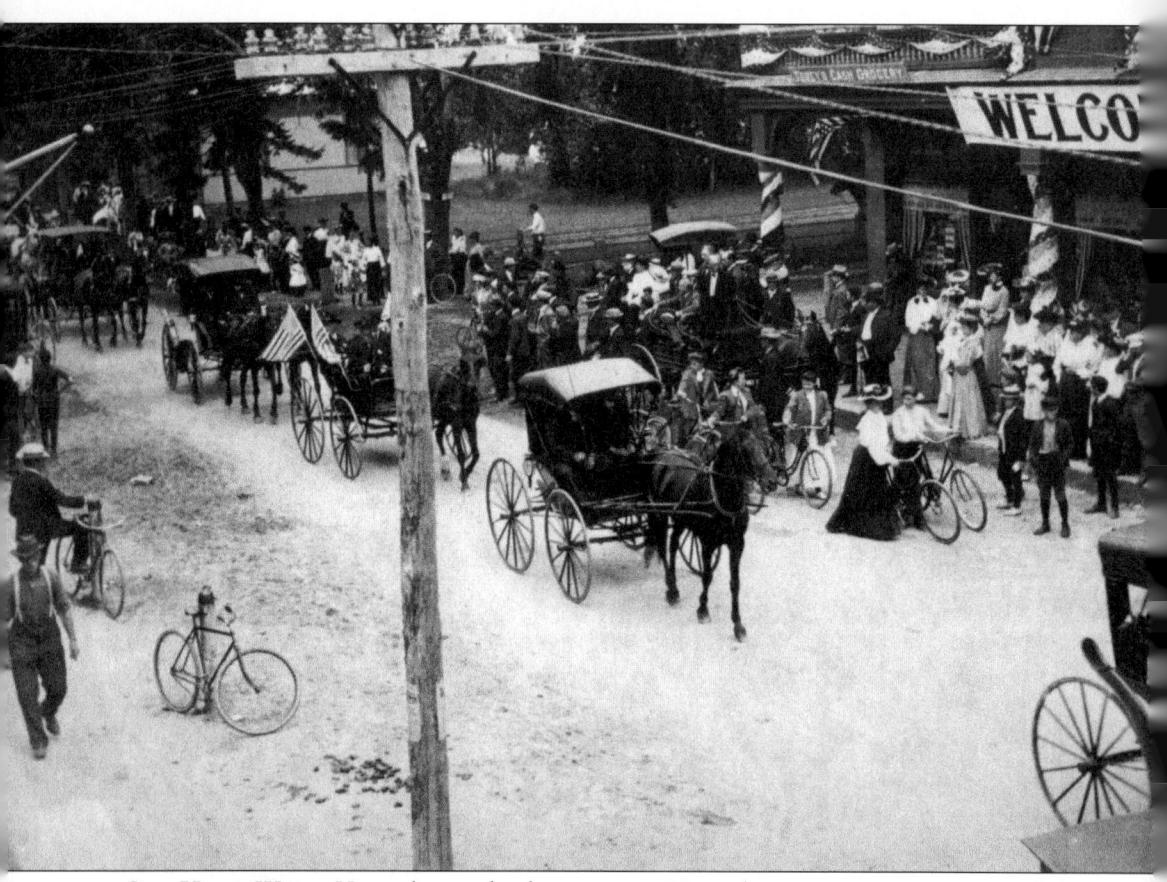

OLD HOME WEEK. Harwich was the first town in Massachusetts to institute a special day to honor the community and its traditions. The festivities included sports contests and a ball at the Exchange Building, but the parade down Main Street was the highlight.

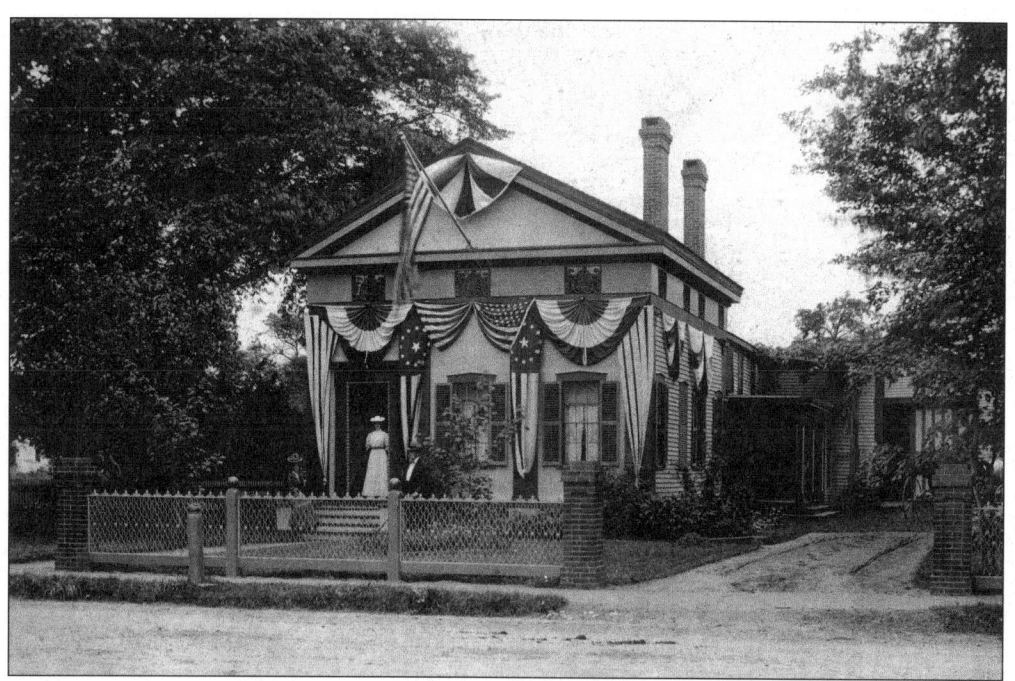

THE ANNIE DUTTON HOUSE DECORATED. Annie Dutton inherited the home of Dr. Franklin Dodge, her grandfather. Houses were covered in bunting for the Old Home Week celebrations.

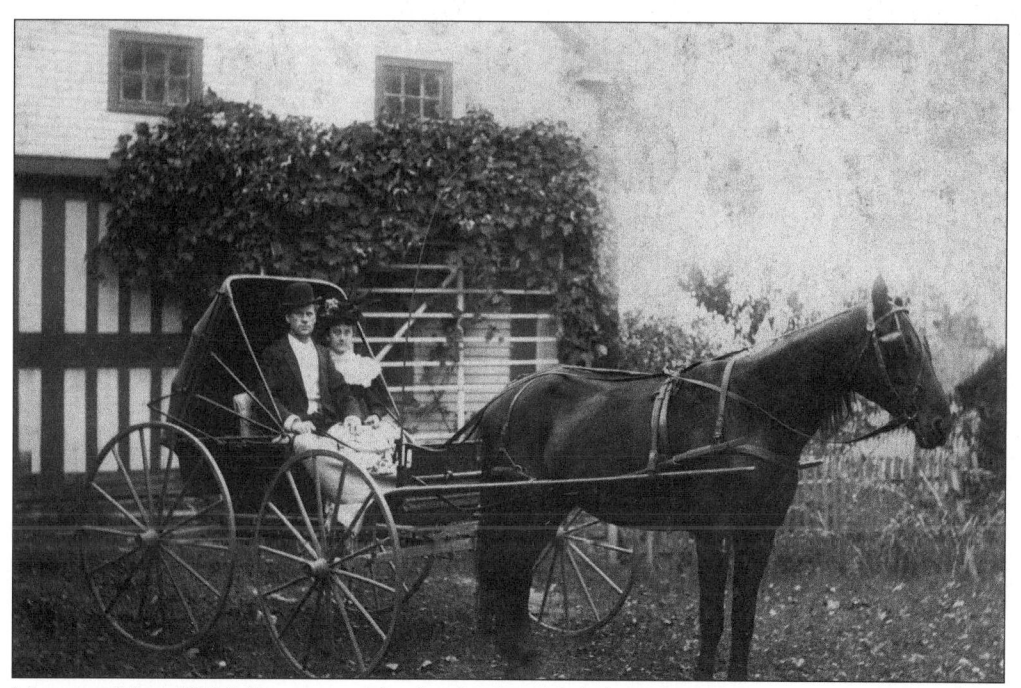

MR. AND MRS. W.M. DUTTON. After her husband failed to return from a trip to Alaska, where he intended to make his fortune, Annie Dutton supported herself by teaching music.

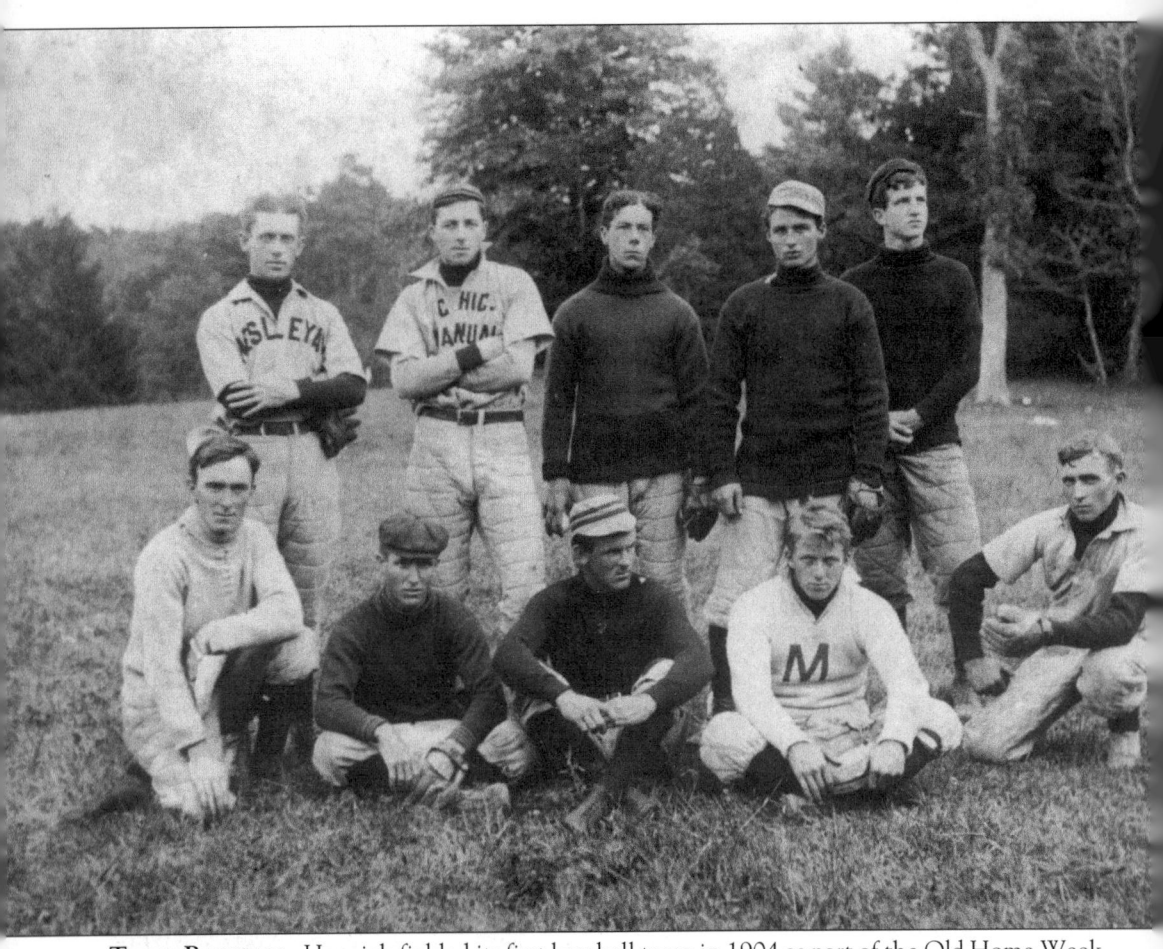

TOWN BASEBALL. Harwich fielded its first baseball team in 1904 as part of the Old Home Week celebrations. Since then, voters have annually approved sponsorship of a town team. Efforts to promote a football team were less successful. The Harwich team was soundly defeated in its first games with Hyannis in 1894. Loyal fans attributed this to lack of knowledge of the rules.

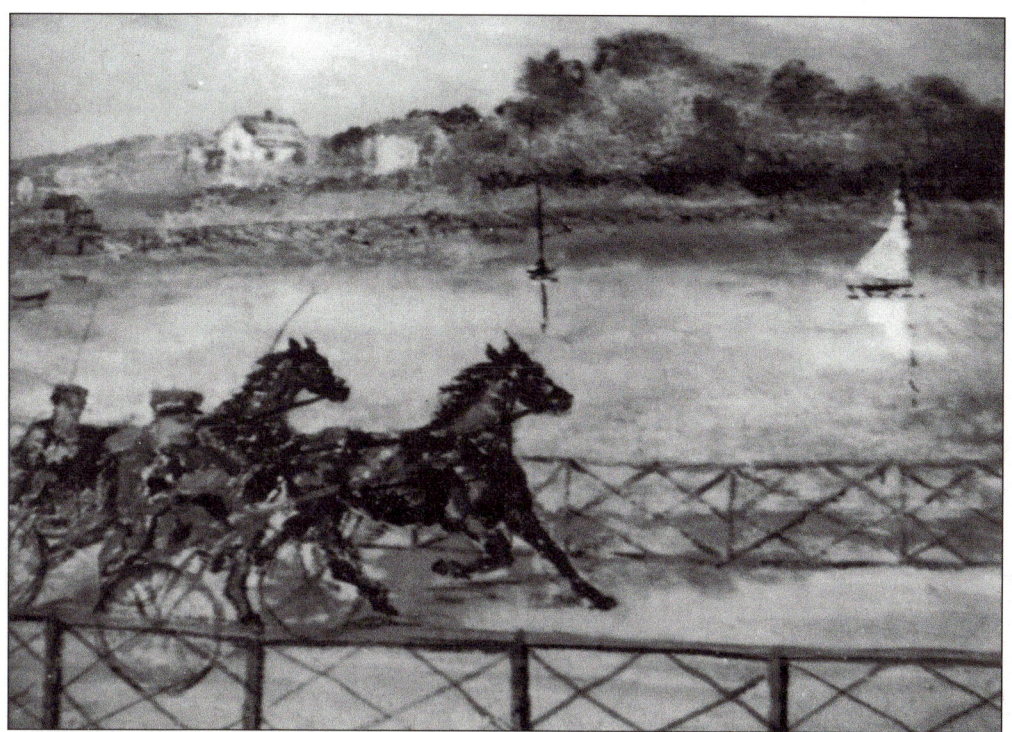

HORSE RACING. Good horses were always prized. As shown in this sketch by Charles D. Cahoon, a racetrack used to circle what is now Wychmere Harbor, and sulky races were well attended and hotly contested. The horse below, owned and driven by an East Harwich man, won track records at the West Dennis Trotting Park.

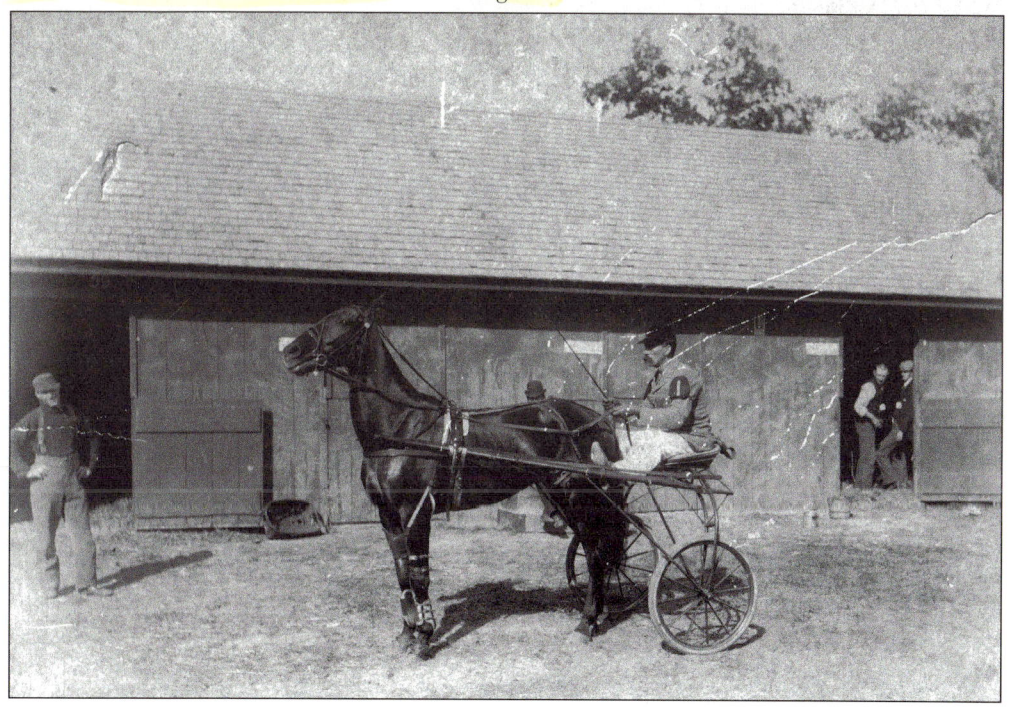

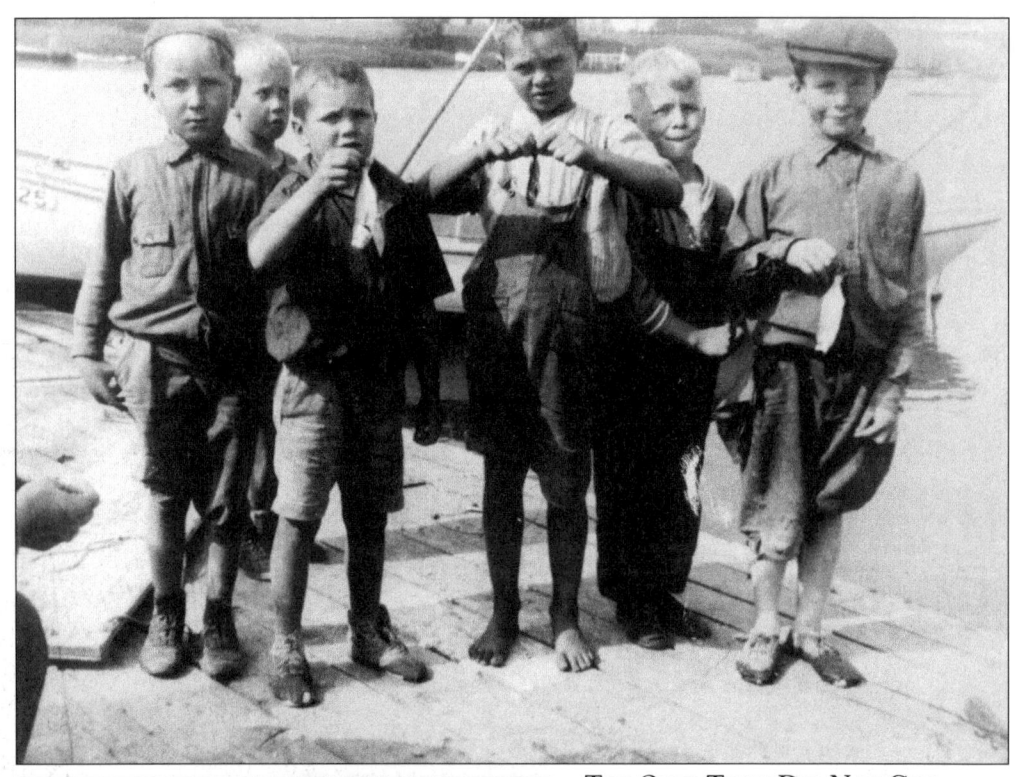

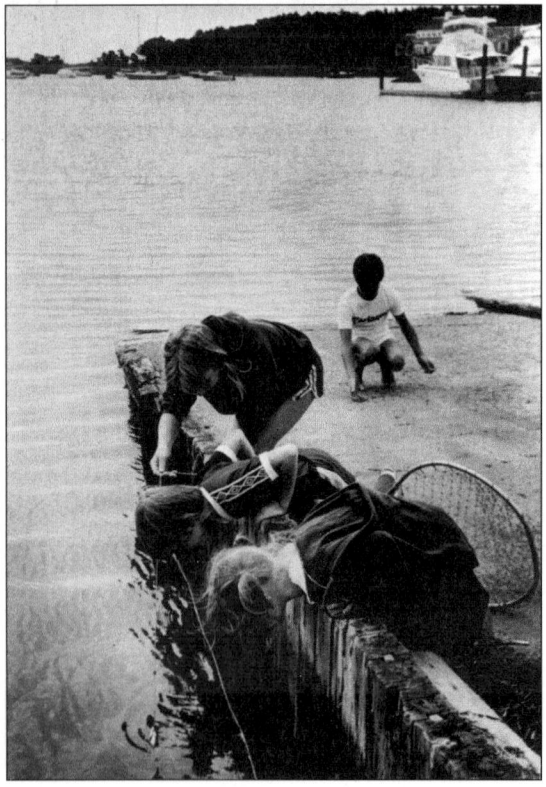

THE ONES THAT DID NOT GET AWAY. If commercial fishing had declined, sports fishing became even more popular. In this photograph, Harwich boys (including future bank president Ralph B. Snow, second from the left) display the day's catch. The other children are less successful.

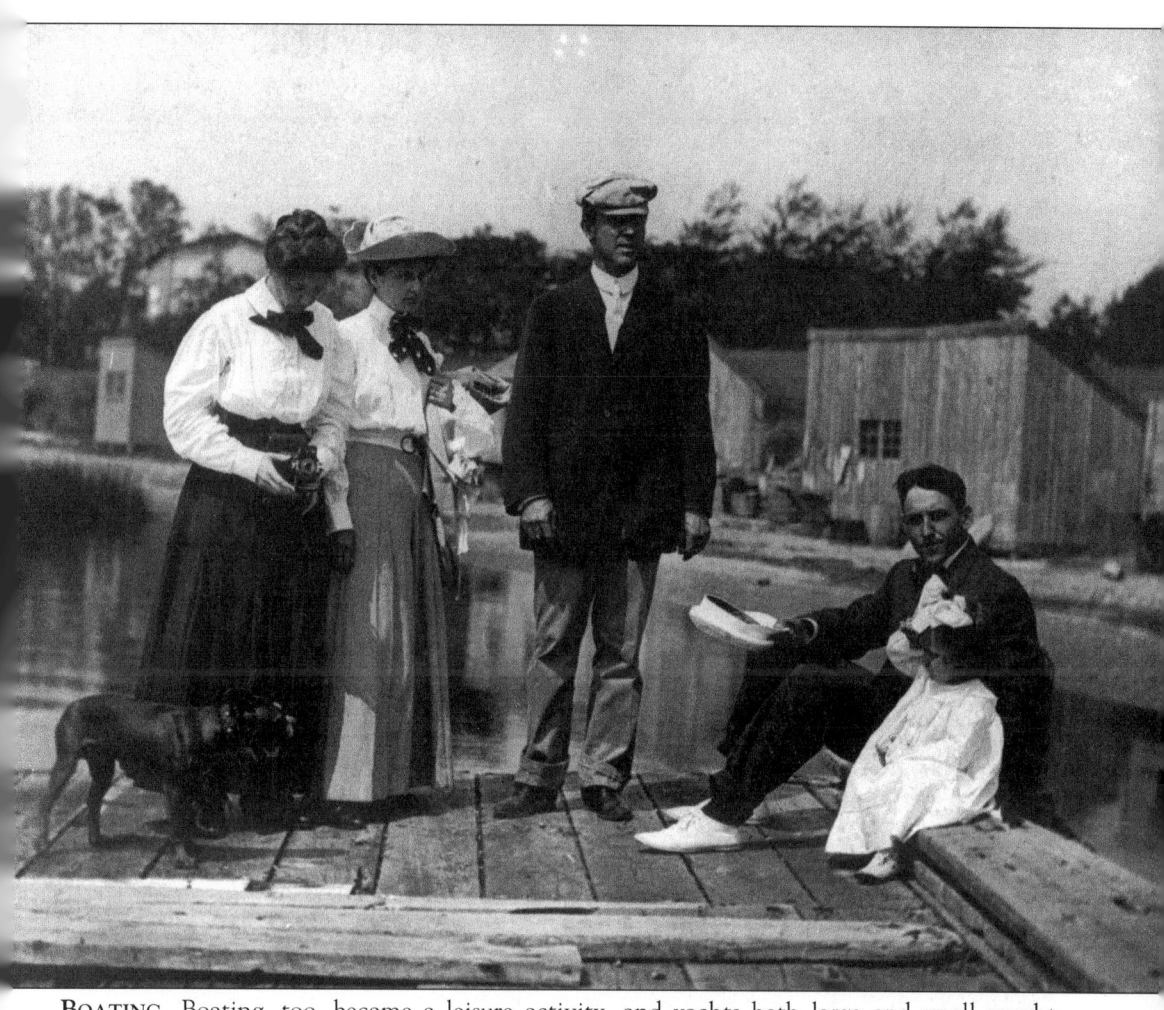

BOATING. Boating, too, became a leisure activity, and yachts both large and small sought berths. Here, Dr. Charles Smyser and his family pause at Wychmere before an outing.

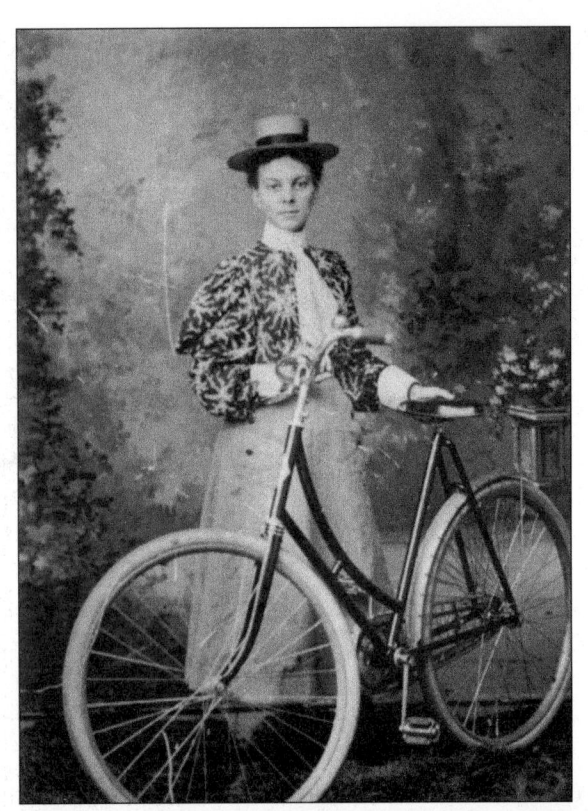

BICYCLING. Bicycling also became a favored activity. Bertha Atkins of Pleasant Lake poses in the studio with a bicycle that looks unfit for use. The children proudly display their own bikes. Local stores were advertising bicycles for $50 and up.

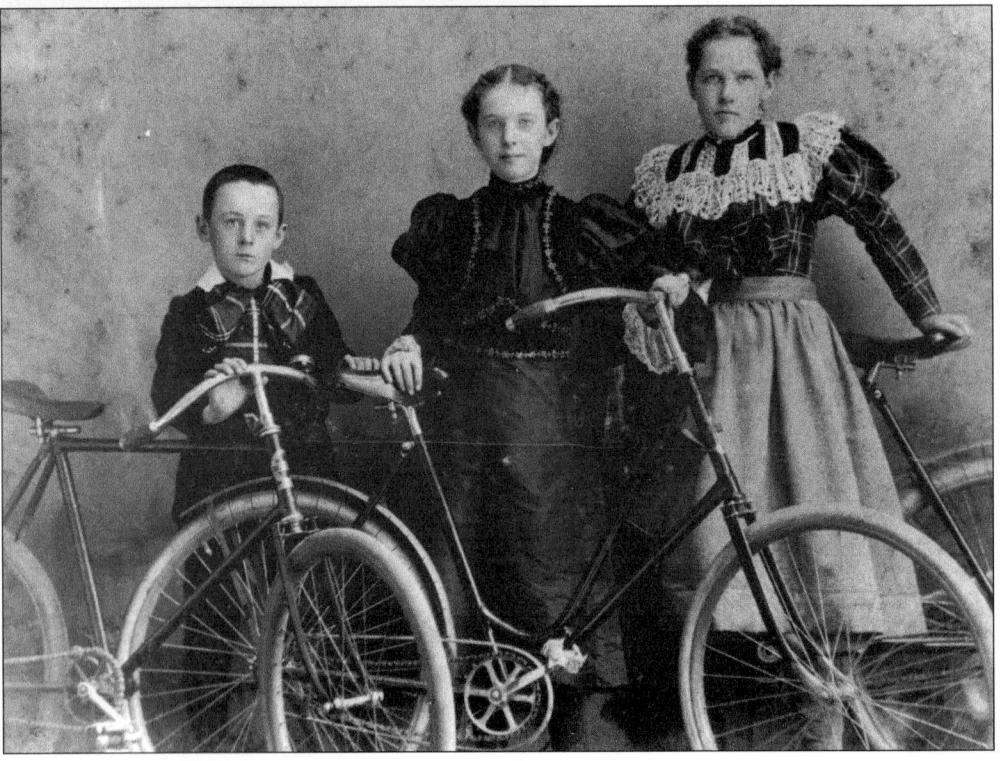

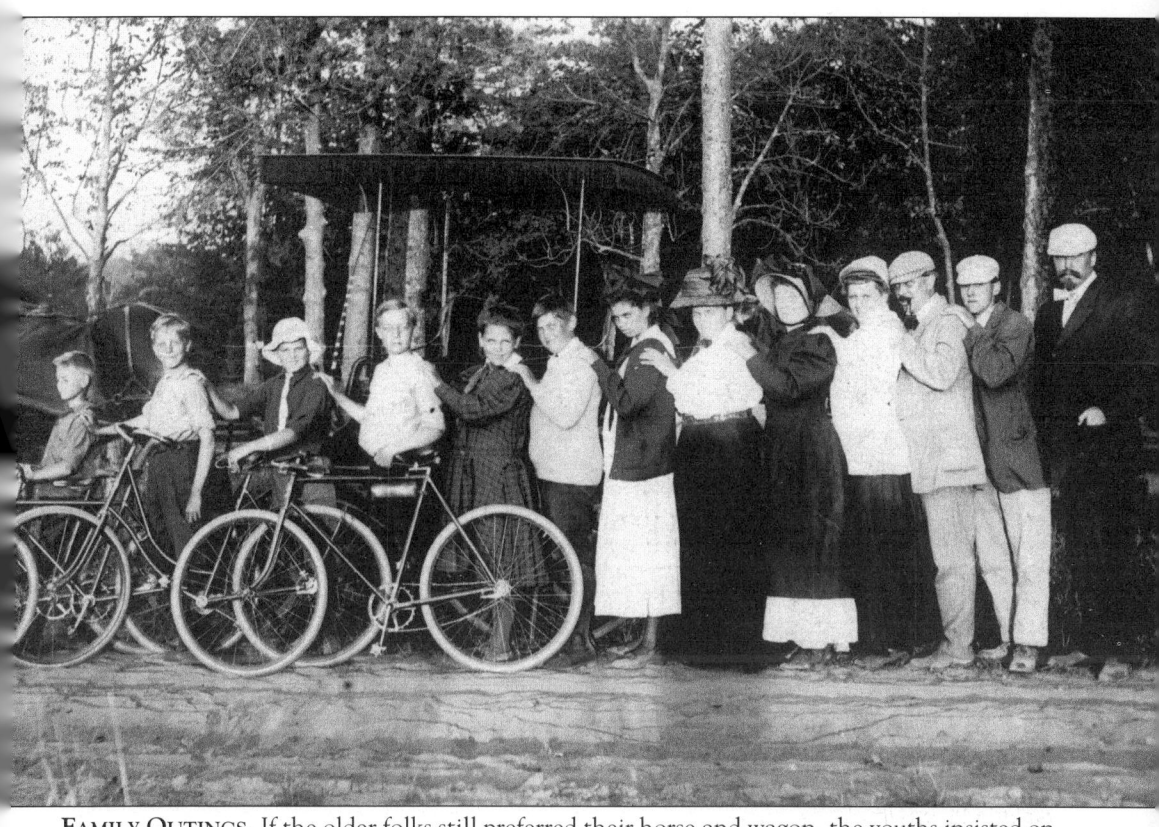

FAMILY OUTINGS. If the older folks still preferred their horse and wagon, the youths insisted on traveling on their bicycles.

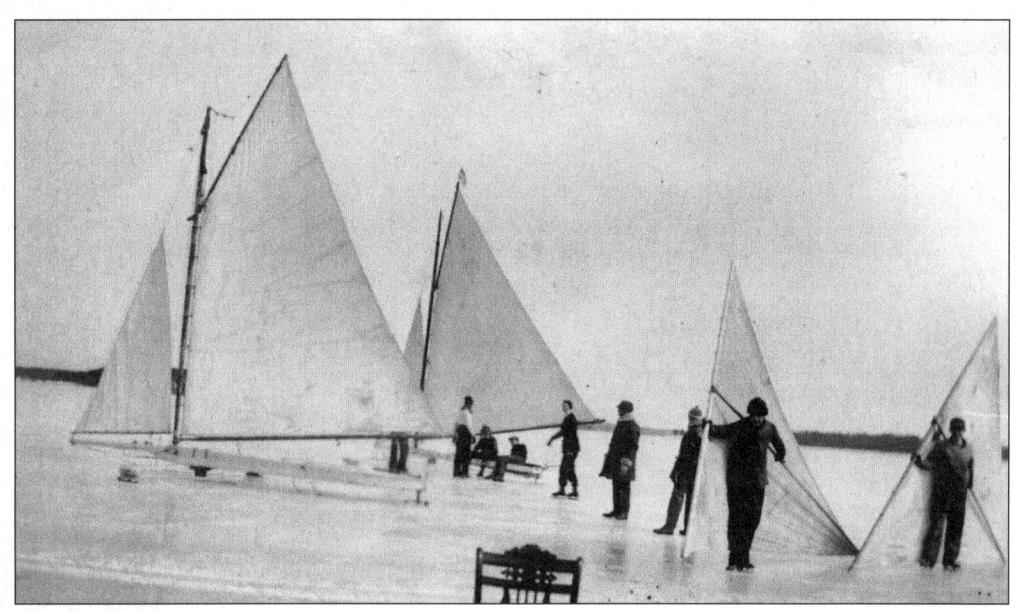

WINTER SPORTS. Ice-skating and iceboating on Long Pond won so many participants that a special excursion train was operated from Boston on weekends.

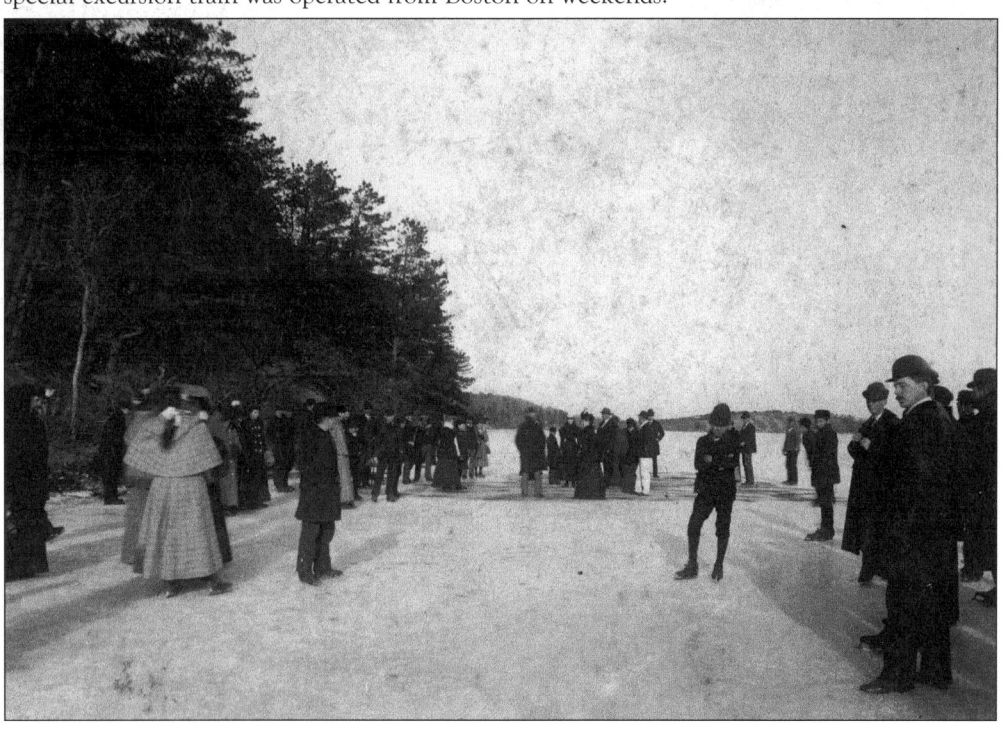

104

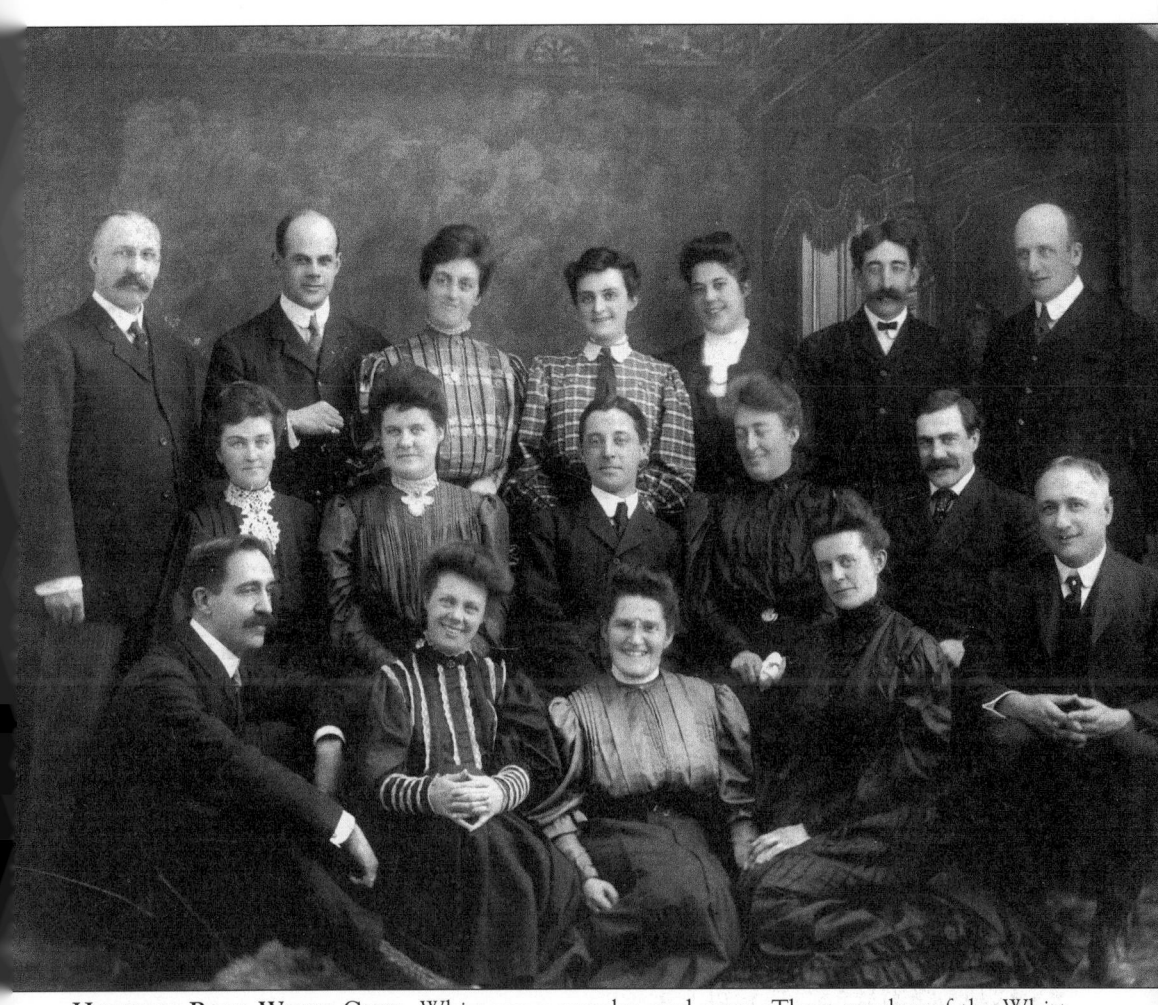

HARWICH PORT WHIST CLUB. Whist was a popular card game. These regulars of the Whist Club include married couples and singles.

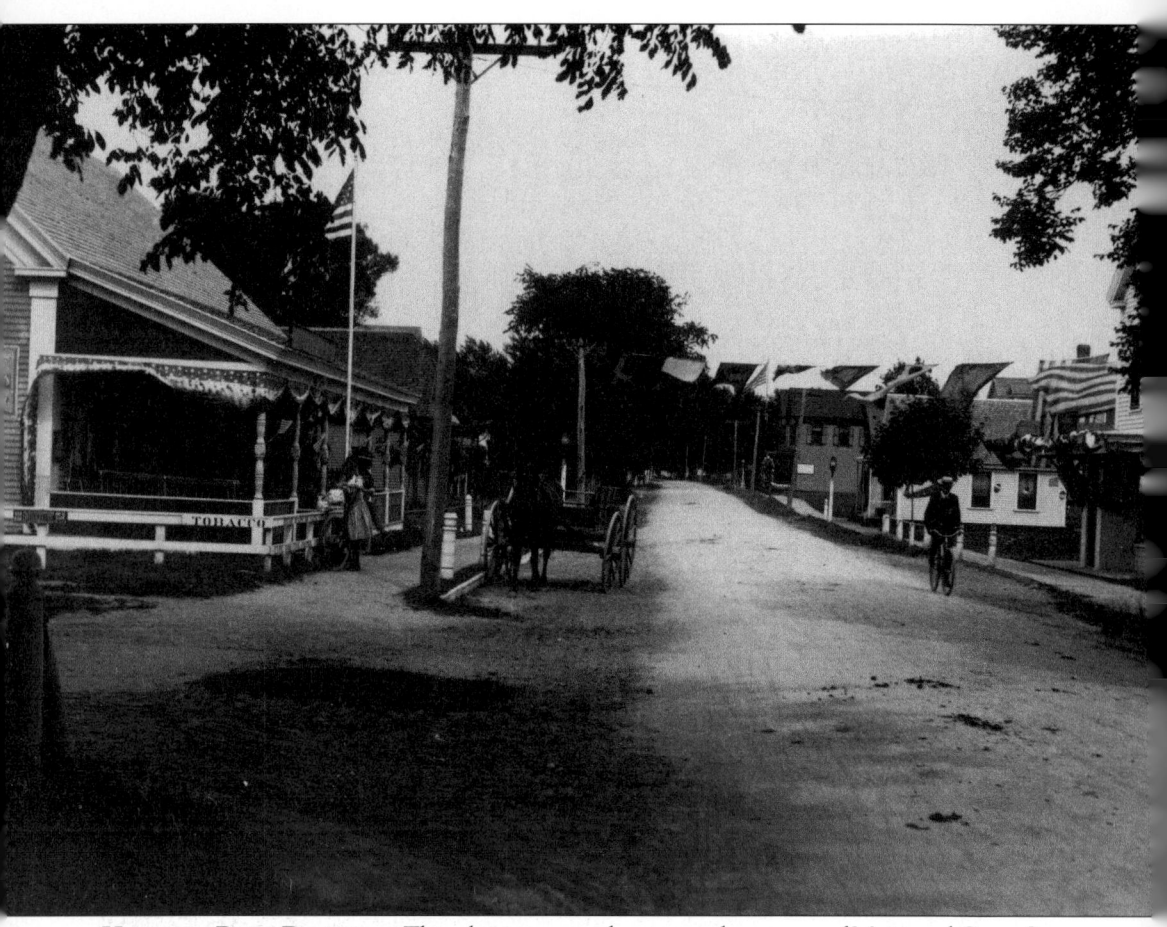

HARWICH PORT DEVELOPS. This almost pastoral scene at the corner of Main and Cross Streets fails to indicate how business was picking up significantly for the local merchants.

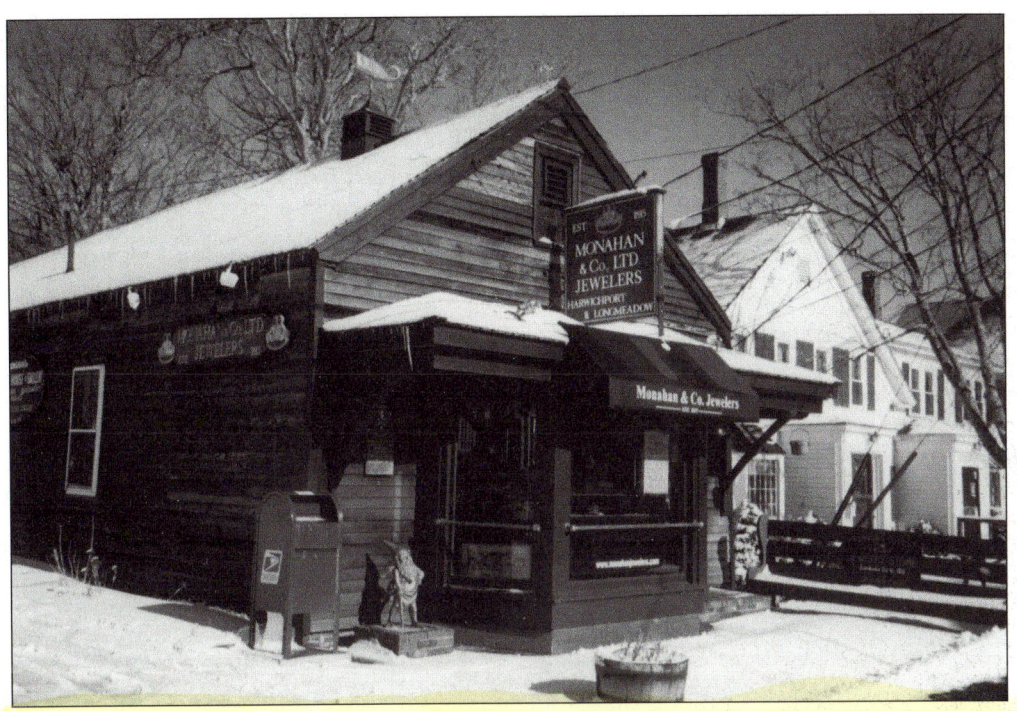

MONAHAN JEWELERS. This building was constructed in the 1850s as an office for Henry Kelley's coal, lumber, and hardware businesses. (Sr. Aureen Rose Behrend.)

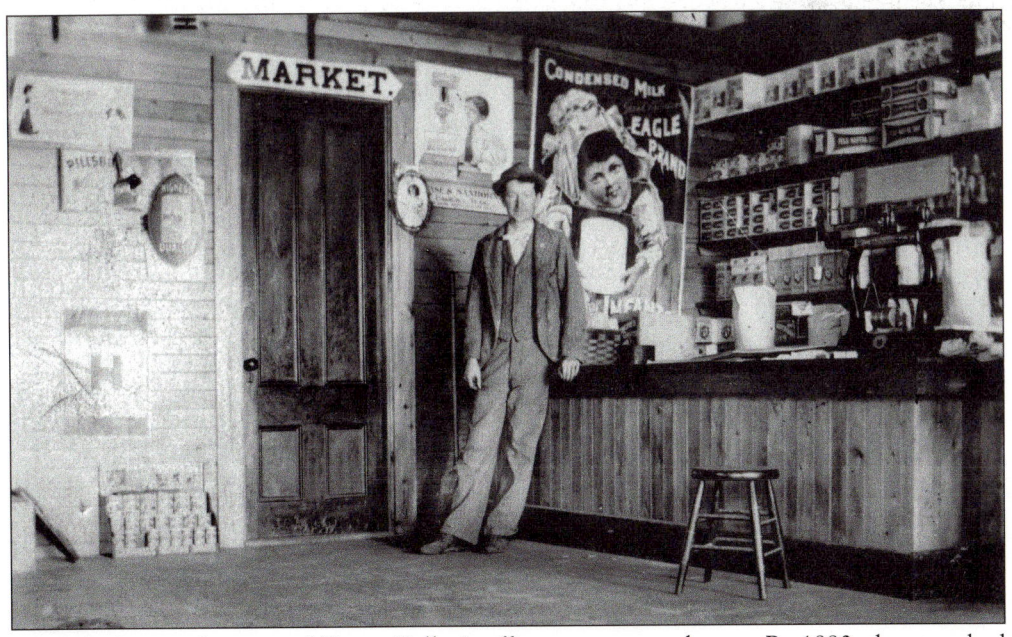

HULSE'S STORE. Just east of Henry Kelley's office was a general store. By 1880, the store had been purchased by James O. Hulse Jr., shown here in 1901 with a small assortment of his wares.

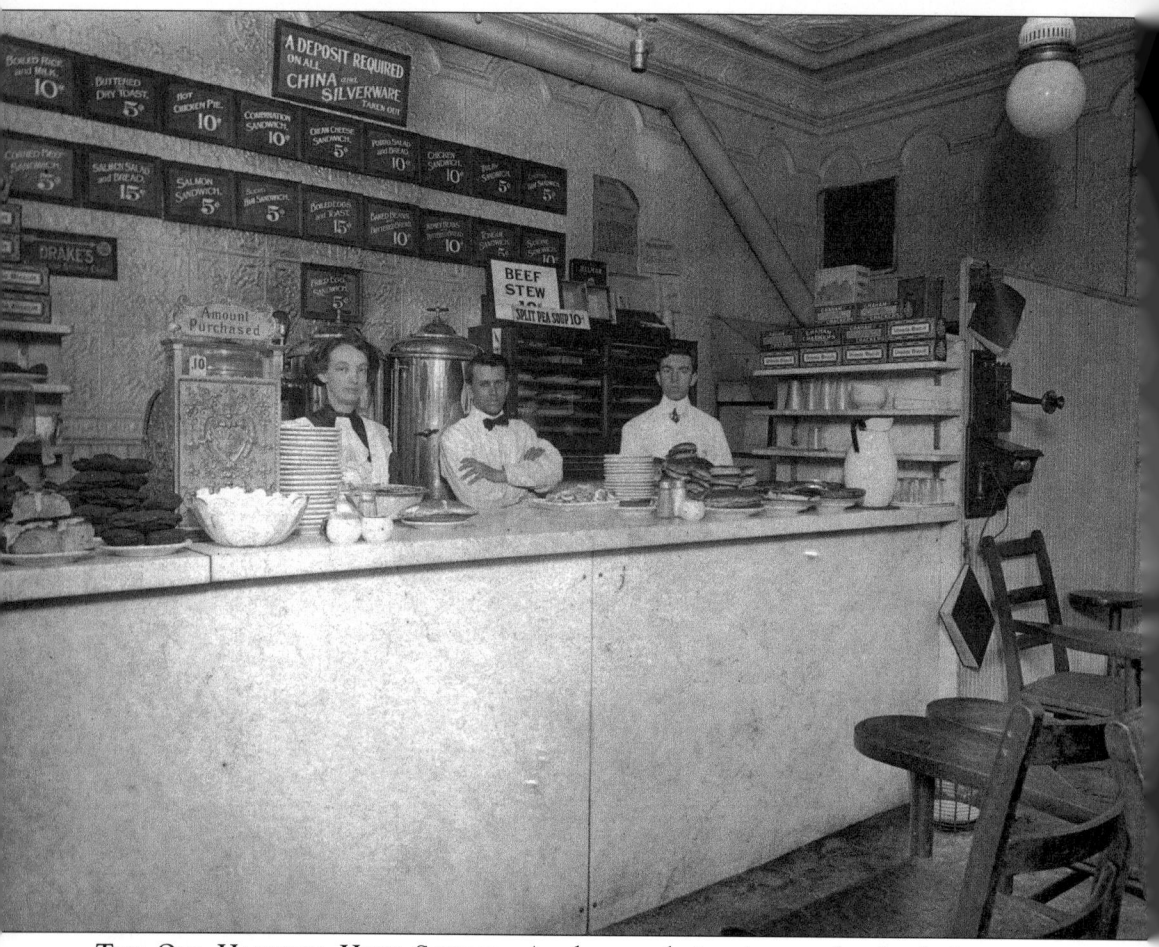

THE OLD HARWICH HIGH SCHOOL. As the population increased, schools became very overcrowded. This cafeteria in the Brooks Academy building was located at the end of the study hall in the area that is now the gift shop.

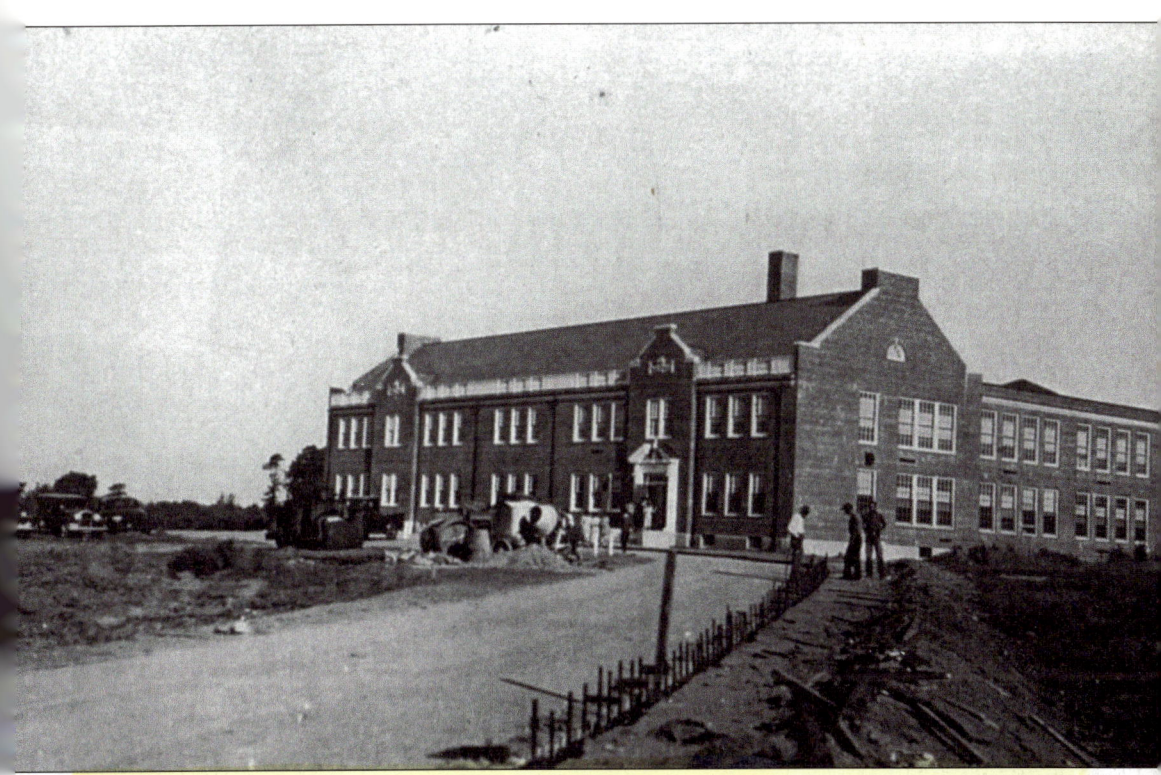

THE NEW HIGH SCHOOL. In 1936, despite the Great Depression, taxpayers endorsed construction of a new junior-senior high school by a 285-0 vote. The school on Sisson Road was constructed for $107,394.

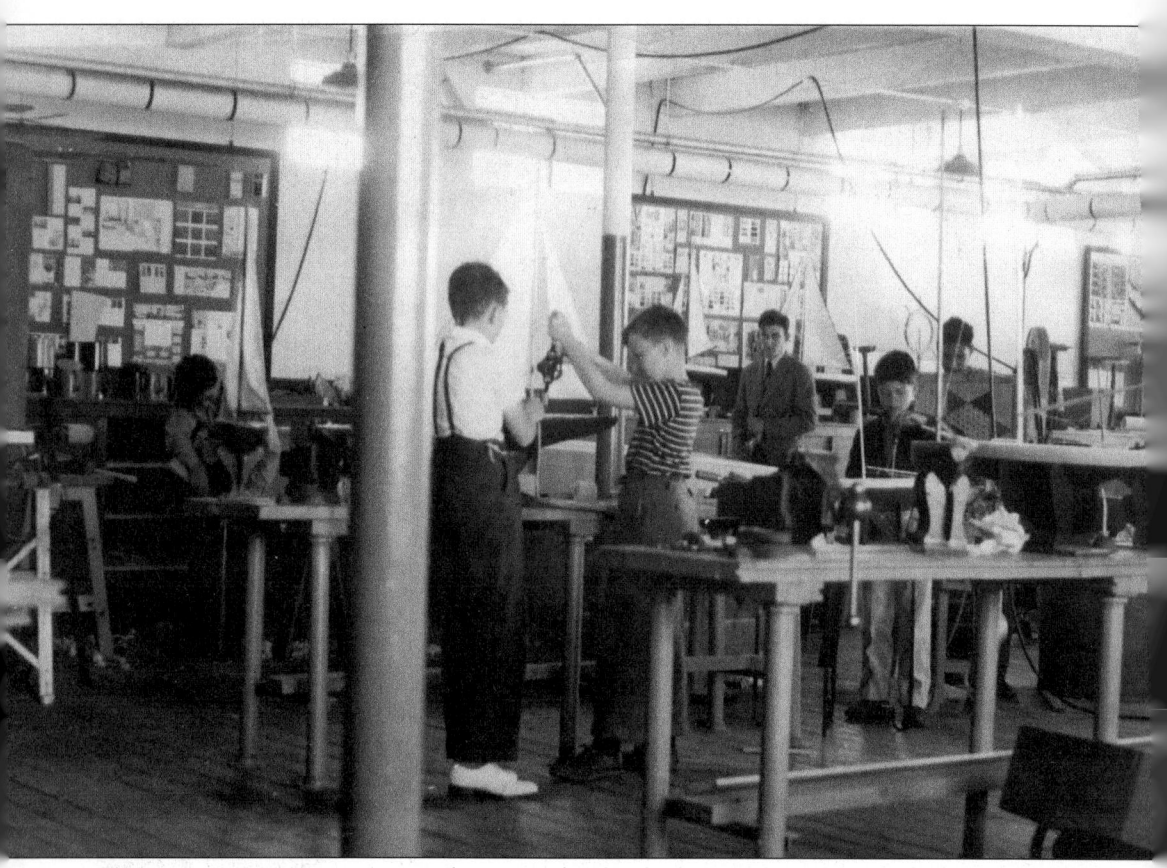

EDUCATIONAL ADVANTAGES. The new school, which was planned to accommodate up to 500 students, opened in 1937. Among its many facilities was this room in which industrial arts was taught.

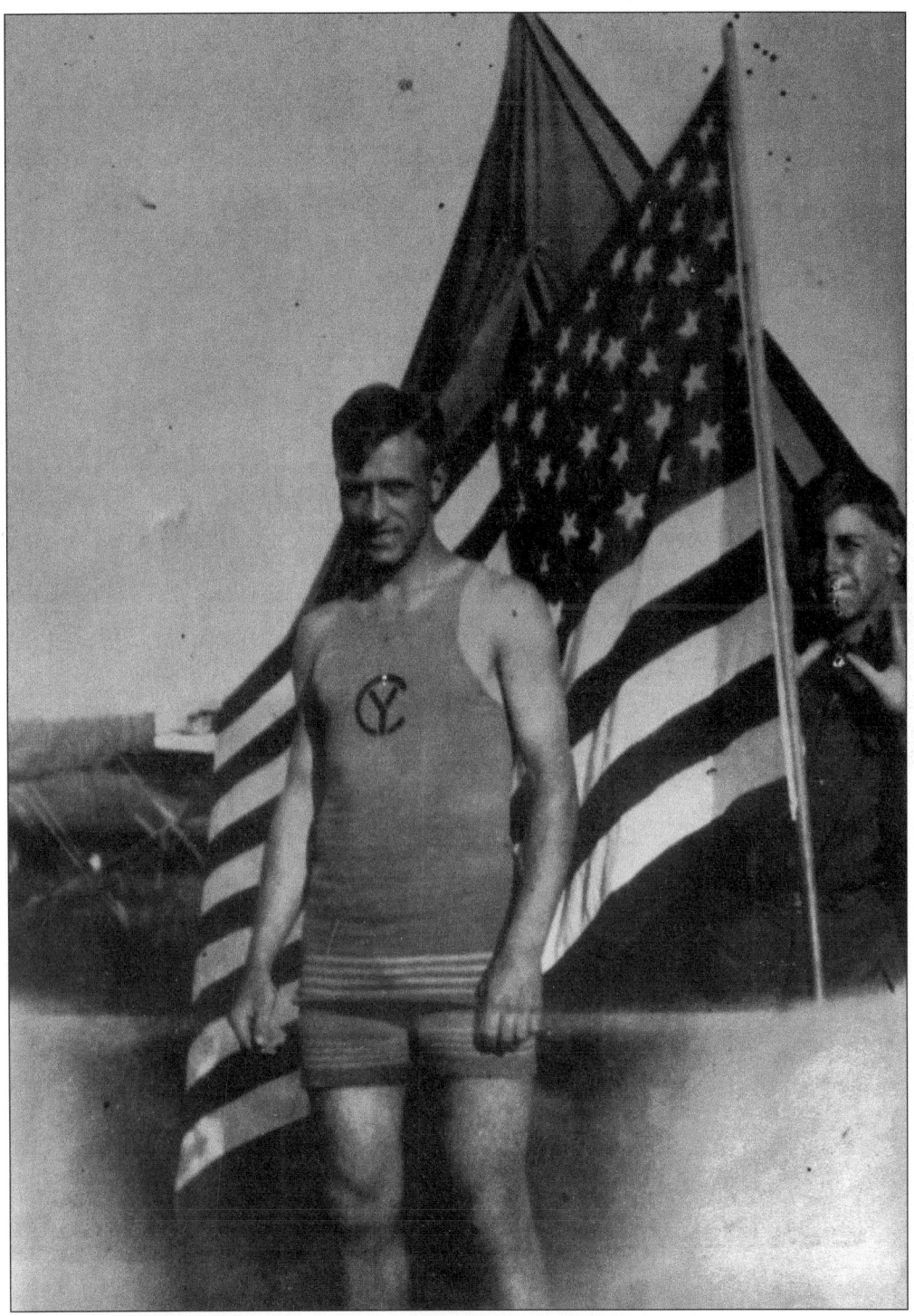

THE 1930S. By the 1930s, Harwich was drawing many vacationers. As late as 1950, however, only three percent of the shoreline was available for public use.

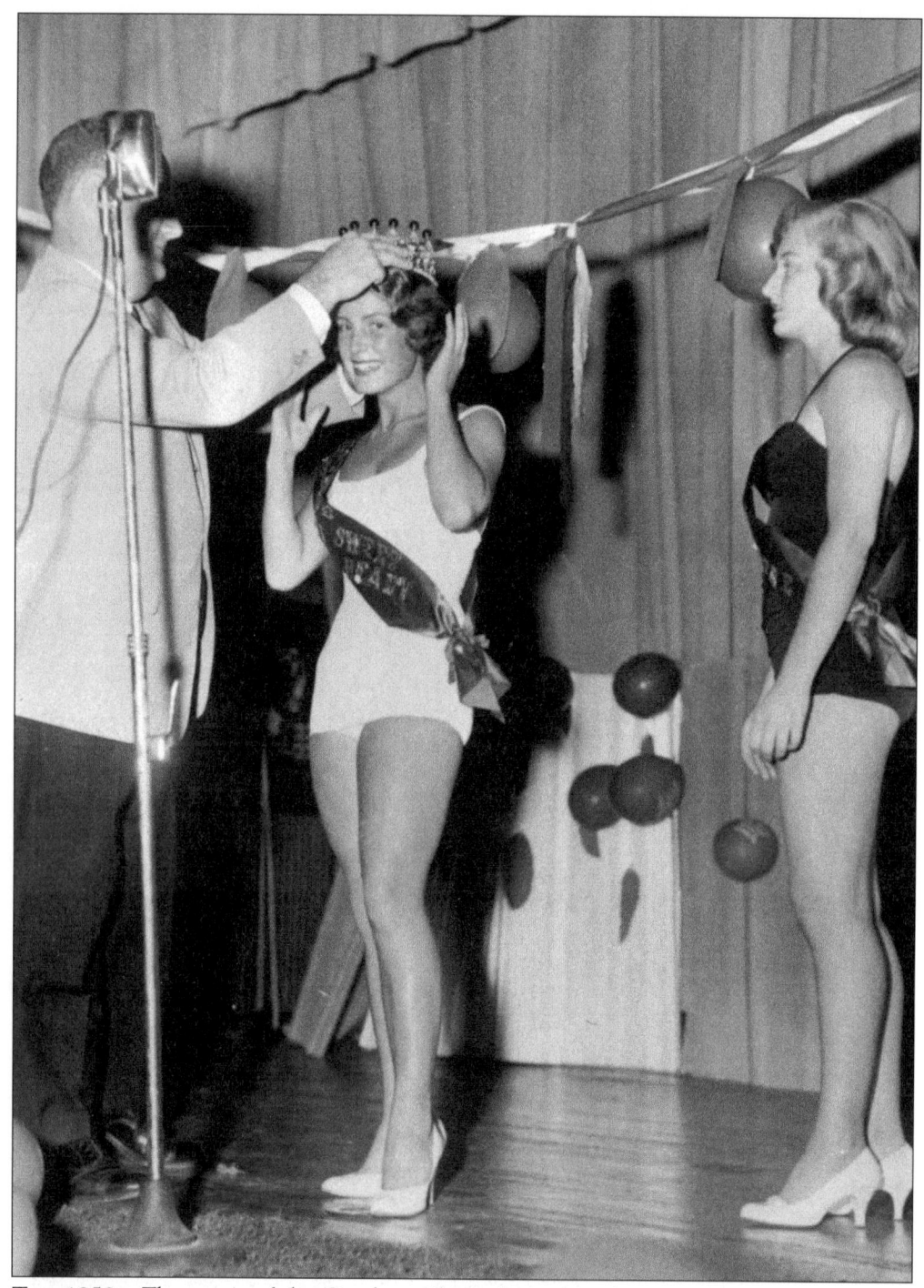

THE 1950s. The queen of the Cranberry Festival is crowned in a ceremony similar to the pageants held in Atlantic City, New Jersey.

Four
HARWICH REMEMBERS

THE JOSIAH PAINE FAMILY. Keeping the past vibrant and passing on traditions assumes many forms and dimensions in Harwich. Josiah Paine—posing with his wife, Polly, and his son John in 1908—was a premier historian of Harwich's earlier days. He passed his passion for collecting and analyzing local documents on to his son. John Paine became an attorney but for many years continued the family's tradition of service to the community by his leadership as selectman.

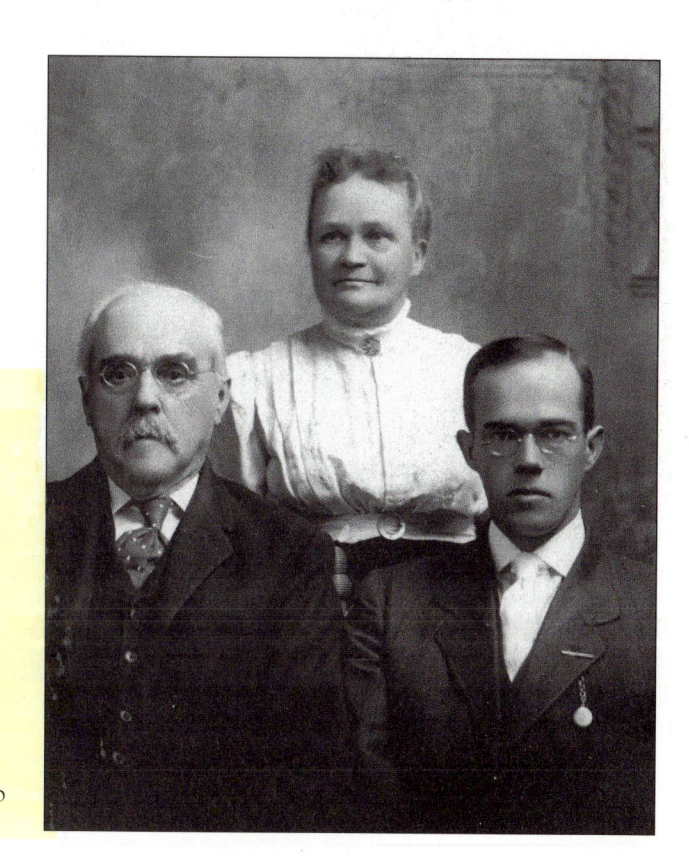

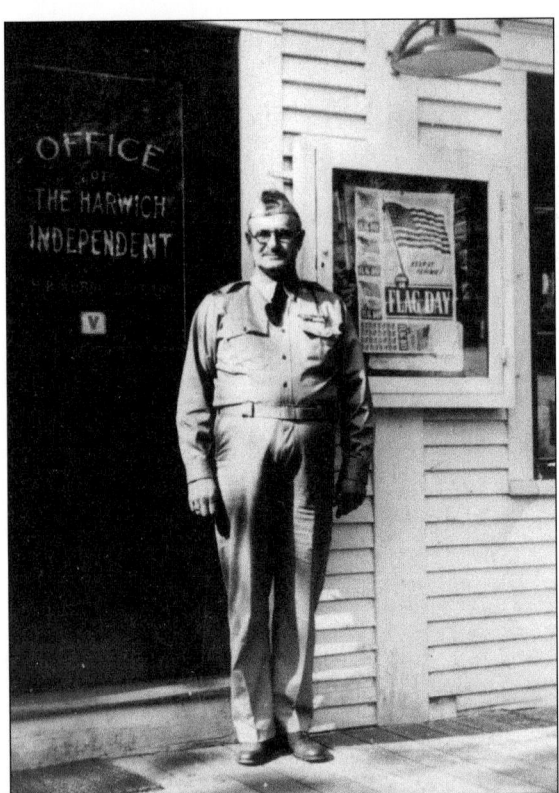

HARRY ALBRO. Favorite son Harry Albro was editor of the *Harwich Independent*. After World War II, he became the first town veteran's officer. He was much respected for his dedication. Albro left his home, located next to the town hall, as a center for Harwich's senior citizens.

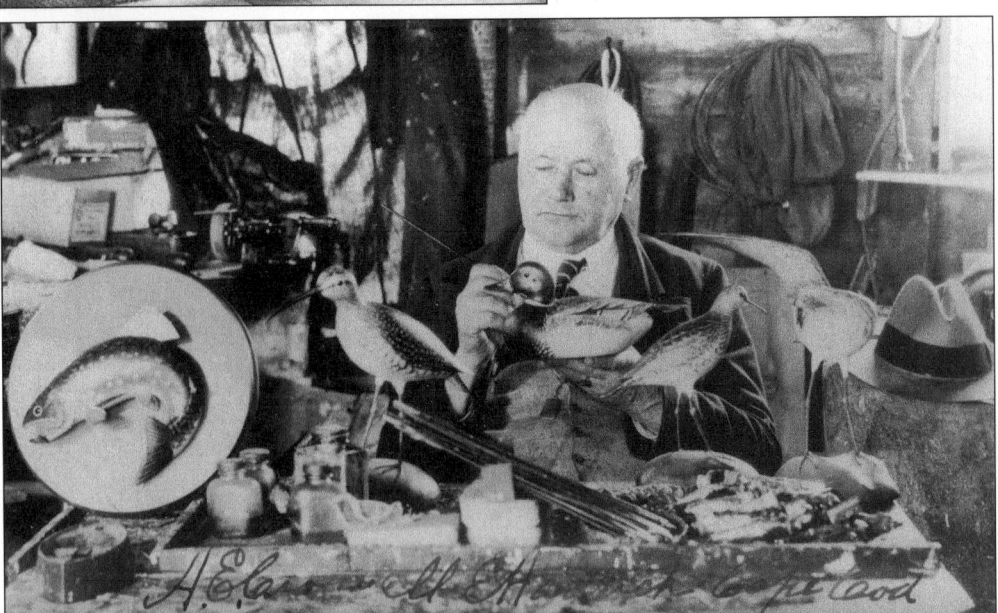

ELMER CROWELL (1862–1951). Among the best-known residents of the 20th century, Elmer Crowell was born and raised in East Harwich. Early in his life, he developed a love of hunting that led him to the carving of bird decoys. His decoys originally sold for $2 to $4. He became foremost in this art form, and his pieces are now highly prized by art collectors and museums. In the mid-1980s, one decoy was resold for $319,000.

114

Betty Pbop. Betty Pbop, a professor at Wheelock College, founded a theater in 1852 to bring its magic to local children. The first productions were staged at the Exchange, providing outstanding training for the children and great enjoyment to their audiences.

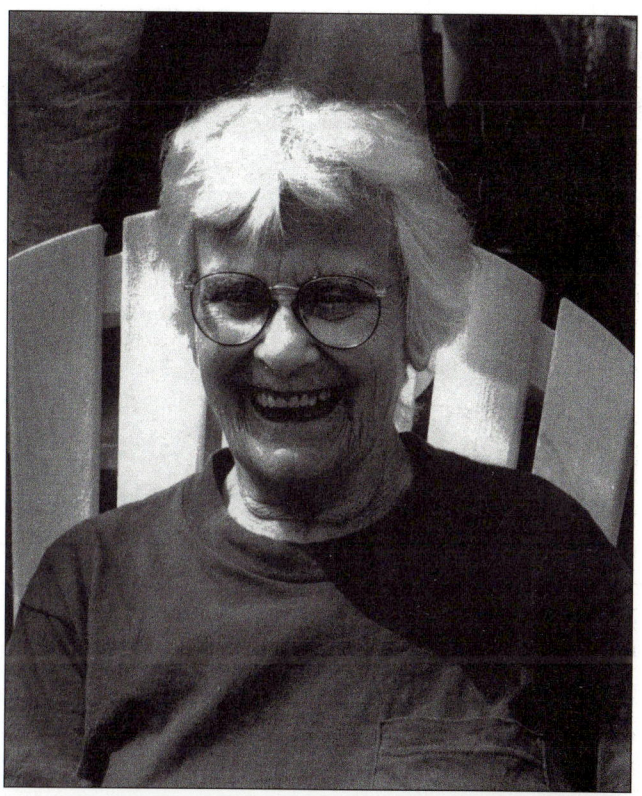

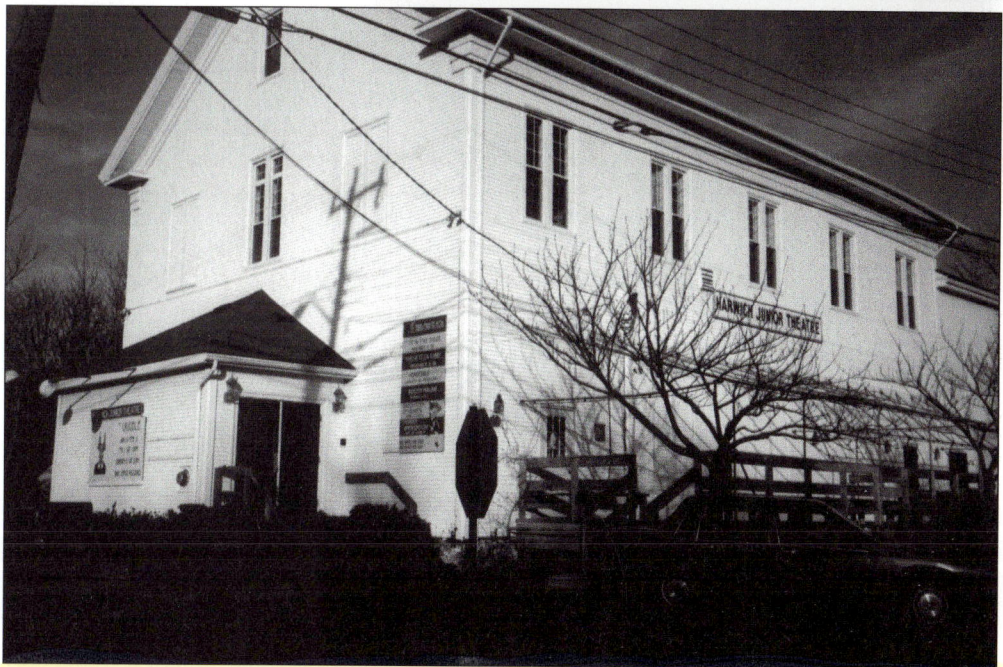

The Harwich Junior Theatre. The Harwich Junior Theatre moved to its own quarters in this West Harwich building, which was built in 1865 as a Masonic Hall. The theater continues to enjoy an outstanding reputation for its productions. (Sr. Aureen Rose Behrend.)

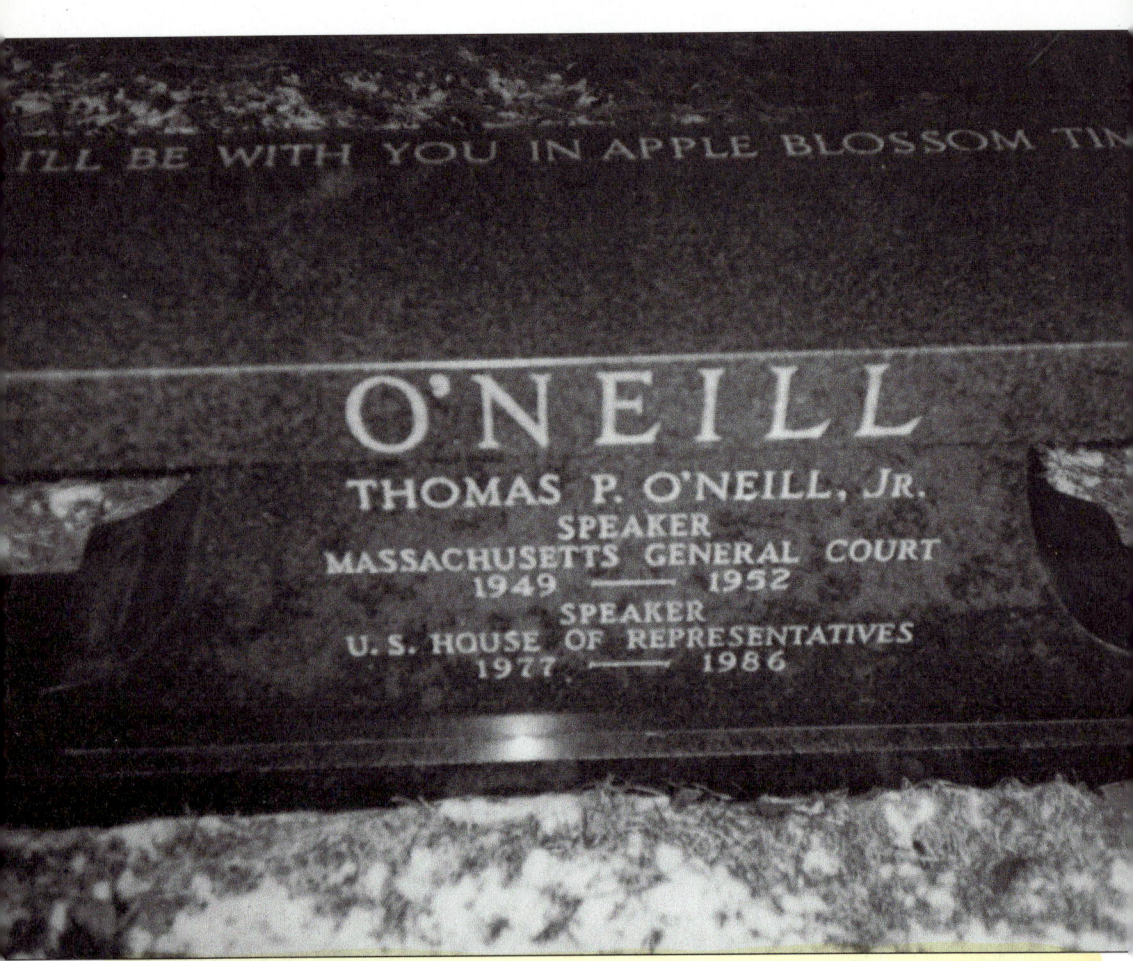

Thomas P. "Tip" O'Neill. One of Harwich's best-loved residents, Thomas P. "Tip" O'Neill was a Cambridge native who chose Harwich as his retirement home. The much admired former Speaker of the U.S. House of Representatives busied himself with many local activities. He was a founder and extraordinary fund-raiser for the Family Pantry and a sponsor of an annual golf tournament. O'Neill asked to buried in Harwich, in this spot overlooking the municipal golf course. (Sr. Aureen Rose Behrend.)

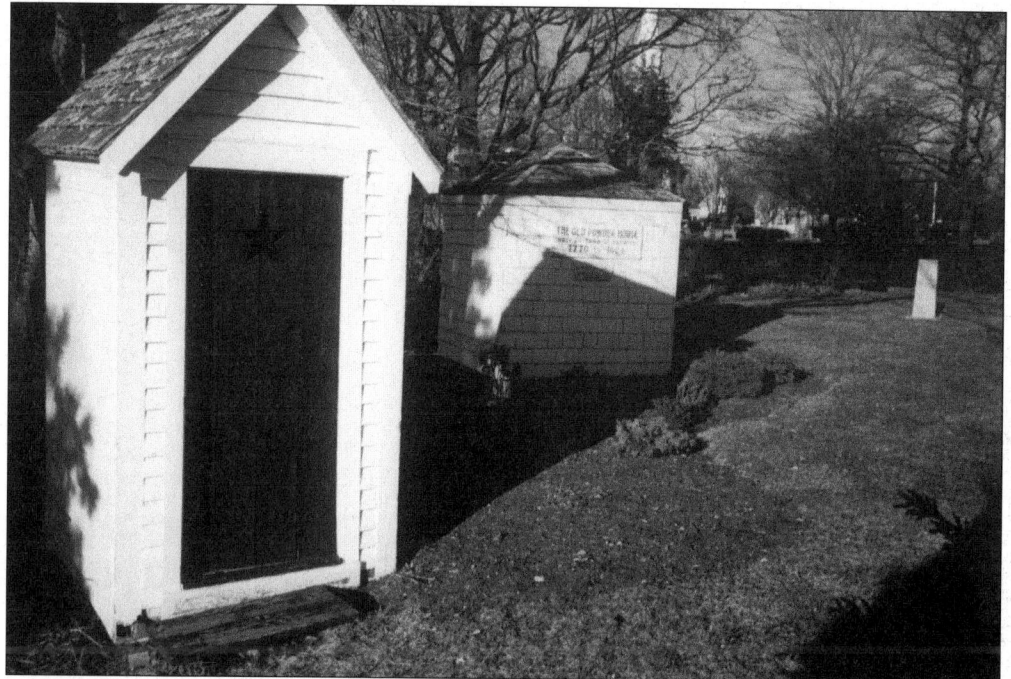

The Powderhouse and the Privy. The Harwich Historical Society's endeavors to preserve the past include the display of the Cape's last surviving powderhouse from Revolutionary days. From 1770 to 1864, the small structure was used for the storage of gunpowder. Next to it, on the grounds of Brooks Academy, is the "privileged privy." Donated in 1990 by Thomas Blute of Crosby's Memorials, the privy was moved to its present site so that children might see an outhouse.

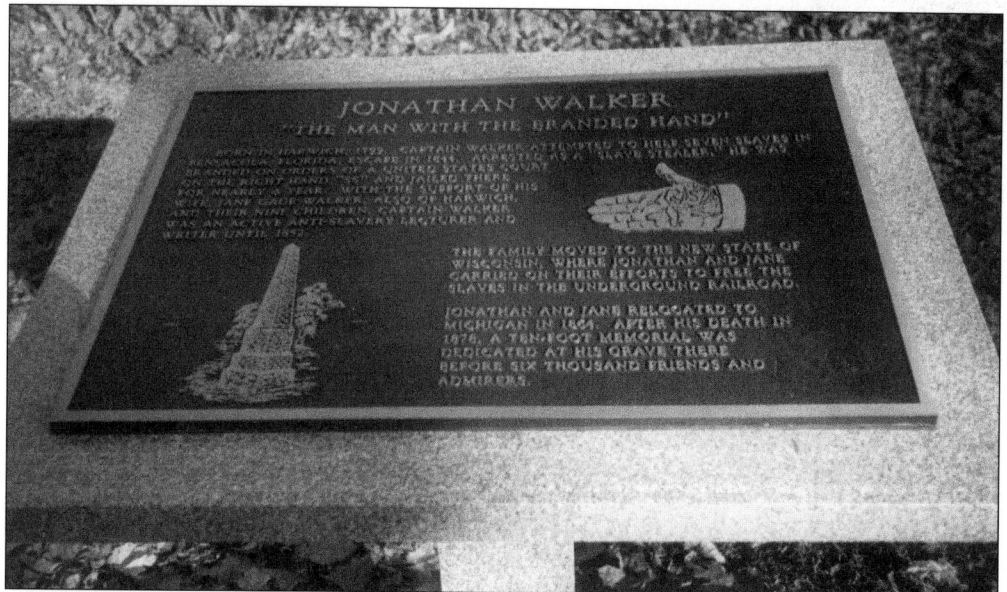

The Walker Plaque. Also on the museum grounds, this plaque honors native son Jonathan Walker, whose hand was branded by Federal marshals with the symbol *SS* because of his efforts to help slaves escape before the Civil War. (Sr. Aureen Rose Behrend.)

117

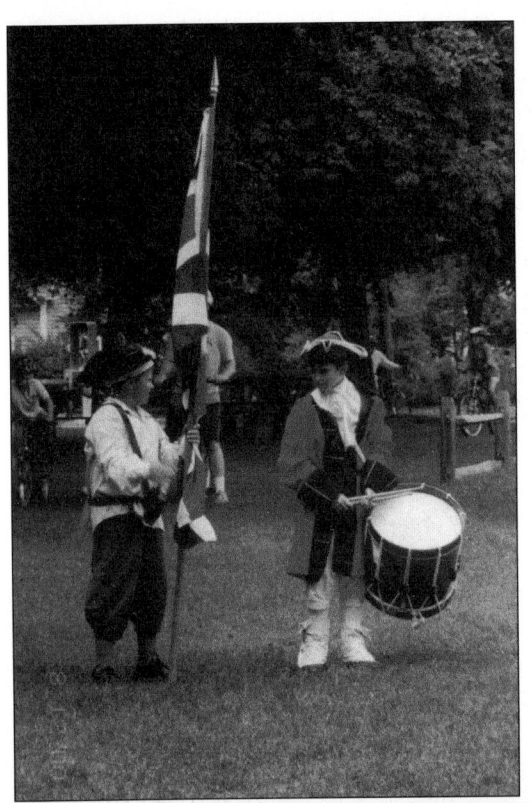

COLONIAL REENACTMENTS. The Harwich Historical Society also sponsors very popular Colonial reenactments in Brooks Park and on the academy grounds. These are conducted by visiting groups of minutemen and their families.

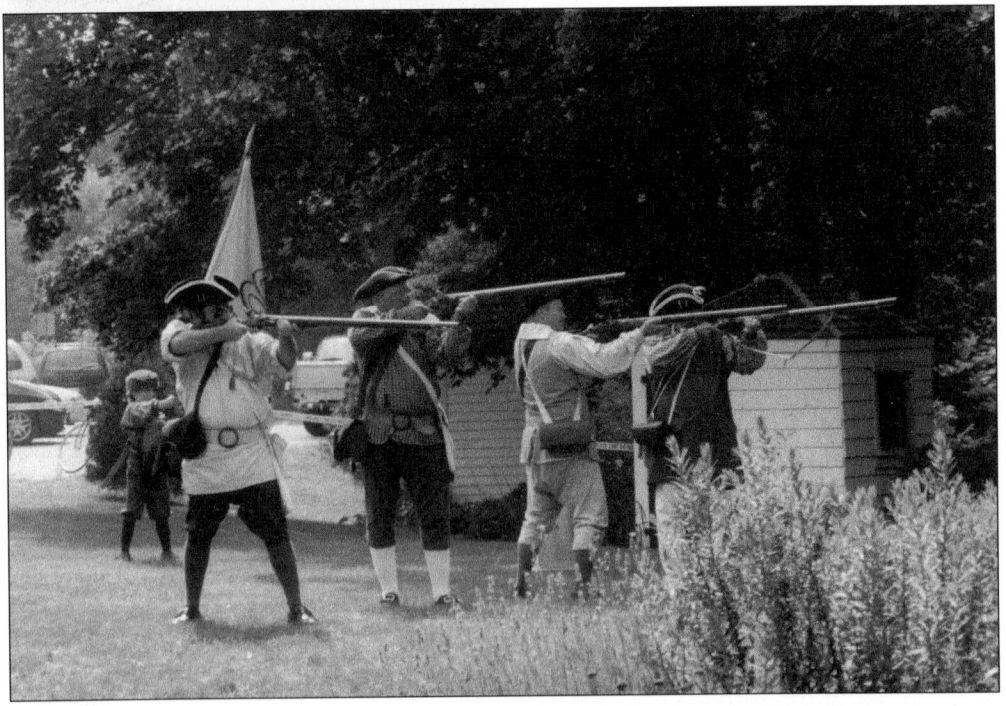

THE PIE FESTIVAL. Each summer, the Harwich Historical Society holds a pie festival, re-creating a favored 19th-century social pastime.

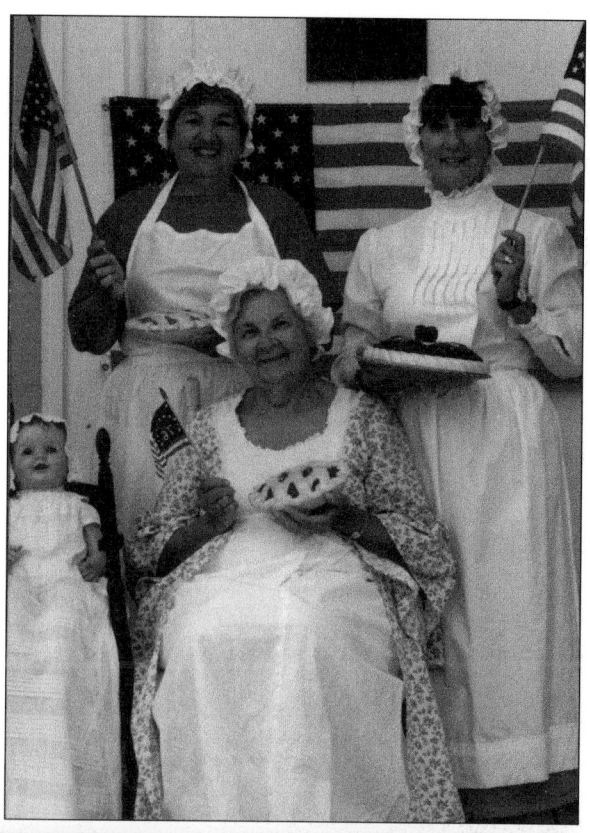

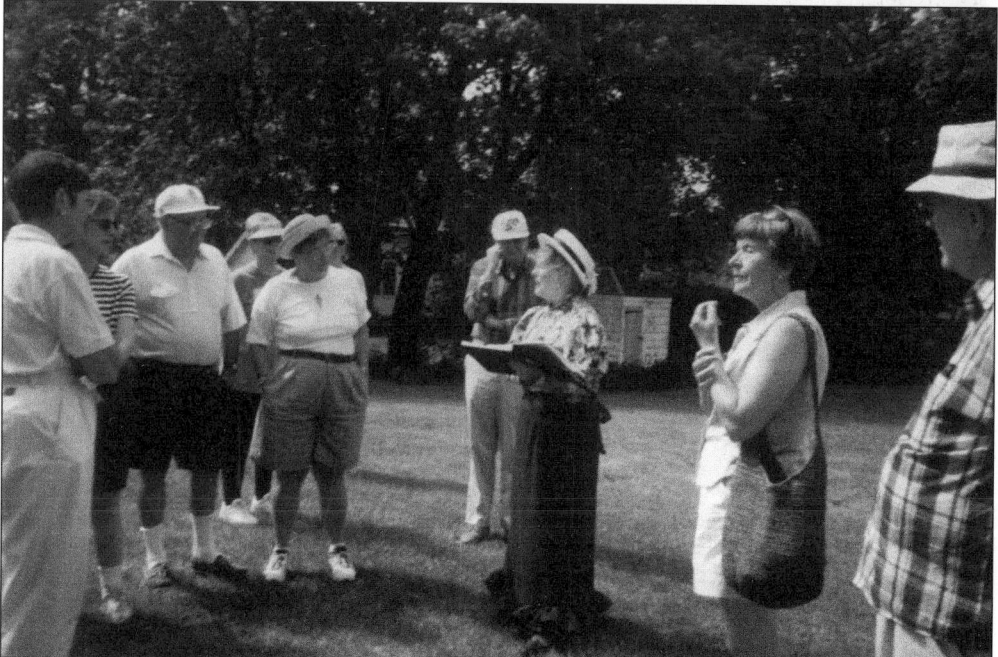

WALKING TOURS OF THE HISTORIC AREA. Another summer activity of the Harwich Historical Society is the walking tour of Harwich Center, led by costumed guides.

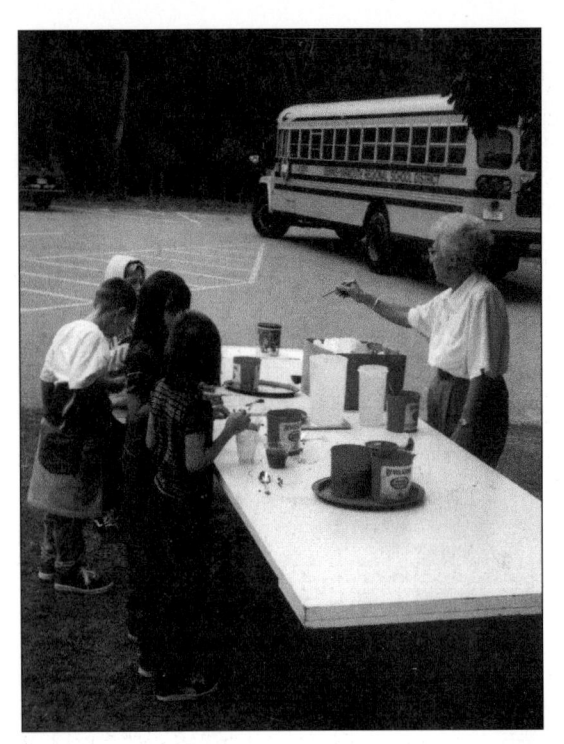

PASSING ON THE LEGACY. One of the most important works of the Harwich Historical Society is teaching the past to visiting schoolchildren. Each fall, classes are taken on tour of a bog, and the children learn the elements by making their own "bog."

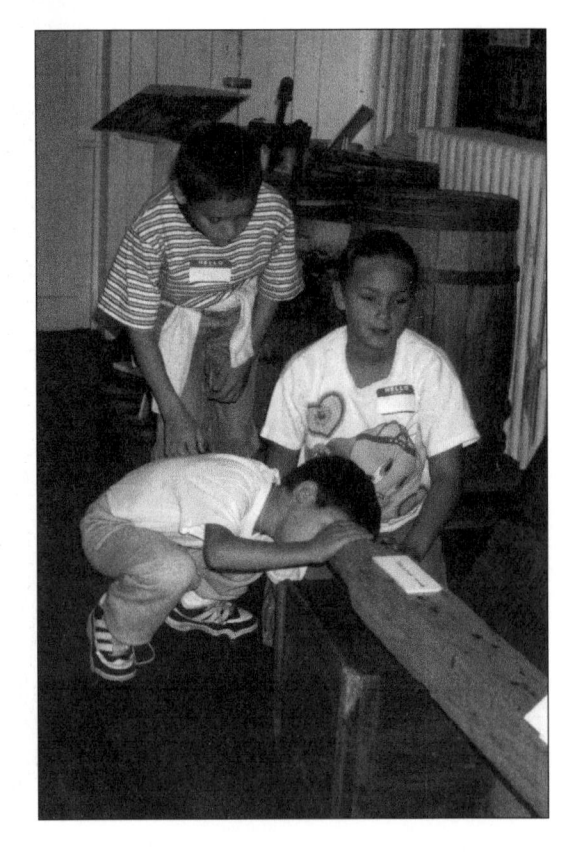

THE CRANBERRY EXHIBIT. The most popular room in Brooks Academy contains a permanent exhibit of the culture involved in the cranberry trade.

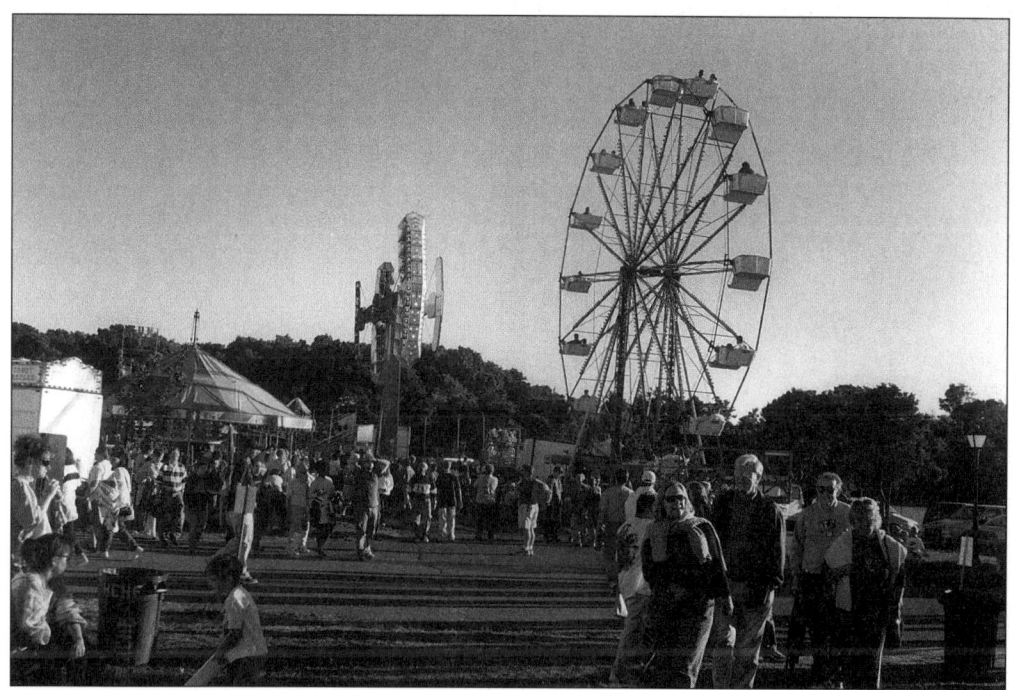

THE ANNUAL CRANBERRY FESTIVAL. Each September, the Cranberry Festival Committee, a group of dedicated volunteers, stages a series of events including a craft show, midway, parades, and beach activities. The celebration climaxes in a fireworks display. The events attract thousands of delighted participants. (Harwich Cranberry Festival Committee.)

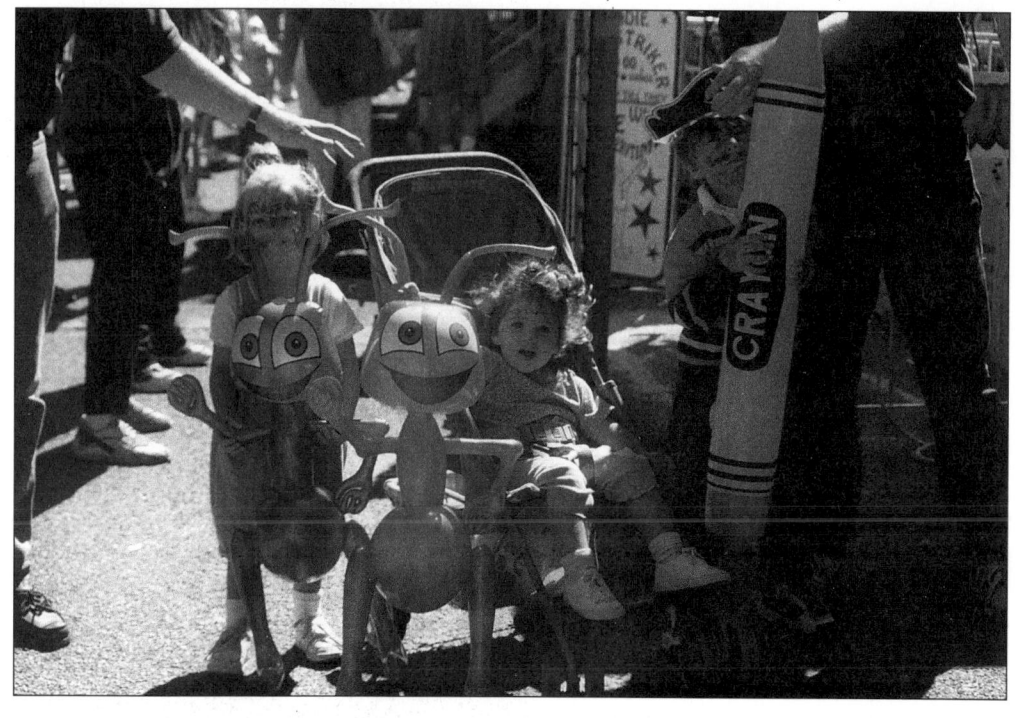

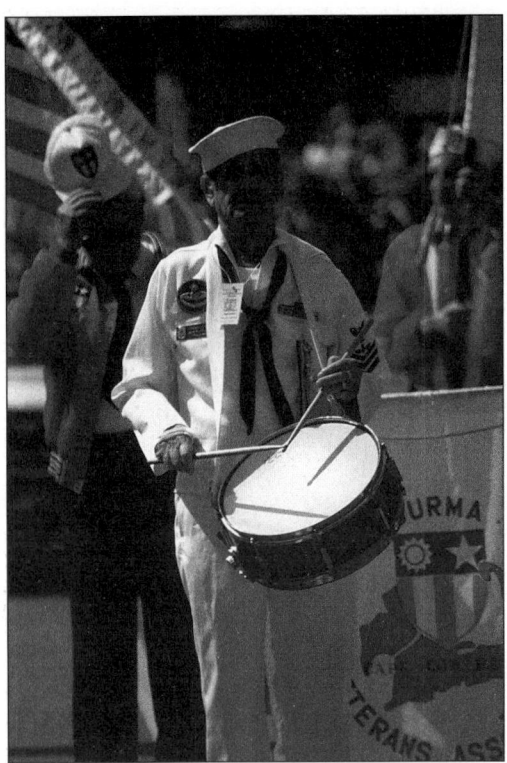

THE CRANBERRY FESTIVAL PARADE. Among recent parade participants was World War II veteran Allyn "Flash" Gordon. Wounded on the USS *Wasp* in 1944, Gordon finally received his Purple Heart 54 years later. His dog, right, clearly aspires to become a parade official. (Harwich Cranberry Festival Committee.)

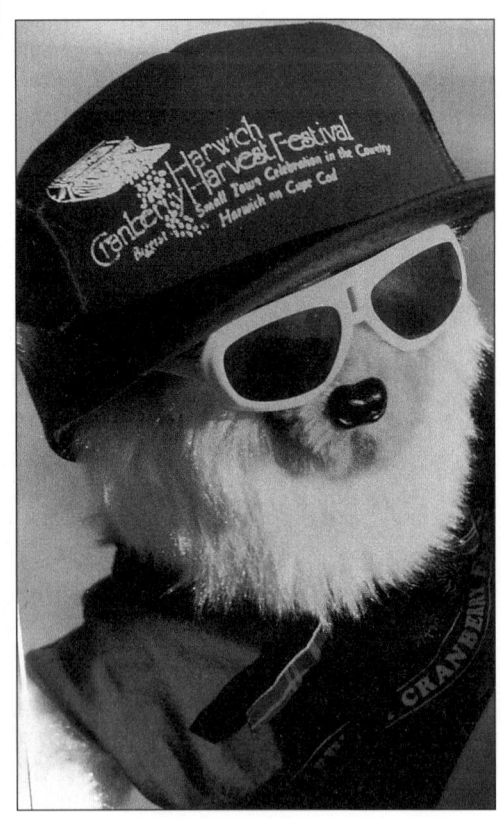

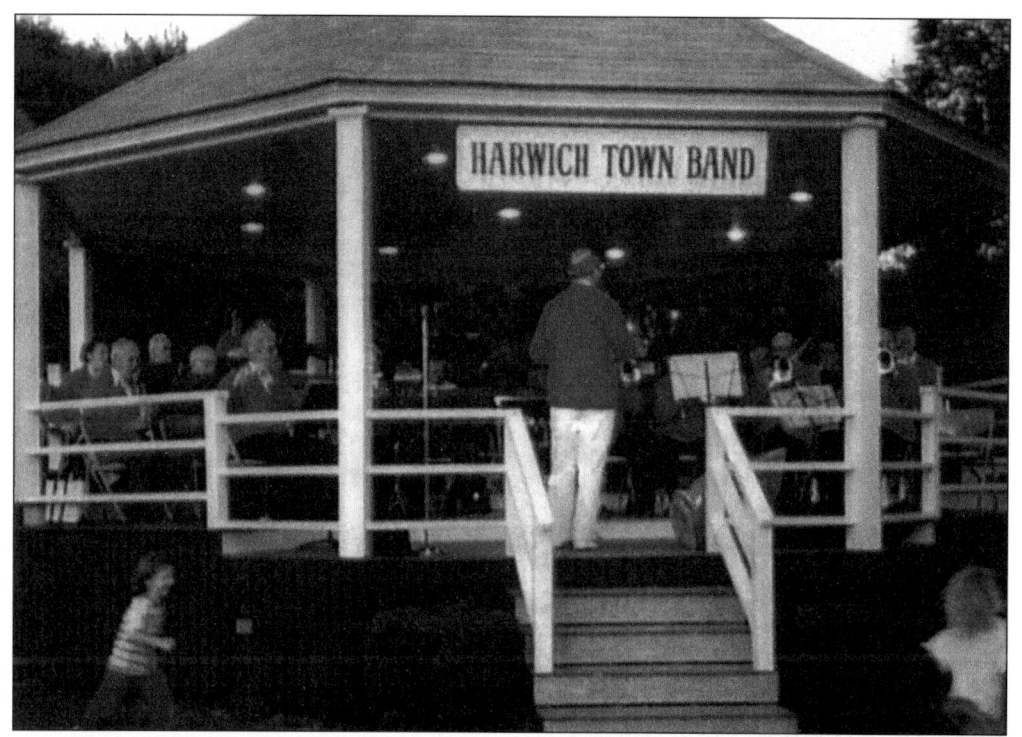

THE TOWN BAND. One of the most popular summer activities is attending the weekly free concerts presented in Brooks Park by the Harwich Town Band.

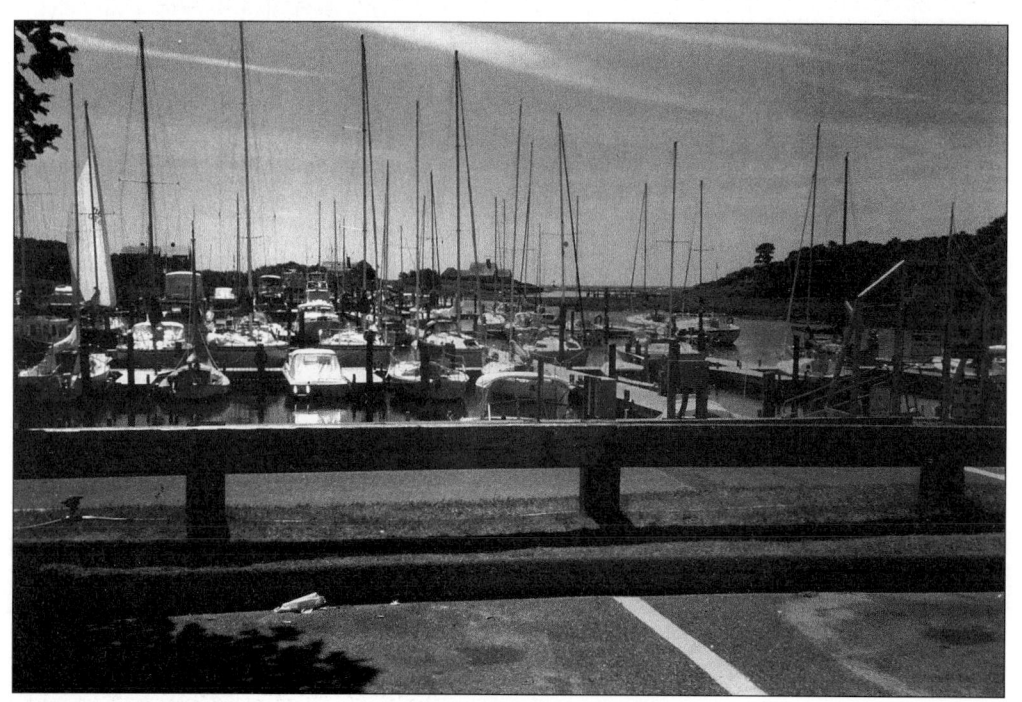

SUMMER AT SAQUETUCKET. Harwich's well-protected harbors are becoming increasingly popular with boaters, as seen in this view of Saquetucket Harbor.

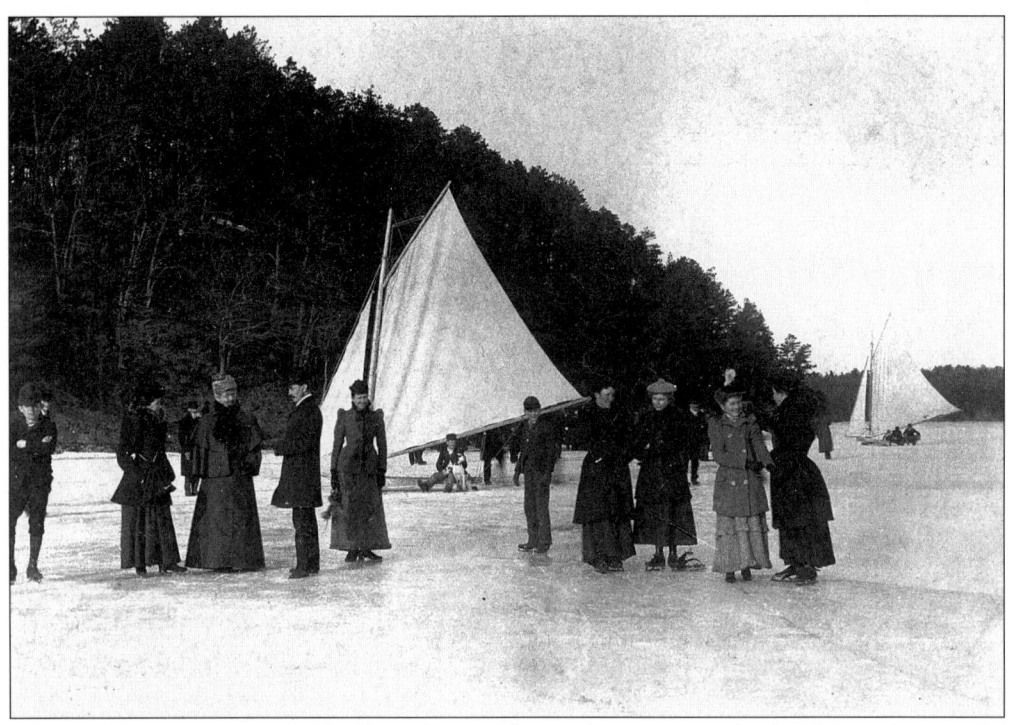

WINTER SKATING. Young and old residents still eagerly anticipate the first heavy freeze. The bogs serve as safe, spacious, and much enjoyed rinks.

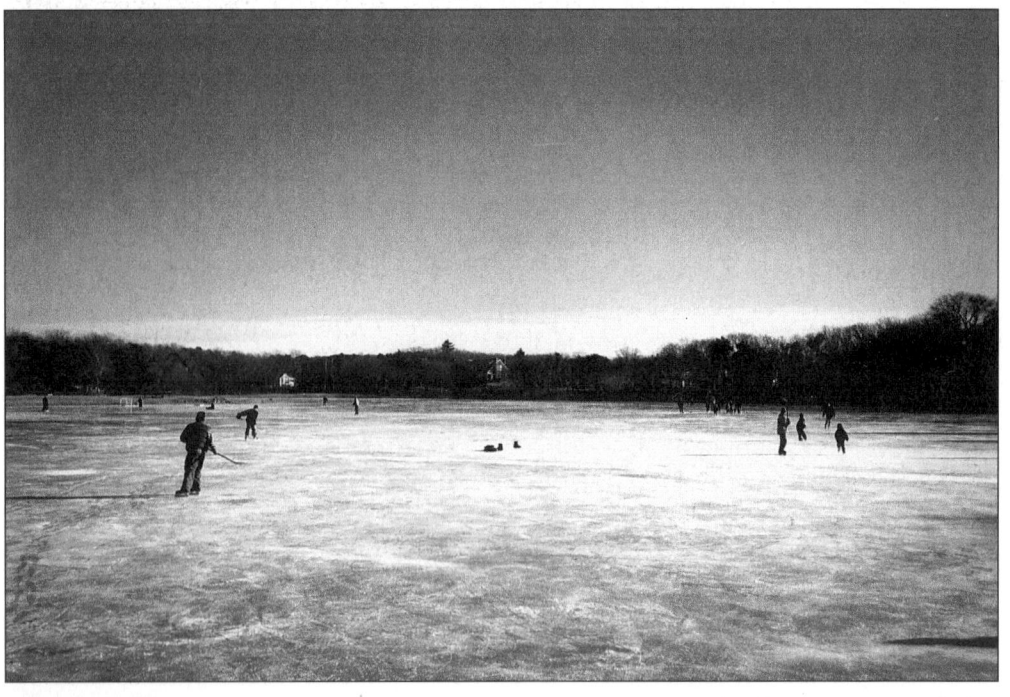

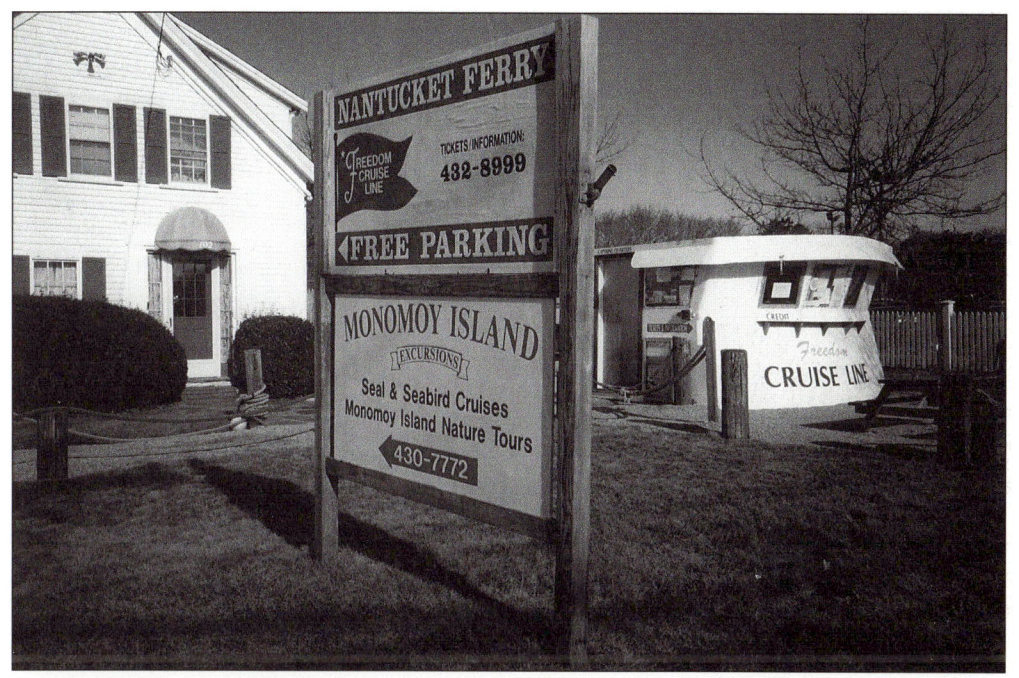

CHANGING HARWICH. Harwich now has its own direct access to Nantucket.

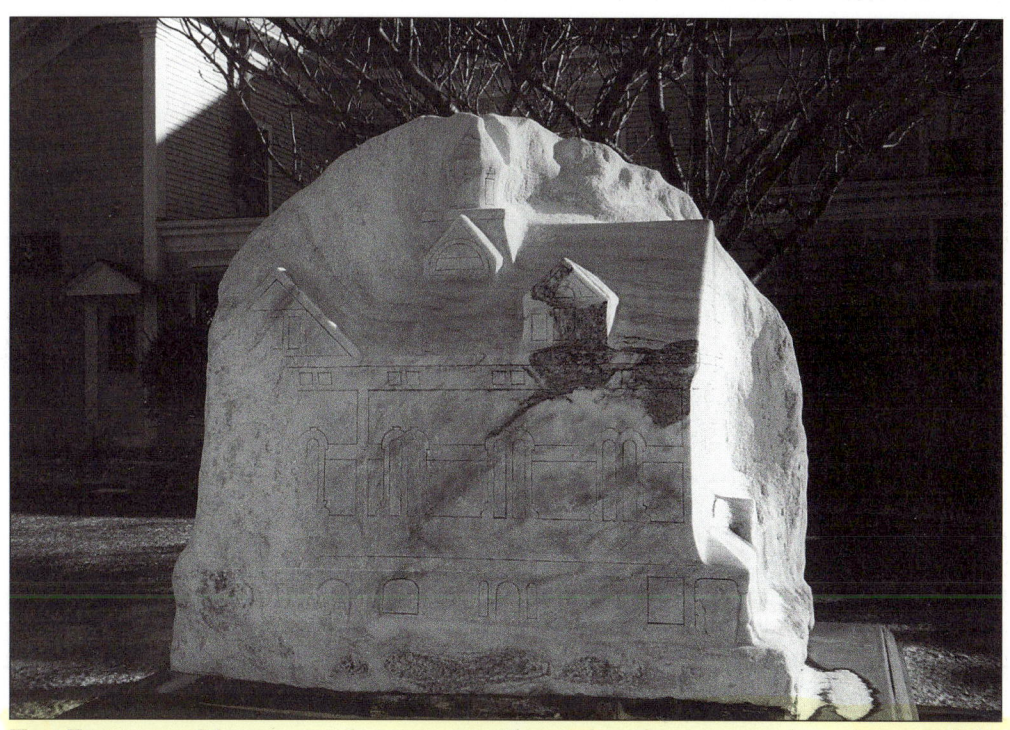

THE EXCHANGE MONUMENT. It is no coincidence that the stone marking the site of the Exchange Building, destroyed in the mid-1960s after voters rejected appropriations for its care, resembles a tomb marker. It is a visible reminder of the need to preserve the past.

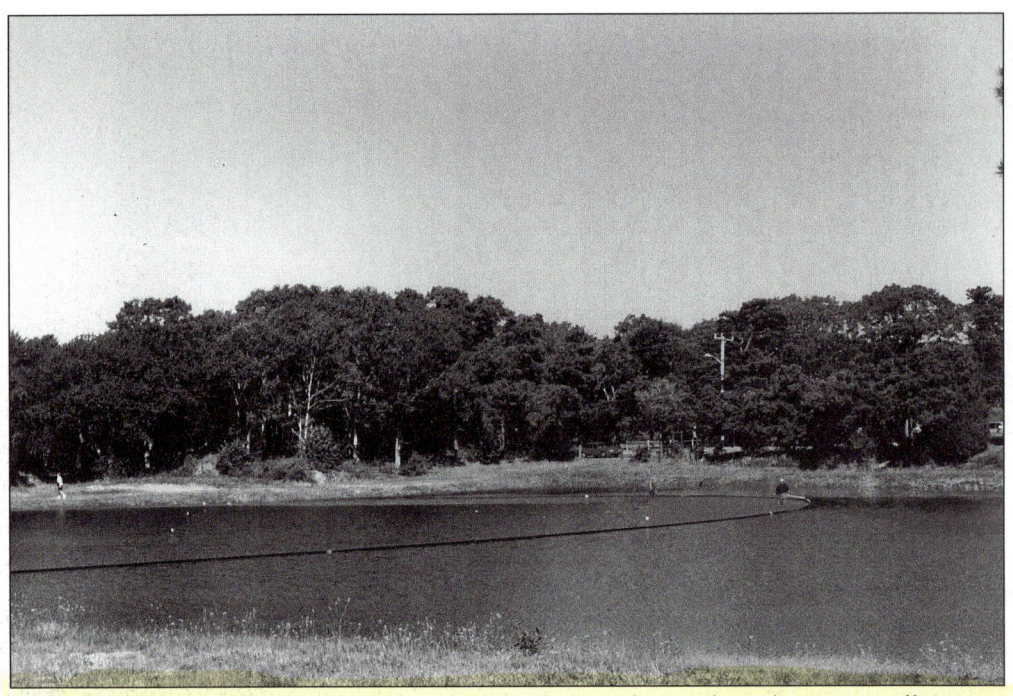

UNCHANGING HARWICH. Even with modern machinery, the cranberry harvest is still a major event that requires skill and cooperative weather.

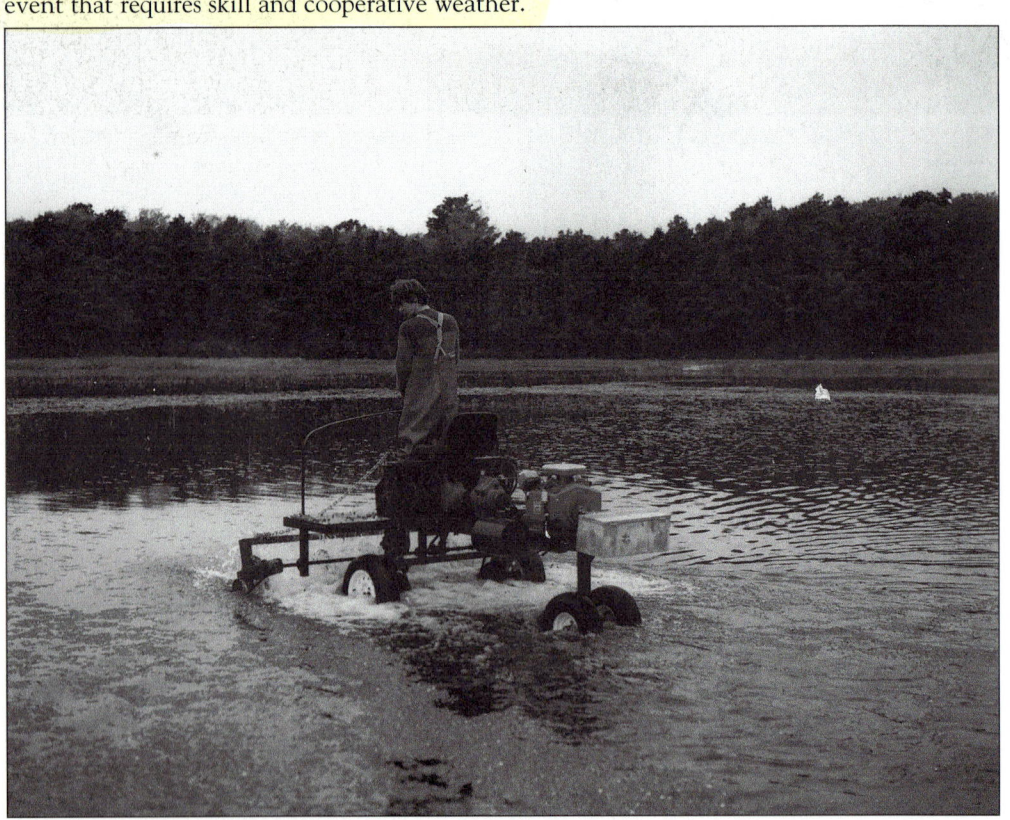

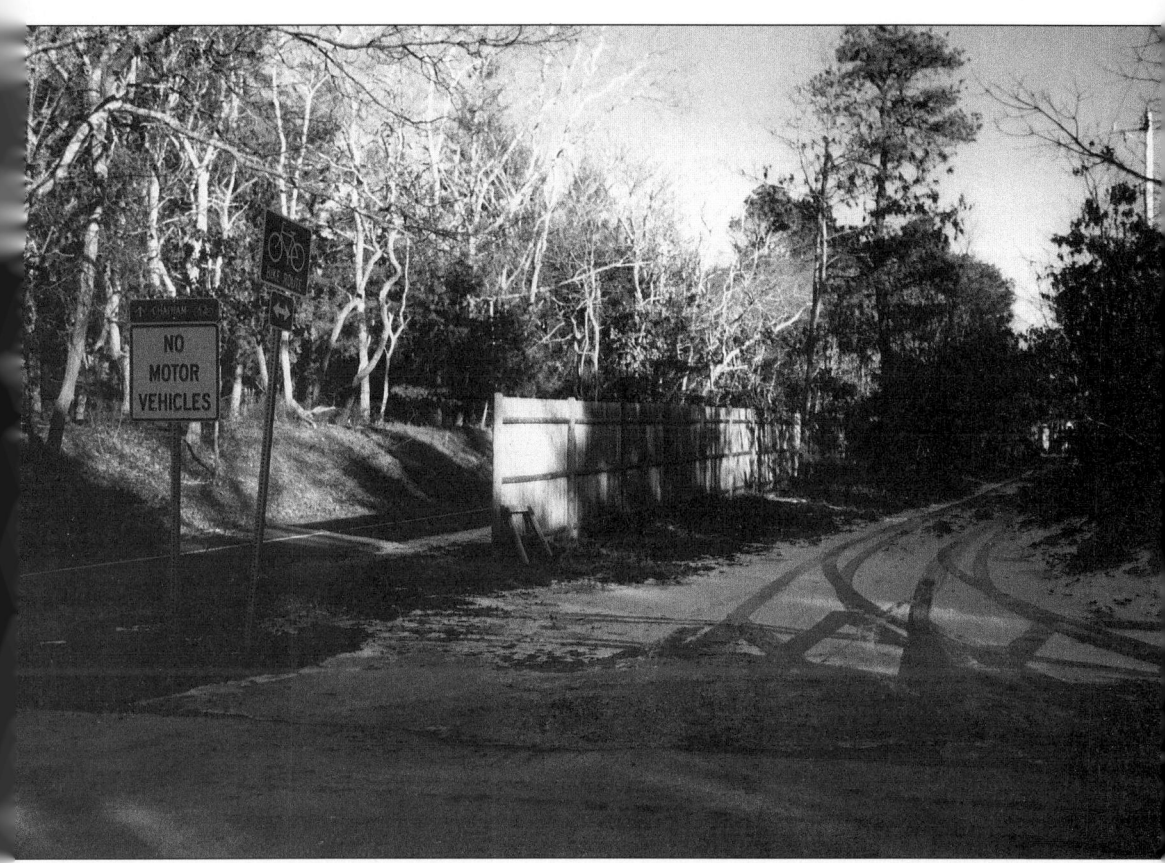

THE RAIL TRAIL. Constructed along the old railroad right-of-way, the bike trail to the left of the fence and the hiking and bridal path to its right symbolize the community's transformation.

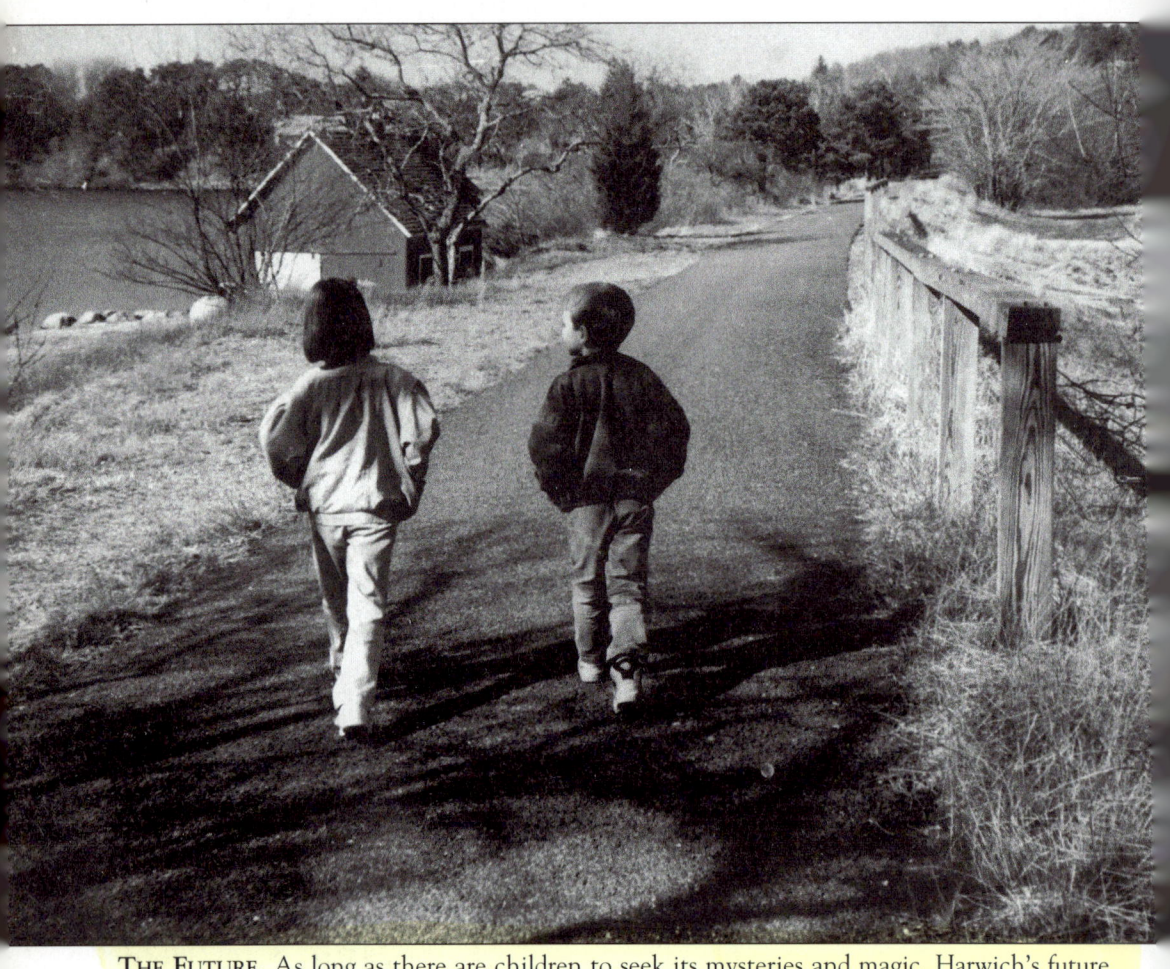

THE FUTURE. As long as there are children to seek its mysteries and magic, Harwich's future is secure.